Bloody Winter

REVISED EDITION

Capt. John M. Waters, Jr.
U.S. Coast Guard (Ret.)

Naval Institute Press
Annapolis, Maryland

First edition published in 1967
by D. Van Nostrand Company, Inc.

© 1967, 1984
by the United States Naval Institute
Annapolis, Maryland

Third printing hardcover, 1989
First Bluejacket Books printing, 1994

Library of Congress Cataloging in Publication Data
Waters, John M.
  Bloody winter.

  Includes index.
  1. World War, 1939–1945—Campaigns—Atlantic Ocean.
2. Convoy—History—20th century. I. Title.
D770.W3   1984   940.54′29   84-18968
ISBN 1-55750-912-3

Printed in the United States of America on acid-free paper ⊗

To those who fought
in the Battle of the Atlantic,
on, over, and beneath the sea

FOREWORD

The submarine is that type of warship which is best qualified for offensive operations in sea areas which are dominated by the enemy. This is again shown in this book.

The Battle of the Atlantic was the longest, fiercest, and—for the outcome of World War II—the most important campaign of the war at sea. The most critical period of it was the "bloody" winter of 1942-43, when the submarine offensive was at its peak, and when eventually the tide was turned by the anti-submarine forces on the surface and in the air who got the upper hand.

This significant period is the subject of this fine book. The author, himself a participant in that battle, and a thorough student of all the relevant war diaries and memoirs, paints such a vivid and accurate picture of the actors, and gives such a stirring account of their actions on both sides of the conflict, that even an old war-horse of that theatre (as I am) is still amazed. It is an exciting story which will appeal not only to the professional sailor, but to everyone.

This book deals with a period which is approximately a year and a half after my active part in the battle was over. Old and new friends of mine on both sides are pictured in this book: my classmates, Siegfried von Forstner and Dietrich Lohmann, my exec of U-99, Klaus Bargsten, and last, but not least, Donald MacIntyre, my old foe and captor and new friend.

It is interesting to see how the tactics developed on both sides. It appears to be a natural evolution—only one thing strikes me today: the frequent electronic emissions by the U-boats as observed by all escorts, which made the HF/DF so effective. In my time, everybody was conscious of the danger of using the wireless transmitter, and I remember that we were very reluctant to use it even when ordered to do so by Flag Officer Submarines. Of course, that U-boat which first sighted the convoy had to signal its enemy contact report, and was later responsible for informing the other boats of the now automatically disbanded patrol line from time to time about the position, course, and speed of the convoy. But all the other boats of the wolf pack remained completely silent.

I have often been asked who was the first to use the term "wolf pack tactics." There is no doubt that Admiral Doenitz, the inventor of the tactics, also coined the term "Rudeltaktik." I remember having been with Doenitz in a train from Berlin to Wilhelmshaven early in the war. I was with some U-boat captains who had dinner with him in the restaurant car. He kept talking about the usefulness of slogans such as General Guderian's for his armoured divisions. Eventually, he took a pencil and wrote something on his table napkin. It was this: *"U-boote sind die Wölfe zur See: angreifen, reissen, versenken!"* (U-boats are the wolves of the sea: attack, tear, sink!)

I am greatly honoured by the author for being asked to contribute a foreword to this wonderful book.

Kiel, 11th July, 1967

OTTO KRETSCHMER, *Rear Admiral, Germany*

PREFACE

This is a story of the bitter six months of fighting that climaxed the Battle of the Atlantic, and ended with the defeat and withdrawal of the U-boat wolf packs from the shipping lanes in the spring of 1943. There was at first the temptation to write a personal narrative of some of these occurrences, for on a trip in USS GEMINI and as a watch officer on the U. S. Coast Guard Cutter INGHAM (WPG-35), I was involved in four of the most crucial battles, around Convoys SC-107, SC-118, SC-121, and SC-122. But as most combat veterans will admit, those actually engaged in the fighting have only a limited view of the whole picture, vivid though it may be. This was particularly true of the convoy battles, which often lasted for days and involved running fights over hundreds of miles of ocean. At any instant, as many as 50 miles might separate an escort, running down a radar contact in the van of the convoy, from a rescue vessel picking up survivors far astern. Furthermore, the battle can only be seen in its proper perspective if the reader is able to view the action from the vantage point of the senior commanders ashore, as well as from the bridges of the warships at sea. To round out the picture of the titanic struggle, it is also essential to take a look from the "other side of the hill," as the U-boat commanders saw it from the conning tower and periscope.

The enemy was seldom seen, though his presence was often evidenced by burning ships, a shadow in the night, a small pip on the radar scope, a returning beep on the underwater Asdic detection gear, or the high-pitched chirp of his radio transmissions. What went on in the U-boats during those nights of fire and blood and terror? Who had fired the torpedoes that blasted a fine ship and 60 men to eternity? What was the reaction of the U-boat crews to our counterattacks as we dropped tons of depth charges that tore the ocean apart while they attempted to evade us 600 feet below the surface? What manner of men were they?

During their days of ascendency, the U-boat men were never far from our wakeful thoughts, but at first we knew little of them, and they at times seemed eight feet tall. Later, when the tide had turned and our superiority in weapons, numbers, and tactics had clearly established a mastery that would not again be challenged, we had learned a great deal about them by studying them carefully, as any good hunter studies his quarry. The wet, dazed, and shocked U-boat survivors fished from the sea were less imposing than we had earlier imagined, yet throughout their terrible two years of agony following their 1943 defeat, the spirit of the Kriegsmarine remained high and until the bitter end they sailed. Their story, as well as that of the escort men who defeated them, deserves to be objectively told.

This narrative is confined to the North Atlantic convoy routes between America and the United Kingdom, for it was there around the great trade convoys that the issue had to be decided. Only by stopping the flow of men and matériel to Britain did the Axis have any chance at ultimate victory. To many old friends who suffered in the terrible weather of the Greenland convoy runs, sweltered in the sticky heat of the Caribbean, or endured the monotony of the Central Atlantic convoys to Gibraltar, I can only plead a certain parochialism, as well as my regret that the scope of this story did not allow the inclusion of the action in those areas.

Likewise, to those who came after May, 1943, I apologize for omitting their role. With the defeat and withdrawal of the wolf packs in May, the dangerous threat to the Allied lifelines was ended, as was the role of the Atlantic as a decisive war theatre. In the months that followed, the weather continued as nasty as before, the days were as long and dreary, and men still died, but most of those dying were German. For the Allies, despite occasional losses, the two years after May, 1943, were the years of the hunter, and they inflicted a terrible revenge on the U-boats.

This, then, is the story of the winter crisis of 1942-43, and of some of the men, ships, and planes who fought through it, turning the spectre of defeat that faced them in March into the victory of the escorts in May. It is also a story of the men of the U-boat fleet, who came within a measurable distance of bringing the Allies to their knees; finally failing to do so, most of them paid with their lives while fighting to the bitter end a battle that had already been decided.

The victory of May was in the main a British, and to a lesser extent, a Canadian one. For reasons explained later, only a handful of American escorts and their crews, totaling perhaps 3,000 men, were engaged in the crucial winter battles. In addition to a few ancient and weary but indomitable 1918-vintage flush-deck destroyers, the American surface detachment on the mid-ocean North Atlantic run consisted of five modern Coast Guard cutters of the HAMILTON class, and these at the time formed the hard core of the American effort. It is around these destroyers and cutters that the narrative centers.

The keeping of personal diaries was forbidden during the war, and it was not until 1946 that I began the notes that later became the basis of this story. They were added to occasionally after spinning sea yarns with old comrades and shipmates. Finally, in 1964, having been assigned to duty in Washington, where I had access to many of the official records, as well as to some of the people involved, I commenced work on the book. Over the next two years, by correspondence and personal visits, I contacted many participants in the battles, both Allied and German, and in nearly every case I received the utmost cooperation. Combining my own observations and notes with those of other participants, and checking all against the official records and documents, the true picture of the battle began to emerge.

These documents included the ship logs and war diaries of individual ships, the action reports of various escort commanders, reports of anti-submarine attacks, reports on interrogation of Allied survivors, and the "post-mortem" reports based on interrogation of captured U-boat crewmen. From the German side, the best sources were the very detailed War Diaries of U-boat Command (*Befehlshaber der Untersee-Booten Kriegstagebuch*), the war diaries of the individual U-boats, and the records of individual torpedo firings. A number of very informative essays and manuscripts were also prepared by German naval officers for the occupation authorities shortly after the end of the war.

In reconstructing what actually happened in the midst of actions involving dozens of ships and U-boats, cloaked usually in darkness, and subject to confusion and sometimes chaos, it is unlikely that we will ever learn the truth concerning many events. Some of the secrets are forever with men long dead, and there they will remain. In the bitter struggle for survival, and of killing or being killed, not all men acted with heroism or even common discipline. The wonder is not that a few failed, but that for the most part the fighting men on both sides acted with courage, dignity, and a long-enduring fortitude under conditions that few men have had to face.

I am especially indebted to Dr. Jurgen Rohwer, Director of the Library for Contemporary History in Stuttgart, Germany, for his painstaking analysis of material which I gathered, for his frank and penetrating criticism of some of my conclusions, and for much valuable data on individual U-boat torpedo attacks.

Himself a former U-boat man, and a widely known writer and historian, Dr. Rohwer is probably the outstanding authority today on the history of U-boat operations in World War II.

I am also grateful to Rear Admiral P. N. Buckley, C. B., D.S.O., Royal Navy (Ret.), and others in the Naval Historical Branch of the British Ministry of Defence for their assistance in providing data, and especially for answering numerous questions regarding the fate of British vessels.

Vice-Admiral B. C. Watson, C.B., D.S.O, Royal Navy (Ret.), was most helpful in providing information from his diary, in recalling many events of those days, and in suggesting improvements which have been incorporated into the manuscript. The opportunity to see the Admiral again years after seeing his ship torpedoed was one of the many highlights of writing this book.

Rear Admiral D. W. Piers, D.S.C., C.B., Royal Canadian Navy (Ret.), made available his records of the actions, and contributed his time and constructive criticism, which were invaluable in deriving an accurate picture of the events.

Vice-Admiral Roy L. Raney, USCG (Ret.), a fine escort commander with whom I was privileged to serve in three oceans, was very helpful in his recollections of the events around Convoy SC-118, and the subsequent rescue of survivors.

For information and background on the late Korvettenkapitän Siegfried Freiherr von Forstner, I am indebted to his widow, Annamaria, now Frau Karl Rapp, and to his only surviving brother, Korvettenkapitän Wolfgang-Friedrich Freiherr von Forstner, German Navy, himself a former U-boat commander.

Mr. Dean Allard, Mrs. Mildred D. Mayeux, and Mr. Harry E. Rilley of the Division of Naval History, Chief of Naval Operations, were most efficient and helpful in providing me with dozens of documents, as well as researching and finding the answers to endless questions which I posed. Without them, the research would have proved impossible to complete.

Captain Joseph R. Steele, USCG, and Mr. Henry Winters, of U.S. Coast Guard Headquarters, contributed many hours of their time in translating German documents and letters, and I am much in their debt.

For her cooperation in digging out photographs from the Archives, I give my thanks here, as on other occasions, to Miss Elizabeth Segedi of the Public Information Division, U.S. Coast Guard Headquarters.

In obtaining information on many aspects of the German side of the picture, I would have been lost without the great help of Captain Helmut Schmoeckel, the German Naval Attaché in Washington. He not only answered numerous technical questions from his own experience as a U-boat commander, but through him I was able to locate many of the former U-boat men in Germany.

During a visit with Grand Admiral Karl Doenitz at his home near Hamburg, I was received with the greatest courtesy and friendliness, and the discussion was most helpful. The Admiral emphasized that his ten years imprisonment in Spandau after the Nuremburg trials had no connection with the manner in which his men fought, and should not reflect adversely on them. His point was well taken. The German submariners fought an unrestricted warfare, but in an almost identical manner with that admitted by their British and American counterparts.[1] Admiral Doenitz was obviously sensitive about the large number of U-boat men lost at sea, which included one of his two sons. The other was lost in an I-boat. Though he realized clearly that the Battle of the Atlantic was lost after May, 1943, the huge Allied resources tied up by a relatively few U-boats at sea mandated that the fight be continued in spite of appalling losses. As the architect of the U-boat war, and later Commander-in-Chief of the Navy, no other figure in the German armed forces exerted such an influence on Allied strategy, or so threatened their final victory.

[1] After thousands of U-boat attacks, only one commander, Kapitänleutnant Eck in U-852, was convicted of attacking survivors. He and his officers were executed by British firing squad on November 30, 1945. The incident provided the background for Gwyn Griffen's best selling novel, *An Operational Necessity.*

Lastly, I am deeply grateful to Rear Admiral Otto Kretschmer, German Navy, formerly Chief of Staff, Allied Forces, Baltic Approaches, for preparing the foreword to the book. The top-scoring submariner of World War II, with over 300,000 tons of shipping, no man is better qualified by combat experience to speak for the men of the U-boat arm. His exploits as a U-boat commander, and his later almost unbelievable escape from a prisoner-of-war camp have been told by Terance Robertson in his book *The Golden Horseshoe*. Captain Donald MacIntyre, Royal Navy, who sank Kretschmer's U-99 and captured him and his crew in 1941, gives this profile of him at the time:

> Otto Kretschmer was the most dangerous enemy of them all. Utterly fearless, supremely confident of his skill as a seaman and a fighter and devoted single-heartedly to his career in the navy, he commanded his U-boat with the iron hand of a martinet, bringing his crew to the highest pitch of efficiency, yet earning their complete devotion. Not for Kretschmer the boastful speeches, the theatrical gestures, the contemptuous over-confidence in the face of the enemy. His equals found him hard to know, nicknaming him "Silent Otto." The hero-worship which was showered on him and the glamour which his name evoked were equally distasteful to him. Compared with his exuberant fellow aces he seemed a sinister figure. Out in the wastes of the North Atlantic he and U-99 were indeed a sinister and deadly menace. . . .

Though at the turning point of the Battle of the Atlantic, Kretschmer was a prisoner-of-war, many of the officers he had personally trained as student-commanders had risen to command of U-boats, and as will be seen in the narrative, several of them tried us sorely.

This latest edition contains the story of Ultra, the amazing code breaking operation of the British at Bletchley Park, which has only been released in part over 30 years after the events.[2] No history of major actions in Europe in World War II can be complete and in perspective without examining the impact of the British ability to intercept and quickly decode the most secret communications of an unsuspecting enemy. This cryptographic breakthrough was a primary factor in the outcome of the war, but due to the highly classified nature of Ultra, only a select few knew the source of this crucial intelligence, and they guarded the secret zealously, even in their own published memoirs, until it was officially released by the British government, beginning in 1976. The revelations of Ultra will force future historians to reevaluate many of the leaders and crucial events of World War II.

In the war at sea, Ultra had a profound effect. But in the crucial period covered by this book, Ultra penetration of the German naval codes was sporadic and at times non-existent. Even when available, the lack of adequate Allied forces to act promptly on the information diminished its value. The most complete knowledge of the enemy's intentions is not decisive without the means to thwart him. Not until mid-1943 did we have adequate ships, aircraft, and equipment to act on the unprecedented intelligence provided by Ultra, and the combination, notably demonstrated by the Hunter/Killer and Support Groups, exacted a terrible retribution from the U-boat fleet in the final two years of the war.

2 See Appendix II, Ultra—Riddle Within An Enigma.

CONTENTS

I

THE ANTAGONISTS

Over the radio came the escort commander's terse order *Raspberry Crack!* and seconds later the first gunflashes broke the early morning blackness, followed by the dull yellow glow of starshells hanging almost motionless in the sky. Many of the merchant ships stood out clearly, and further away from the dozens of starshells and flares others loomed as shadows in the night. The convoy of 50 ships, seven miles across the front and two miles in depth, moved slowly but relentlessly onward, while around them in a protecting cordon, the men-of-war of the escort raced in a preplanned pattern, attempting by the dim light of the starshells to locate the U-boats that had struck still another blow at their charges.

Five miles astern, the convoy rescue vessel, screened by a patrolling corvette, was picking up the oil-covered survivors of a sunken tanker. The rescue crew worked with a speed born of desperation, knowing that life for a swimmer in the cold waters of the winter North Atlantic is measured in fractions of an hour, and the tanker was only one of several ships that had been hit. Other survivors were in the water ahead, and those not fortunate enough to be in lifeboats or rafts had little time remaining.

The escort commander, fully aware that men with whose safety he was charged were dying in the night astern of the convoy, had made his harsh and agonizing choice—he would send no other escorts back to help. To further deplete the screen around the merchantmen would invite even greater losses, for the U-boats, greatly outnumbering his force, were hanging onto the flanks of the convoy, seeking an opening to dash in and launch more torpedoes. For three days the fight had raged, with quarters neither given nor asked, and no end was in sight. When the starshells died out and darkness again enveloped the convoy, the escorts resumed their stations in the protective screen, their radars sweeping, underwater sound-detection gear probing the depths, and lookouts straining for a view of a low-lying silhouette that could be a U-boat running on the surface.

This bitter fight had no name, only the convoy designation and number, and a position marked by latitude and longitude. Most historians call the great series of actions the Battle of the Atlantic, while a few designate them collectively as the Battle of the Convoys. In nearly six years of fighting, extending over thousands of miles of ocean, 2,828 merchant ships, 158 Allied warships, and 781 German U-boats were to meet their death, carrying with them over 45,000 Allied merchant and naval seamen and 32,000 men of the Kriegsmarine, a toll greater than all the other naval battles of the past 500 years combined.

When the fighting reached new heights of fury in March, 1943, the losses in the trade convoys rose to such terrible proportions that serious doubts arose as to whether the convoy system was still effective and should be continued. If the great merchant convoys, carrying the food, oil, and munitions from the New World to the Old were to be terminated, where would the Allies turn? No one knew, but the implications of such a step were far-reaching and terrible, for this complex system of trade protection had twice in a quarter of a century saved the Allies from defeat, and until the catastrophes of the winter of 1942-43, its abandonment would have been unthinkable.

Convoys are not new; the British used them as early as the thirteenth century to protect their cross-channel shipping. Some of these early convoys consisted of 200 sail, escorted by up to two dozen men-of-war, and directed by two King's officers: the commodore of convoy, in charge of the merchant vessels; and the escort commander, in command of the warships. But even at that early date, merchant sailors and the ship owners were reluctant to sail their ships in convoy, and Edward III had to forbid independent sailings by Royal Edict.

In the sixteenth century, the losses of galleons between their overseas colonies and Spain became so serious that the Spanish also instituted convoys. Covered by powerful warships, known as the Indian Guard, these convoys were so effective that privateers were never able to capture the convoyed treasure ships. They did, however, succeed in taking many vessels sailing independently.

The Anglo-Dutch wars of the seventeenth century saw both sides using convoys, covered often by the main fleets, and the attempts of the British fleet to interfere with Dutch convoys led in nearly every instance to major actions.

Convoy was an accepted practice in the Napoleonic wars and was obligatory for all English ships; Lloyd's would not insure those sailing independently. The huge convoys were conducted in accordance with carefully developed instructions and procedures, many of which were still applicable a century later. The necessity for convoys was unquestioned by naval officers as the Napoleonic era ended in 1815.

For nearly 100 years after that, no major sea wars were fought, and with the possible exception of the threat occasioned by a few Confederate raiders against Union shipping, the need for convoys never arose. In the absence of an immediate and compelling threat, convoys—with their inconveniences and the connotation of a defensive strategy—slipped into an undeserved disrepute. To replace them, the Royal Navy evolved new and untested theories for protection of merchant shipping. In all fairness to the naval thinkers of those peacetime decades, they were not confronted with the submarine, which had not yet developed as a usable weapon. Planning was concerned with the threat of a small number of surface raiders operating against merchant shipping, and limited by the necessity to coal at frequent intervals. With the numerical superiority of the British fleet unchallenged, and possessing secure bases around the world (which no likely opponent had), it would only be a matter of time before British cruisers would run down and eliminate the raiders. Some losses were expected, but were deemed of little consequence in comparison with the administrative and tactical problems caused by convoys.

The opponents of the convoy system, and this included the majority of naval officers in the years immediately before the First World War, had developed a number of arguments to support their views. Some were difficult to refute, for the long years of peace had precluded the acid test of new naval theory—combat at sea.

Arrival of large numbers of ships at one time would, they maintained, overcrowd port facilities, resulting in congestion and long delays. Convoys sail at the speed of the slowest vessel, and faster vessels would have to dawdle wastefully along with the others. Finally, few naval planners of the era thought that sufficient number of warships could be mustered to adequately escort the large number of convoys that would be required.

Because of the loss of revenue, the shipping companies themselves were reluctant to accept the slow speeds and long periods in port awaiting the make-up of convoys. Merchant seamen—an independent group jealous of their prerogatives—resisted being subjected to naval discipline and the many demands and constant alertness required during a convoy operation. Everyone desired a system of protection that would keep the merchant vessels moving as in peacetime with a minimum of interference from both their own and the enemy's navies.

In such an atmosphere, it was natural that the concept of patrols "keeping open the sea lanes" by sweeping the oceans should be quickly accepted, not only by the merchant marine but by naval officers, who naturally gravitated to an "offensive" concept rather than one in which warships were tied down to the unglamorous task of defending slow-moving convoys. In dealing with submarines such a concept ignored the fact that after the warship on patrol had swept through an area of ocean the water was as unprotected as it had been before. Few would admit that, despite the patrolling ships and the distant presence of the main fleet, such a system offered no direct protection to a merchant ship.

The coming of the submarine invalidated this new strategy even before it was applied, but the anti-convoy school of thought refused to acknowledge the changed situation. In what may appear to the modern reader to be classic naïveté, an implicit reliance was placed on the Rules of War as laid down by the Hague Convention. These rules denied the right of any warship to sink an unescorted merchant ship without warning, and without insuring that the crew had a safe means of reaching land. Compliance would, of course, so handicap a submarine that its usefulness in a war against commerce would be severely limited.

As a result of this unwarranted faith in the patrolling of sea lanes, and the failure to fully appreciate the U-boat's potential as a commerce destroyer, Britain entered World War I with no preparations for convoying nor any intentions of so doing. Fortunately, the Germans were no more enamored with the U-boat's potential than the British, and they entered the war with just 28 U-boats and only vague ideas on employing them against merchant shipping. Because of its desire to avoid trouble with the neutrals, Germany until the end of 1916 did, in fact, observe many of the principles of the Hague Convention. Most merchant ships sunk by U-boats were stopped on the surface and the crew allowed to abandon ship. Yet, even under these restrictions, a relatively small number of U-boats had succeeded in sinking over 1,300 ships by the beginning of 1917. Thousands of Allied warships, blimps, and aircraft patrolling the sea lanes in offensive sweeps during the same period had managed to sink only four submarines. The failure of such tactics to blunt the U-boat offensive was painfully clear, but merchant shipping losses were still in the acceptable range, and enough supplies were still arriving in Britain to postpone a crisis.

With an intensified building program, and few losses, the U-boat fleet by 1917 had been increased to 100 operational U-boats. Finally, on February 1, 1917, all restrictions were removed, and an all-out campaign began in order to starve Britain into submission. The result for the Allies were catastrophic.

In the three months after the start of unrestricted U-boat warfare, 800 ships totalling 2,000,000 tons were sunk. In the black month of April, 1917, a total of 420 ships of 881,000 tons were lost. The grain reserves in the Islands were down to six weeks, and the government put the limit of endurance as November 1st at the latest.

The First Sea Lord, Admiral Sir John Jellicoe, warned the War Cabinet that they must face the fact that the Navy had neither command of the sea nor even a reasonable measure of command. "If we do not recognize this," he declared, "it is my firm conviction that we shall lose the war by the starvation of our people and the paralyzing of our Allies by failing to supply them with coal and other essentials." Yet, in the face of the appalling situation, the Admiralty still resisted the introduction of convoys. One of the prime reasons was their contention that insufficient escorts were available to cover the arriving and departing vessels, estimated at 2,500 each way, weekly. In actual fact, the figure was some 130 ocean-going vessels weekly, a fact discovered by two junior commanders in the Admiralty. The larger figure had been based on all vessels of 300 tons and over, even including ferries. That such a miscalculation could occur when the nation's very existence was at stake was a damning indictment of the lack of "homework" by the Admiralty.

In the worsening crisis, the ship owners and the Merchant Navy should have been vocal supporters of the demand for close protection of merchant vessels. In fact, they proved to be as reluctant as the Admiralty. Part of the blame can be laid to the government's insurance scheme, which made good all losses by private shipping companies resulting from enemy action. The government had replaced Lloyd's as the prime insurer, and without the pressure of increased insurance rates, there was no economic coercion to sail in convoy.

It remained for the French to supply the impetus needed. Being vitally concerned with and dependent on the cross-channel coal trade, they demanded that the colliers be sailed in convoy, and the Admiralty agreed to do so. With the start of these convoys in February, 1917, the colliers, which had been suffering heavy losses, gained almost complete protection. In the North, Admiral Sir David Beatty, commanding the Grand Fleet, obtained grudging permission from the Admiralty to commence escorting convoys to Scandinavia, and losses on that route dropped radically.

Despite the critical situation, and the obvious success of the two convoy routes already in operation, the Admiralty refused to extend the system. It remained for Prime Minister Lloyd George, armed with information supplied by junior officers at the Admiralty, to force the issue. He advised the First Sea Lord that he would come to the Admiralty for a discussion of the matter, and the note left little doubt as to his intentions. The Admiralty had a change of heart, and when the Prime Minister arrived, recommended widespread instigation of the convoy system.

The results were dramatic. Losses in convoy promptly dropped to 10 per cent of those suffered by independent ships. By the turn of the year, though much hard fighting was ahead, the crisis was past.

The lessons of 700 years of sea convoys had been reaffirmed and were not quickly forgotten again. In 1939, convoy plans were ready and were quickly implemented on the outbreak of World War II.

But Allied planners had almost completely disregarded the tremendous benefits to be derived from aerial protection of convoys. Of 257 ships sunk in convoy in World War I, only five were lost when aircraft augmented the surface escort. Despite the obvious conclusions to be drawn, World War II found the Allies unprepared to provide long-range air coverage for convoys, and hundreds of fine ships and thousands of seamen were lost due to this lack. Not until 1943 were the necessary aircraft provided, with startling results as we shall see later.

Another lesson of World War I which failed to carry over to the second conflict was the futility of sweeping and search operations by warships in the open ocean far removed from convoys. By its very nature and ease of concealment, a submarine which is concerned only with its own safety is a very difficult creature to locate and kill. The Royal Navy began anti-submarine operations in September, 1939, with a division of effort. Some escorts were assigned to convoy protection; but many others were diverted to hunting operations in the open sea. With the exception of a couple of perhaps over-confident U-boat commanders sunk in the first weeks, no kills were made by these ocean sweeps. The exposure of valuable fleet units in this wild goose chase had a predictable outcome, and the aircraft carrier COURAGEOUS was torpedoed and sunk in September by a U-boat. Another carrier was saved from a similar fate only because of faulty U-boat torpedoes.

The proponents of convoy had failed to sell one obvious truth —that the close escort of a convoy by screening vessels is not a defensive tactic alone. One of the most successful British escort commanders of World War II stated: "Convoy is the essence of offense, for instead of dispersing your forces in search of an enemy whose object is to avoid them, it forces the enemy to scatter his forces in search of your shipping and when he finds it either to fight on your own ground and your own terms in order to reach your shipping or to remain impotent." [1] Hunting of submarines is most productive where large numbers of them are

---

[1] P. Gretton, *Convoy Escort Commander* (London: Cassell & Co. Ltd., 1964), p. 199. The view was nearly identical with that expressed by American Admiral W. S. Sims nearly fifty years before.

concentrated, and around the convoys is "where the boys are." Once this basic truth was accepted, warships were withdrawn from area-sweeping operations and assigned to the convoys. The kill-rate of U-boats immediately rose. Not even the most daring U-boat commanders desired to attack strongly-escorted convoys, for the risk was too great. The top aces such as Kretschmer, Schepke, and Prien made most of their kills against ships sailing independently or in weakly-escorted convoys.

No one realized this difficulty better than Admiral Karl Doenitz, Flag Officer, U-boats, and himself once a top-flight combat U-boat commander. Describing his experiences in World War I, he said:

> In the First World War, the German U-boat arm achieved great successes; but the introduction of the convoy system in 1917 robbed it of its opportunity to become a decisive factor. The oceans at once became bare and empty; for long periods at a time, the U-boats operating individually would see nothing at all, and then suddenly up would loom a huge concourse of ships—thirty or fifty or more of them— surrounded by a strong escort of warships of all types. The solitary U-boat, which most probably had sighted the convoy purely by chance, would then attack, thrusting again and again and persisting, if the commander had strong nerves, for perhaps several days and nights, until the physical exhaustion of both commander and crew called a halt. The lone U-boat might well sink one or two of the ships, or even several, but that was a poor percentage of the whole. The convoy would steam on.[2]

During the first three and a half years of World War II, the convoy escorts were in most cases inadequate in number, and escort commanders could seldom spare ships to stay with and work over a U-boat contact until it was destroyed. The defense of the convoy took priority. By early 1943, however, enough escorts were available to form up special Support Groups, which reinforced threatened convoys, but were not directly charged with their close defense. Operating in the vicinity of the convoys

[2] Karl Doenitz, *Memoirs of Ten Years and Twenty Days* (Bonn: Athenaum-Verlag Junkerund Dunnhaupt, 1958), p. 4.

and freed from the necessity of maintaining a close screen, they were able to hit at the gathering U-boats and stick with the contact to destruction. The toll of U-boats mounted steadily. Before the war ended, large numbers of these Support Groups (called Hunter-Killer Groups by the Americans) were roving the oceans. But conspicuous success was obtained only by those which operated in the vicinity of convoys, or were able to move into concentrations of submarines which had been located by radio intelligence.

The convoy system in itself was not the answer to the U-boat, but it did provide a means within which scientific developments, new tactics, increasing forces and, above all, the tremendous effort and courage of the personnel of the Allied Navies and Merchant Marine finally defeated the U-boat. It was a battle that came near to disaster before the final victory.

That it did not was due to the surprising unpreparedness of the German Navy for a war which it had neither expected nor desired. The Kriegsmarine, forbidden by the Treaty of Versailles from having U-boats, did not build the first of its new underseas fleet until 1935. When war broke out four years later, it possessed a mere 46 boats ready for action, only 22 of which were suitable for service in the Atlantic. With time required for maintenance and passage to and from the patrol areas, an average of only six U-boats on station at sea were available to wage war on Allied merchant shipping.

While much of the blame for this unpreparedness rested with Hitler and his myopic continental strategy, the situation was not improved by the inability of the German Navy itself to reconcile many conflicting views as to the use of U-boats in war and the type of boat required. Consequently, the building program was repeatedly postponed, and in the three years before the outbreak of war, only 28 U-boats were built. For a nation embarked on a road of aggression, and facing as a probable enemy the world's greatest maritime power, the failure to heed the obvious lessons of the First World War seems incomprehensible.

Sir Winston Churchill's post-war judgment was that "The U-boat attack was our worst evil. It would have been wise for the Germans to stake all upon it." [3]

But if the obvious was lost on Hitler and the government, it had in no way escaped Admiral Doenitz, who had impatiently bided his time during the years after the First World War when Germany had no submarines. When U-boat construction began again, he was the logical man to entrust with the new arm. A single-minded naval genius, passionately believing in the U-boat as a decisive weapon, he threw himself body and soul into the build-up of the U-boat arm. Frustrated by indecision in the government and Navy in building up a numerically adequate force, he turned his abundant talents toward its training and tactics. By 1939, the small U-boat force was superbly trained and its boats were ton for ton the best in the world. From this small group of operational U-boat men would come the high-scoring "aces," and the men who would form the cadres for new boats coming out of the building yards. They were highly-trained, dedicated professionals with high *esprit de corps*. The rapport between the Admiral and his U-boat commanders was exceptional, and loyalty was strong "up and down." [4] It was so through their days of triumph in the "happy times" of 1940, and it was to remain so with their ebb of fortune and final crushing defeat.

The confidence of Doenitz and his young men was not shared by others in the Navy. The convoy system had proven a very effective antidote for the U-boat threat in the First World War, and conditions did not appear to have improved for the submariners in the intervening years. In fact, the Royal Navy had in the post-war years perfected a new underwater detection de-

[3] Winston Churchill, *The Second World War*, Vol. IV (Boston: The Houghton Mifflin Company, 1950), p. 125.

[4] Even today, his former commanders speak of him with admiration. One, recalling the personal messages from the flag officer, U-boats, to his commanders at sea, told of the radio message sent by Doenitz to his leading ace, Korvettenkapitän Günther Prien, on the birth of Prien's daughter. It read, "Ein U-boot ohne Schrehr ist heute angekommen." (A submarine without periscope arrived today.)

vice called *Asdic*, whose secret was guarded carefully, but which was reputed to be many times more effective than the earlier hydrophone listening equipment, and able to pinpoint the position of a submerged submarine at a range of several thousand yards.[5] To many profound thinkers in the realm of naval science, the submarine was obsolete.

Using the tactics of the Kaiser's war, it may have been. But Karl Doenitz had no intention of fighting the same type of war. Since 1918, he had believed that the best means of attacking a convoy was by hitting it with large numbers of U-boats simultaneously, preferably on the surface at night. A U-boat, with its low silhouette, was extremely difficult to see in darkness, and in most cases could see and avoid an escort before being detected itself. By running on the surface, the U-boat could travel at high speed, whereas a submerged boat was forced to travel so slowly that it was for all practical purposes immobilized. A surfaced boat had a further advantage; it could not be detected by the escort vessel's Asdic equipment, and radar was still in the future.

There was much work to be accomplished before such theory became standard operating procedure, and when the first new U-boat flotilla was commissioned in 1935, development of group night surface tactics took priority. Night surface attacks had been conducted by a few enterprising skippers in 1918, and had proven feasible and effective. But the submarines of that day had such poor communications equipment that it was impossible to exercise control of a large number from a central command post. When a convoy was sighted, other boats could not be contacted and directed to the convoy. But by 1938, naval maneuvers had proved conclusively that a large number of U-boats could be directed by improved radio onto a convoy, where they could attack by night on the surface with devastating results. In 1939, Doenitz published a book, *Die U-bootwaffe,* in which he clearly advocated this form of attack. Strangely enough, it appears to have made little impression at the time in British naval circles.

[5] See Appendix I, page 239.

The first year of the Second World War found the U-boats operating singly, much in the fashion of the previous conflict. Not until the early fall of 1940 did Doenitz have enough boats available to put his new tactics to use. They were immediate and deadly in their effect. The British were caught unprepared and convoy after convoy was slaughtered by concentrations of U-boats running swiftly through the columns on the surface. The months that followed were known in U-boats as the "happy time." The concentrations of U-boats were called "wolf packs" by the Allies, and by the Germans, *Die Rudeltaktik*.[6] Its principle was described by Doenitz as "being as strong as possible in the right place at the right time." [7]

It was against these men and tactics that the battles of the convoys were fought. The tide of conflict surged to and fro with no quarter given or asked. The wolf packs played havoc with shipping, and England was more than once pushed to the edge of defeat. Though most of the convoys somehow fought through, losses were appalling. With 1941 came radar, able sometimes to detect the surfaced U-boats at night. Mid-year saw increasing American help, and the flow of supplies, though diminished, continued. The entry of America into the war brought a second "happy time" for the U-boats as they rampaged along a nearly undefended American coast and in less than six months sank over two-and-a-half million tons of shipping, equal to half of the total tonnage of the American merchant marine. A mere handful of U-boats manned by less than 600 men inflicted incomparably greater damage than did the mighty Japanese Mobile Fleet during the same period at Pearl Harbor, the Coral Sea, and Midway. Yet the Germans, caught unaware by the Japanese attack at Pearl Harbor, were unprepared for warfare off the American coast, and were never able to mount a concerted campaign before the Americans rallied their forces and drove the U-boats away in

---

[6] Literally "herd or pack tactics."
[7] Which was akin to Confederate General Nathan Bedford Forrest's, "Git thar fustest with the mostest."

mid-1942.[8] Had they been forewarned and able to deploy a major portion of their boats on station prior to America's entrance into the war, it is highly likely that they could have effected a total blockade of the east coast and effectively closed every American port.

The inability to deal with even the small group of U-boats off our coast was a damning indictment of the complete lack of American ASW preparedness; two years of submarine warfare in Europe and the Atlantic should have given ample warning. Only after four months of slaughter did we institute coastal convoys, scrape up the required ships and aircraft, and finally force the U-boats to seek greener pastures. It was a black and unforgivable episode in our military history, and few of the key participants emerged unstained.[9]

But the crisis was still to come. The rising manpower and war products of America had to be transported to Europe and most of it would be in the great merchant and troop convoys. U-boat Command possessed the only means of stopping them. As 1942 arrived, Germany threw all its shipbuilding resources into a mighty U-boat build-up. Ninety new boats joined the fleet between July and October. Doenitz believed that with 300 U-boats he could win the Battle of the Atlantic. The battle had become a race between the German build-up and the construction of Allied escort vessels and aircraft, between the merchant tonnage sunk and new construction replacements, and between the introduction of new equipment and tactics by one side, and countermeasures by the other.

The decision lay ahead on the stormy North Atlantic convoy lanes. October, 1942, to May, 1943, would see the Battle of the Atlantic reach its ultimate fury. It was to be remembered as the Bloody Winter.

---

[8] The Germans opened the attack with only 5 U-boats on station and never mustered more than 12.

[9] Naval planners today, faced with a potential enemy having far greater submarine resources and the ability to deploy before hostilities, would be well advised to restudy in detail the 1942 East Coast debacle.

II

OCTOBER / PRELUDE

TO DISASTER

On October 20, 1942, the Convoy and Routing Section of Commander in Chief, U. S. Fleet (COMINCH), transmitted an encrypted secret radio message to British authorities concerning the forthcoming sailing of Convoy SC-107, due to depart New York on October 24th for England. The pre-sailing conference of ship captains, the convoy commodore, and the escort commander was scheduled for the following day in New York.

The conference was held as scheduled. Another conference, hurriedly called, met the same week, not in New York, but at the Headquarters of the German U-boat Command on the Avenue Maréchal Maunoury in Paris. The subject of both conferences was the same—the sailing of Convoy SC-107. U-boat Command had the complete deciphered message on routing and composition of the convoy!

The compromise of the secret Allied code was not due to treachery, but to the highly efficient German Navy *Beobachter Dienst* or Observation Service (B-Service) which monitored Allied radio traffic and tried to decipher it. Created during the thirties, and working on the British Fleet's outmoded system of hand ciphering which was used to handle large volumes of radio traffic in the Abyssinian crisis and the Spanish Civil War, B-Service cracked the relatively simple British codes early in the game. During the early months of the war, the Germans held a commanding lead in code breaking until the British changed to machine-ciphered fleet codes in 1940, and the brilliant British Ultra team began its inroads into the German's Enigma machine ciphers. Unfortunately, the British made no change to their British and Allied Merchant Ship (BAMS) code until 1943, and for nearly four years B-Service was privy to the most detailed convoy composition and routing secrets. This terrible and still unexplained lapse generously supplied the U-boats with abundant prey and SC-107 was to be only the latest burnt offering. Although the speed of advance of Convoy SC-107 could vary, and tactical diversions from the course might be made, Admiral Doenitz had already had a look into his opponent's hand. To the south of Greenland and off the foggy Newfoundland banks, he figuratively had 15 trumps. Their collective name was U-boat Group *Violet*.

It was as well for the peace of mind of the captains of the convoy vessels that all this was unknown to them as they gathered for the sailing conference on the afternoon of October 21st. Of the 28 masters and commanding officers gathered in the room, all ages and types were represented; many were in civilian dress, and the rest were in a variety of uniforms representing five nations and numerous shipping lines.

After the confidential books and documents were passed out, the briefing took nearly an hour. As he completed his presentation, the young U. S. Navy briefing officer re-emphasized certain points:

> Don't dump refuse; it could give away the fact that the convoy has passed that spot. Try to keep your smoke at a minimum during daylight; it's a sure giveaway to any U-boat within 25 miles. Be sure that no lights are showing at night, and that includes the captain's cigarette. Above all, gentlemen, maintain a proper station within the convoy. I know it is crowded, but collisions are second only to the Jerries as a cause of ship losses.[1] If you are inclined to chuck it all, and romp or straggle where you have more room, don't! It is a very likely way to buy the farm. Good luck and smooth sailing.

Next, the escort commander of the Western Local Escort, a young Royal Navy commander, the skipper of the destroyer WALKER, briefed them. His job was to escort them to a position off Newfoundland, where the mid-ocean escort would take over. The escort commander would be in overall command

---

[1] During the war, one-fourth of all ship losses were due to collision, foundering, and marine casualties not directly attributable to enemy action.

of the convoy, both warships and merchantmen, and his was the ultimate responsibility for their defense and safe arrival.

British and Canadian escort commanders were also captains of their own ships. An American escort commander, on the other hand, usually rode on a warship commanded by another officer, leaving him free to carry out his duties without worrying about handling the flagship. The American escort commanders also tended to be more senior than their British counterparts, often being four-stripe captains.

As he finished, the young British officer smiled and said, "Some of you are perhaps thinking that you have been past more light-houses than we Navy chaps have telephone poles. I will try to stay out of your hair as much as possible. Let me assure you that if I demand something, it will be for a good reason."

The last to speak was the convoy commodore, Vice-Admiral B. C. Watson, C.B., D.S.O., Royal Navy (Ret.). Quickly he covered how the ships in the convoy would be run, and their movements coordinated. The commodore was responsible for the administration and discipline of the merchant vessels within the convoy, keeping them closed up on station, and maneuvering them as a body when the escort commander decided course changes or emergency evasive turns were required.

The commodores of the Atlantic convoys were usually retired admirals of the Royal Navy, called back from the security of retirement to what was often a trying and thankless job, or experienced captains of the Merchant Navy. Theirs was a proud and gallant record and 21 convoy commodores died at sea—more casualties than suffered by admirals on the active list of the Royal Navy. Not only was the duty arduous and dangerous, but the commodores found themselves under the orders of escort commanders many years their juniors in rank and age.[2] There was, of course, a good reason and a necessity for this. The escort

[2] On the forthcoming convoy, Vice-Admiral Watson would be subject to the orders of the escort commander of the mid-ocean escort, Lieutenant Commander D. W. Piers, RCN, 24 years his junior and who had served under him as a lieutenant while the Vice-Admiral was commanding at Greenock.

commander had the fighting vessels, communications, and information required to defend the convoy, and by virtue of this, was in the best position to exercise overall command, seniority notwithstanding. (The necessity for the arrangement is well understood by naval officers, and generally works without friction if normal courtesies are observed.)

As Admiral Watson prepared to sail on his sixth trip as a convoy commodore, he could look back on a long and distinguished career at sea, starting as the navigator of the Harwich Cruiser Force under the famous Tyrwhitt in World War I, and between wars including commands of a sloop in China, a destroyer flotilla and a cruiser in the Mediterranean, and a battleship in the Home Fleet. In 1938, he was appointed Admiral in Command of Submarines, where he served until 1940, when at the age of 53 he was promoted vice-admiral and retired. Promptly recalled, he was assigned as flag officer in command of naval bases on the west coast of Scotland, with his headquarters at the big escort base at Greenock. After two years in this command, he began service as a convoy commodore—a far cry from the usual peace of retirement.

At that time, there was a surplus of commodores in New York, and the Admiralty ordered the convoy to also take a vice-commodore. SC-107 drew Captain Pat McKay, Royal Navy (Ret.), for the job. He was to prove a fortunate addition.

The commodore would be sailing in the SS JEYPORE, a big P&O cargo liner, which before the war had been employed in the eastern trade. The local escort, consisting of only three ships, would be under command of the young commander in HMS WALKER, and overall responsibility would be his for the first few days at sea. When the convoy reached the vicinity of Cape Race, Newfoundland, it would be joined by other merchantmen from Halifax and St. John's, and the local escort would be relieved by a mid-ocean escort group for the trans-Atlantic run.

An aerial view of a convoy at sea in the North Atlantic. USCG/National Archives

Karl Doenitz, Vice-Admiral Commanding U-boats, and the foremost tactical genius in submarine history. He was later promoted to Grand Admiral and Commander-in-Chief of the German Navy.

Two troop ships, CRISTOBAL and WAKEFIELD, loaded with troops for Europe, plow ahead at high speed through heavy seas. Virtually immune from U-boat attack because of their high speed, and heavily protected, the troop convoys escaped the terrible punishment suffered by the slow trade convoys. USCG/National Archives

The USS GEMINI (AP 75). Built in 1919, the ancient 2000-ton vessel was taken over by the Navy and converted into a transport. Slow and with no watertight compartmentation, it was a risky vessel in which to carry hundreds of troops. USN

While the staffs in New York and Paris were busy with the larger matters of convoy SC-107, the lower echelons were innocently going about their preparations. In Boston, trucks pulled into the South Boston Army Base and began to unload passengers on the pier alongside the USS GEMINI.

For the passengers, 12 Coast Guard officers and 255 Army officers and troops, the day had dawned gray and dismal; and the GEMINI blended in with the mood. An ancient Great Lakes freighter of World War I vintage that had been taken over by the Navy as a transport to help fill in the void caused by the U-boat blitz of 1942, her very appearance should have been an omen of evil times to come. This ancient scow was ample proof that we were digging deep for tonnage. She had been commissioned on August 4th and for over two months had lain alongside the pier without venturing out to sea. Her maiden voyage was to be Convoy SC-107, with an untried crew consisting mostly of new reservists.

Like the assembling passengers and crews of many of the other convoy vessels, those on GEMINI were mercifully unaware, yet there were many indications that day that things on the Atlantic were grimmer than most people ashore realized. Nearby lay the big transport WAKEFIELD, gutted by a fire at sea. During the morning, a tanker limped into the harbor, nuzzled along by four tugs, with a torpedo hole the size of a barn door in her bow. The previous day, a big HAMILTON-class cutter had pulled into an adjacent pier, her bearded crew showing the strains of weeks of relentless convoy action. But each week, the newspapers duly carried a stereotyped notation that "the Navy announced that during the past week, two medium-size freighters were sunk on the North Atlantic." The Navy was, by necessity, lying through its teeth.

The entrance of America into the war in December, 1941, had found the U. S. Navy woefully unprepared to deal with the submarine menace. Despite the disastrous and nearly fatal experience with U-boats in 1917 and 1918, and the bitter battle between the U-boats and the British after 1939, American measures to meet the threat were hopelessly inadequate. The Navy's eyes were on the Pacific.

In the entire Atlantic, thanks to the increasing number and quality of escort vessels, the British loss rate in merchant vessels during 1941 had been much lighter than in the last half of 1940. But beginning in January, 1942, Doenitz deployed six U-boats to the East Coast of the United States, and turned it into a slaughter pen for coastal shipping. Our unpreparedness and ineptness could have seemed ludicrous had it not been so tragic. There was no coastal convoy system and little effective anti-submarine effort. Not until April was the first submarine sunk by an American surface vessel, the USS ROPER, followed shortly thereafter by the sinking of U-352 by the Coast Guard Cutter ICARUS, and U-157 by Cutter THETIS.

In the same month, authorities belatedly began enforcing a blackout along the coast, and merchantmen were finally able to sail coastwise without being silhouetted against the shore lights as easy targets for waiting U-boats. By June, 360 merchant ships totaling 2,250,000 tons had been sunk along the American coastline at the cost of only eight U-boats. Finally, coastal convoys were organized, escorts and aircraft were belatedly scraped up, and in July, the Germans began deploying to the Caribbean or back to the North Atlantic due to the tougher defenses being evidenced in the American coastal areas.

While the pickings were easy in American coastal waters, Doenitz had stationed only a few boats on the trans-Atlantic route to keep the escorts honest, and sinkings in the high latitudes dropped drastically during the first half of 1942. But as the U-boats moved back to the northern convoy lanes in mid-summer, the losses there rose rapidly. August and September were bad months, and the area of heaviest losses once again became the North Atlantic. With a rapidly increasing number of new U-boats reporting into the Atlantic operational areas from the

Baltic training grounds, the Allied outlook grew darker. That the all-out U-boat blitz was making up was now a certainty; only the timing remained in doubt.

But these matters of large import were locked up in the conference rooms of London, Washington, Berlin, and Paris, and the junior officers, not being privy to the big picture, could enjoy their last hours on shore. There were few sad hearts among them as they made ready to sail for the big adventure.

But all was not joy in Boston. GEMINI was scheduled for Iceland, and in addition to a general cargo, and the small group of Coast Guard officers destined for the escort cutters of Task Group 24.6 operating from that strategic mid-ocean escort base, she was carrying a contingent of Army troops for the Iceland garrison. It was not preferred duty, but the troops, like troops everywhere in every war, tramped aboard with resignation to endure the trip in an unfamiliar environment. The Coast Guard passengers, mostly new Academy or OCS[3] graduates, with a sprinkling of experienced lieutenant commanders, were at least going to assignments of their own choosing. The Army men had not even that compensation. But Army, Navy, and Coast Guard alike, they were all approaching the end of innocence.

After reporting aboard, they were assigned to bunk rooms below decks, not the type of accommodations naval officers usually have, but the best the ship had to offer, and the trip would be of only two weeks' duration. Late in the afternoon, GEMINI cleared Boston Harbor, for the first time in many months feeling the motion of the sea as she headed for New York to join the convoy.

Three days later, the convoy formed up as it departed New York Harbor, the little blue and white camouflaged destroyer and corvettes working like sheep dogs rounding the flock into some semblance of order, and hurrying to finish the job before darkness. The destroyer steamed down the lanes of the convoy with its blinker light flashing and signal flags whipping in the

---

[3] OCS—Officer Candidate School for training reserve officers.

wind as the escort commander made a last bed check for the night. The rust-streaked veteran of numerous convoys was a welcome sight for the Naval and merchant crews lining the rails of the 22 convoy vessels, and the name WALKER was one to inspire confidence in anyone who knew her history. In March, 1941, she had teamed up with HMS VANOC to sink U-99 and U-100, skippered by Kretschmer and Schepke, two of Doenitz's top three "aces." During the same week, HMS WOLVERINE had sunk Prien, the third of the top trio. Weak though the escort was numerically, the presence of WALKER indicated that some of the first string were in the game. The old pros—the Royal Navy— were still delivering the goods after three bitter years of relentless struggle. Their losses had been heavy, and at times the battle had hung in the balance, but they had always come through in the crisis, due to the dogged tenacity of the British and Canadian escorts as they met attack after attack. American reinforcements were still of a token nature on the North Atlantic, and it would be over a year before their full weight was felt.

As the "tin can" came up the last column and moved out with a bone in her teeth to take up night screening station several thousand yards ahead of the main body, the other two escorts— a minesweeper and a corvette—could barely be seen on each side of the convoy. One on either beam, and a destroyer ahead, a weak escort for a 22-ship convoy! But this was only the local escort. The mid-ocean group would undoubtedly be stronger.

An SC convoy, operating from New York to Great Britain, was supposed to make good a speed of only seven knots. The faster merchantmen went in the nine-knot HX convoys.[4] After leaving New York, the convoy was escorted for the first several days by the small local escort group, reinforced on the third day by another destroyer. On Thursday, October 29th, when north of Sable Island, an escorting aircraft dropped a white flare ahead of the convoy—the signal that a submarine had been sighted. The

---

[4] In actual practice, most convoys were about one or two knots slower than their scheduled speeds.

convoy made an emergency turn to port, and the two escorting destroyers hurried out over the horizon to the southeast. It proved to be a wild goose chase. The aircraft and ships were unable to maintain communications with each other, and after dark the two destroyers rejoined. All night, the northern horizon provided a brilliant display of the Aurora Borealis, with long flickering streamers turning the night almost into day, but the convoy was not molested.

Just after noon on October 30th, the destroyer HMCS CO-LUMBIA, 22 miles astern of the convoy, sighted a surfaced U-boat on the same course as the convoy, but chased it down before it sighted the merchantmen.

As the convoy passed close under Cape Race to take its departure from the American continent, 6 merchantmen from Sydney and 16 from Halifax joined up, swelling the convoy to 42 ships. The same afternoon, the mid-ocean escort arrived and took over from the local escort for the trip across.

The mid-ocean group was disappointingly weak for so large a convoy. In addition to the destroyer HMCS RESTIGOUCHE, the only fast vessel, there were four small FLOWER-class corvettes capable of only 16 knots.

The corvette, despite its tradition-laden name borrowed from the days of sail, was not a true man-of-war, but an offspring of the small whaling vessel. During World War I, a number of escort officers had observed that submarines had much in common with whales. They often surfaced and made off at high speed; they turned quickly under water, and a highly maneuverable vessel was required to pursue them; furthermore, they frequented rough and stormy waters, and a chaser had to be seaworthy. Shortly before World War II, a somewhat larger adaptation of the whaler was designed, and came to be known as the "patrol vessel, whaler type." By 1939, two prototype vessels had been built and tested. They were the forerunners of the famous corvettes. The design reached Canada only three days after the war began, and the decision was made to build them in Canadian as well as British yards, and man many of them with Canadian crews. The decision was easier made than implemented. Canada had neither the yards nor the technical personnel to undertake such a program. Neither did she have the trained officers and men to man the ships, assuming they could be built. But despite the overwhelming handicaps, the program was launched, and it involved a revolution in Canadian industry. As the ships began to come off the ways, they were manned by the rapidly expanding Royal Canadian Navy, but the nucleus of experience was pitifully small. Most of the crews of these small ships were men from the interior provinces of Canada who had never even seen the sea until they reported aboard.[5] Their mistakes were many, but as time passed, they learned in that most unforgiving and thorough of schools, the sea. In the end, the Royal Canadian Navy, expanding from less than 4,000 officers and men in 1939, to a wartime strength of over 90,000, proved to be one of the most important factors in keeping the North Atlantic sea lanes open. Had they failed, the results would have been catastrophic. In their expansion, the emphasis was at first on numbers rather than quality, and their mistakes as they learned were sometimes painful; but any sailors who cruised those waters in the year of crisis should gratefully salute the Royal Canadian Navy ensign whenever they see it.

The escort for SC-107 was far from battle-ready. The young escort commander, acting Lieutenant Commander Desmond W. Piers, RCN, was an experienced escort officer, but the responsibility he was assuming was one that would have proved crushing for a far more experienced and older officer.[6] ARVIDA and AM-

---

[5] There is an oft-told story of two Canadian corvettes, both commanded by rather green reserve officers, meeting in mid-Atlantic after losing contact with their convoy. "What's our position?" one asked. The other replied, "Beats me. I'm a stranger here myself."

[6] For which awesome responsibility he was paid $7.50 per day. Commissioned sub-lieutenant in 1937 after five years training with the Royal Navy, he had served in RESTIGOUCHE as a watch keeper, then executive officer, and from 1941 as commanding officer. At the time, he was 28 years old, but had ten years' service as a cadet, midshipman, and officer. Due to the peculiarities of the Royal Canadian Navy pay system and bonuses paid reserve officers, the escort commander was receiving less pay than his navigator, engineer, and medical officer.

HERST had new commanding officers.[7] Nearly all ships had had a high turnover of crew members, as the more experienced sailors were pulled off to form the nucleus for new construction. But aside from the slow and small vessels in the group, the greatest weakness was lack of experience in working together as a group. Anti-submarine tactics call for a high degree of coordination between ships, and this can only be obtained by repeated practice while working under one group commander. It was a weakness that plagued the Allied escort forces until enough ships were made available to allow the formation of permanent groups. Until then, an escort commander would have to make the best of the strange and assorted units given him for each crossing. It would inevitably result in slow and uncoordinated reactions to attacks, even when the ships of the group were, as in many cases, well trained individually. But on October 30th, as Piers deployed his ships around SC-107, there was little opportunity to exercise.

Lying somewhere ahead in the fog were 15 U-boats of Group *Violet*, stretched out in a north-south patrol line, and spaced 15 miles apart. Piers and his five little vessels were overwhelmingly outweighed. Not only were they outnumbered three to one, but U-boat Group *Violet* was under the immediate control of Admiral Karl Doenitz, Flag Officer, U-boats, and undeniably the foremost tactical genius in submarine history.

Group *Violet* was waiting in the area through which the convoy was expected to pass. As the convoy moved through the patrol line, the first U-boat to sight it would transmit a sighting report to U-boat Command in Paris, giving the position, course, and speed of the convoy. U-boat Command would then order other boats to converge on the contact boat, which would trail astern of the convoy and send out frequent progress reports, and radio signals on which other U-boats could home. When enough boats had gathered, they would move in on the convoy after dark

---

[7] ARVIDA was named indirectly for Arthur Vining Davis, American industrialist and Chairman of the Board of Aluminum Company of Canada. The town of Arvida in Canada, the site of one of the company's plants, was named for Davis, and the ship took her name from the town.

and attack. The low-lying U-boats, being difficult to see at night, would remain on the surface whenever possible to take advantage of their higher surface speed. During daylight, submerged attacks could be made as opportunity presented itself, but the main emphasis was on night surface attacks. Once in contact with the convoy, Doenitz emphasized one cardinal principle—freedom of action! The actual attack was left to the initiative of his experienced skippers, with a minimum of interference from ashore.[8] The entire plan had the stamp of genius and simplicity.

In warfare, as in other endeavors, luck plays a large part. U-boat Group *Violet* had a big break when the coded message of October 20th was deciphered, giving the routing of convoy SC-107 after passing Cape Race. The Group had been deployed astride this route in ample time to meet the expected convoy, but as they were short of fuel, Doenitz ordered them to shorten their patrol line and move westward.

On the afternoon of October 30th, the U-boat men got a second break. U-522 was south of Cape Race running on the surface. On the bridge were the officer of the watch and four lookouts, alertly scanning the seas and skies around the compass. Suddenly, the starboard bow lookout shouted, "Smoke, two points on the starboard bow!"

The watch officer quickly checked the bearing, then shouted down the hatch, "Commander to the bridge!"

Seconds later, Kapitänleutnant [9] Herbert Schneider climbed up to the bridge, pulling on his leather jacket and looping the strap of the binoculars around his neck. For several minutes, he

---

[8] Although, before attacks, Doenitz was prone to sending out "inspirational" messages, exhorting his commanders to more and greater achievements. A captured U-boat commander told of Korvettenkapitän Rainhard "Teddy" Suhren calling on Doenitz after a patrol where he had received a number of such messages from the Admiral, urging him to "pursue relentlessly and attack fiercely." In the course of the interview, Suhren told the Flag Officer, U-boats, that he considered the signals unnecessary and insulting. Doenitz was momentarily taken aback by the impudence, but recovered in time to seize Suhren by the neck, lay him across the table, and administer a few well-placed whacks to the "naughty boy."

[9] Equivalent to lieutenant commander, U. S. Navy.

scanned the horizon through his binoculars, then said to the OOD, "We'll close and have a better looksee."

"Hard astarboard, steer 315, both ahead full."

U-522 picked up speed and began shuddering from the drive of the Diesels, occasionally burying her nose in the long westerly swell.

Twenty minutes later, the smoke was clearly visible, as well as the masts of several ships. Then the watch officer sang out, "Corvette, one point, port bow."

Three pairs of binoculars focused on the escort riding two miles on the starboard wing of the convoy. Due to the U-boat's low silhouette, there was little chance that the corvette had seen it yet, but the range was closing rapidly.

Kapitänleutnant Schneider was an experienced commander and an aggressive one.[10] Only three months later, this aggressiveness would lead to his death at the hands of HMS TOTLAND, lending a little more weight to the adage, "There are old commanders and bold commanders, but there are no old, bold commanders."

But now, Schneider's first and overriding task was not to attack, but to get out a contact report on the convoy to U-boat Command and shadow it until other boats could home-in. To Schneider, his course of action was clear—find what the convoy was doing and get out the sighting report. Best play it safe.

"Alarm!"

The watch officer and four lookouts scrambled down the conning tower hatch.

"Dive! Dive! Dive!"

The harsh blast of the klaxon echoed throughout the boat as Schneider dropped through the hatch, and as he finished dogging it closed, the levers in the control room were pulled, opening the main vents to the sea. As the air hissed out, U-522 sank be-

---

[10] Schneider was an aviator until September of 1940. Feeling that action was to be had in U-boats, he entered U-boat training that month, and got his first command, U-522, in June of 1942 at the age of 26. He sank over 50,000 tons of Allied shipping.

neath the surface, continuing the descent to 100 feet while the trim was worked out.

"Periscope depth, Chief, if you're ready."

"Boat at periscope depth, sir."

"Thank you. Let's take a look."

Schneider climbed onto the seat of the attack periscope, raised it carefully and took a quick sweep around the horizon, then a slower, more careful look. Next, he made a careful sweep of the convoy vessels, and quickly lowered the scope.

"Two escorts, fourteen ships, five of them tankers."

From his low periscope, Schneider had seen only part of the convoy, but it was enough. Turning to the hydrophone operator, he asked, "What have you got?" [11]

"Noise bearing 010 to 030. Many screws."

"O. K., don't lose them and keep the bearings coming. Steady on 345, slow ahead together."

U-522 began easing toward the convoy for a closer look. Schneider raised the thin attack periscope for a brief moment.

"This is the corvette. Bearing, mark. Range, 6,000. Bow angle, starboard sixty, speed twelve."

For the next hour, he took periodic quick periscope observations, calling out the information to the quartermaster busy running the plot. As darkness approached, U-522 had dropped six miles astern of the convoy, and Schneider had all the information he needed on SC-107 for his sighting report. It was quickly drafted, encrypted, and handed to the radio operator.

"Up periscope." Schneider took a long, careful look around the horizon with the large search periscope, checking both the sea and the sky overhead.

"Sound room?"

"Noise bearing 035 to 050. Good distance off, sir."

---

[11] The hydrophone was able to detect the propeller noises of ships at great distances when the U-boat was submerged. It was a primary means of detecting convoys out of sight over the horizon.

"Very well. Down periscope. Stand by to surface." The look-outs gathered below the hatch, ready to go on deck.

"Surface!"

U-522 started slowly up.

"Conning tower clear, sir."

The Diesels were started, the hatch opened, and Schneider jumped out onto the bridge, took a look around the horizon, then called down, "Bridge party on deck."

"Blow out main ballast by Diesel."

"Full ahead, together. Steer 050."

With both Diesels roaring, U-522 picked up speed, heading after SC-107 in the gathering darkness ahead.

"Let's get out that message now."

The radio operator began tapping out the sighting report at 1624, and fifteen minutes later, it was acknowledged by U-boat Command. Orders came back from Flag Officer, U-boats, to maintain contact and report every two hours. Next came a message, U-boat Command to all boats of Group *Violet,* to close U-522. Acknowledgments were quickly received from U-520 and U-521, "Closing full speed."

Throughout the night, others reported in by high-frequency radio. As U-522 transmitted radio homing signals, the wolf pack responded to the call, and the ring tightened around SC-107. An RCAF Canso sighted U-522 and forced her to dive, but less than an hour later, she was again running on the surface and following the convoy.

During the time U-522 was passing down the starboard side and taking frequent quick periscope observations, SC-107 steamed along in an atmosphere of lessening alertness. Even in times of danger, alertness wanes with time, and there was no apparent danger here. Nearly a week at sea had passed and nothing of any significance had occurred. In the wardroom of GEMINI, two bridge games were in progress as well as the inevitable game of cribbage. The passenger officers had no assigned duties or watches, and could sleep, eat, read, or play cards. On this gray

Friday afternoon, tiring of reading, several donned sweat gear and went aft to the poop deck to do calisthenics. After working up a good sweat, they leaned over the rail and looked out over the gray rolling water.

The North Atlantic is not a pretty sea. Cold and threatening, its dark, gray-green color is a depressing contrast to the clear blue waters of the Caribbean and Gulf Stream. Far out on the port beam was a small corvette, pitching and frequently burying her nose as she maintained station. There were no other escorts in sight, but this seemed no cause for concern, for the convoy stretched out as far as the eyes could see, and the other escorts were undoubtedly patrolling in the van and on the other beam. The prospect of action appeared remote, and there were no signs of a war except for the ready gun crew standing its watch on the after three-inch mount and some troops lying unwarlike around the well deck.

On RESTIGOUCHE, things were also quiet. Earlier in the day, she had carried out a required escort routine, making a sweep astern to urge three stragglers to close up. There were always the chronic stragglers astern of the convoy, tempting targets for a trailing U-boat commander to pick off, and covering them required a further spreading of the already thin escort. To RESTIGOUCHE's urging to "please close up," came an almost standard reply, "Am making best possible speed." It was always surprising how their speed could increase when the first depth charges were dropped.[12]

Several times during the day, RESTIGOUCHE also made signals warning of excessive smoke coming from vessels in the convoy. Rising high above the convoy, smoke was a convenient sign post in the sky for distant submarines, and it had betrayed SC-107 to U-522. But with the many old ships and green engineers, it was hard to enforce smoke discipline, and even the

---

[12] Sometimes an escort would drop a depth charge astern of a straggler to frighten him into more speed. But you had to be careful. One British destroyer did so, and the nervous merchant crew promptly abandoned ship.

JEYPORE, on which the commodore was riding, was smoking badly. During the night, several Diesel-powered vessels had also been making sparks from their funnels, and at the slow speed the convoy was running, the Diesel vessels found it a difficult thing to prevent.

The commodore had taken advantage of the light seas during the morning to exercise the convoy vessels in turning movements. Admiral Watson was well aware that this odd conglomeration of merchant and naval auxiliary vessels represented all levels of experience and training, and he was taking every opportunity to work them out before an emergency occurred that might require turning them by signal in the darkness. The simultaneous turn of 42 vessels is a difficult maneuver. One ship failing to turn on time can throw the entire convoy into confusion, or cause a collision and the possible loss of one or two vessels. At the conclusion of the morning exercises, the commodore was pleased. His charges were doing better than expected.

On RESTIGOUCHE, the HF/DF (high frequency direction finder) operator was methodically cycling the frequencies.[13] Occasionally, he had been able to get a radio bearing, but there was nothing close by. At 1624, a radio signal began coming in loud and clear. Quickly, he retuned the frequency and read the bearing off the scope. This baby was close by and lying west of the convoy. He leaned over and blew into the voice tube.

"Bridge, aye," the OOD answered.

"Bridge from DF. U-boat signal, strength five, bearing Red one six oh."

"Very good, DF."

The message was relayed to Piers, who climbed up to the bridge, feeling a familiar tightening of the stomach at this first chirping warning of impending trouble.

---

[13] The shipboard HF/DF was an instrument used to determine the bearing on which a radio signal was being transmitted. The range could not be determined. However, if two ships were able to obtain bearings on a transmission, the bearings could be plotted; the point of intersection of the bearings would give the approximate position of the radio sending the signal. See Appendix I, p. 246.

The U-boat signal had also been picked up by the shore HF/DF net,[14] and Commander in Chief, U. S. Fleet (COMINCH), transmitted a message to RESTIGOUCHE reporting the position of the radio emission near the convoy.

RESTIGOUCHE closed JEYPORE and sent a blinker message to the commodore, reporting the probability that a U-boat had made contact. After discussing the situation, a decision was made to alter the convoy course after dark to try to throw off the U-boats. With U-boats already trailing, Piers decided to break radio silence and request aircraft for first light. If the U-boats were converging, air cover was the best defense. Aircraft could hit the U-boats running on the surface or, at least, force them to submerge where their reduced speed would hinder the concentration. Unbeknownst to RESTIGOUCHE, an RCAF aircraft had already attacked U-520, the first boat to answer U-522, and sank it as it was racing toward the convoy. An hour later, an aircraft of RCAF Squadron No. 145 blasted U-658 on the surface. Two were down—not a bad beginning—but 13 more remained.

The following morning dawned gray and foggy, but the night had been a quiet one, the only strain being that of keeping station in greatly reduced visibility and darkness. But the escort commander was gravely concerned. During the night, 35 U-boat radio signals had been heard astern of the convoy, and there could no longer be any doubt that a wolf pack was forming. COMINCH also sent another urgent warning to RESTIGOUCHE that radio intelligence indicated a sighting report had been sent and that SC-107 was being shadowed. The pattern was alarmingly familiar. The high-pitched chirping of the U-boat radio signals were not unlike a rattler's warning before it strikes, but it was at least a warning. Again before noon, COMINCH warned that the convoy was being trailed by an increasing number of U-boats.

The convoy plowed on toward the northeast, and Piers

---

[14] The shore HF/DF net worked on the same principle, and from stations located around the Atlantic basin, U-boats throughout the ocean could be plotted.

searched the sky anxiously for the promised air cover, but all flights had been cancelled because of weather. He also asked HMS WALKER, which had not departed with the rest of the local escort group, to remain with the convoy as long as possible in view of the threatening attack. There was, he concluded, nothing else to do but wait.

Little of the ominous news reached the merchantmen within the convoy, and their crews and passengers passed another boring and uneventful day. There was an unusual lack of tension and worry, and on GEMINI not even emergency drills were carried out. There had been few abandon-ship drills, despite the fact she was newly commissioned and still in a state of training. It was, remarked one of the Army officers, another phoney war.

The conversation in the wardroom was animated and gay; the sea stories flowed, the wind and waves getting stronger and taller with each story. A Coast Guard officer was telling of the rum war at sea during prohibition days, and Lieutenant Commander K. C. Phillips remarked that it had been a helluva lot more action than this convoy. Less than two years later, he was to go down with his ship, which was blown in half by a U-boat torpedo. A newly married Army lieutenant related the difficulties of his oft-postponed honeymoon, the first half of which was spent with a mother-in-law in attendance, the rest interrupted by frequent field maneuvers. It was topped off with rush orders to report to Boston and the GEMINI. The reservists and the "trade school" boys were engaged in their usual friendly exchange of insults, as was common at that early stage of the war. There was little talk of submarines and convoys; so far there was nothing to talk about. It was a boring and routine crossing.

While the passengers relaxed below, the bridge watch of GEMINI was working full time, learning the art of station keeping and the secrets of seagoing in general. They were having enough troubles without interference from U-boats. Given a little time, they would be reasonably proficient, but it was now rapidly running out. The timekeeper was Kapitänleutnant Heinsohn in U-438, who had taken over the contact keeper's job from U-522 that day. Heinsohn braced himself against the bridge casing and trained his glasses on the smudge of smoke and the masts ahead and waited. He was in no hurry. By the next night, the wolf pack would be concentrated around the convoy, and SC-107 would be entering the Greenland air gap—the Black Pit—out of range of covering Allied aircraft.

As the Kapitänleutnant climbed down the ladder, and began pulling off his oil skins to turn in for a night's sleep, the trap was closing according to plan. He could afford to be patient.

III

NOVEMBER /SLAUGHTER
OF THE INNOCENTS

For the North Atlantic, Sunday, November 1st, dawned as a fine day, brisk, partly cloudy, and with good visibility. In that latitude, sunrise came late, and most of the crew members up-and-about were able to see the sunrise through broken clouds. For many, it would be their last.

Admiral Watson was up early on the bridge of the JEYPORE, perusing the messages received during the night. After finishing, he estimated that as many as eight U-boats were following the convoy. It was a remarkably accurate guess, for during the night U-402, U-522 and U-89 had latched on. U-89 was the eighth arrival.

Lieutenant Commander Piers had been on the bridge of RES-TIGOUCHE before dawn, checking the convoy and scanning the sky for the promised air cover. The convoy was well closed-up after the night's cruising. HMS WALKER was still in the screen, but would have to be released during the forenoon due to her low fuel state. After her departure, the thin screen of escorts would be stretched even further.

Piers had a numbers/distance problem. Current doctrine required escorts to screen the convoy at a distance of 5,000 yards during darkness, and at this distance, the screening perimeter around the convoy covered a distance of 25 miles; with five escorts, there was only one for each five miles. But the detection range of the Asdic underwater detection gear was not over 2,000 yards under the best of conditions, and an escort, even with aggressive patrolling, could cover an arc of not over three miles. Radar range on a trimmed-down U-boat on the surface was not much better.

The convoy was, in terms of effective screening, only about half covered. The only solution was more escorts, but in the northwestern Atlantic, no more were available. The North Atlantic escort groups had been depleted badly by withdrawals for an event that was still nearly two weeks away—*Operation Torch,* the invasion of North Africa. While many of the northern escorts were being withdrawn, U-boat Command had not yet reacted with a countermove, being still unaware of the pending African invasion. It was to prove a fortunate break for the invasion forces, but one that would be paid for in blood by SC-107, which was destined to lose as many ships as the combined African invasion fleets.[1]

A Canso flying boat finally arrived from Newfoundland shortly before noon and flew low overhead, but soon lost sight of the convoy due to the low clouds and was unable to find it again. The lumbering seaplane was far offshore and, after a half-hour of futile searching, was forced by fuel shortage to return to Newfoundland. By nightfall, the convoy would enter the Greenland air gap, beyond the range of friendly aircraft based on Newfoundland and Iceland, and there would be no more air cover until it emerged on the Iceland edge.

Doenitz's strategy was working according to the books. In the latter part of October, he had two patrol lines deployed in the North Atlantic. One was on the western approaches to England; the larger one was off the Grand Banks of Newfoundland, where

---

[1] During the time the invasion fleet was approaching the African coast and the attention of U-boat Command was focused on SC-107, another convoy—SL-125 —en route from Sierra Leone to the United Kingdom, was detected, and all boats off Morocco and Gibraltar were rushed south to attack it. Through the resultant U-boat gap, the invasion forces sailed without even being reported. The loss of 27 ships from the two convoys was, in the large scheme of things, a cheap price to pay for the safety of the great invasion fleet; but it was of little immediate consolation to the men who had acted as chance and unwitting "decoys."

eastbound convoys could be detected well before they entered the Greenland air gap. An early contact would allow time to concentrate the pack around the convoy before it entered the "Black Pit," [2] and attack as it crossed the gap without fear of Allied air intervention. Stationing of the U-boats so far west placed them in an area of heavy Canadian air coverage, and U-520 and U-658 had paid the price on October 30th. But now, with the convoy located and concentration completed, Group *Violet* was ready to go to work as soon as darkness fell. For the next three days, there would be little to worry about from the skies.

The pack members were all hungry, for most had been at sea since the first week of October, and except for U-704, which had sunk a 5,000-ton freighter on October 16th, none had attacked

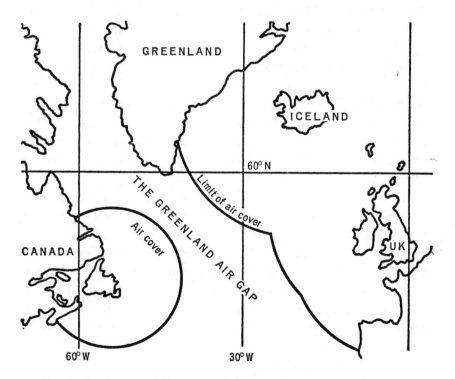

[2] Also known by the U-boat men as "The Devil's Gorge."

a target. Short on fuel though they might be, they were not short on either torpedoes or desire. Heinsohn in U-438 was even more eager than the rest and didn't wait until dark. Shortly after noon, he sighted a straggler, worked into position ahead of it, and dived for a submerged approach. The torpedo, fired at long range, missed. Neither the straggler nor the escorts were aware of the attempt.

WALKER broke off in mid-morning to return to Halifax, carrying out an anti-submarine sweep astern on her way back. She saw nothing. As evening approached, the weather cleared, and the sea subsided even more. It promised to be one of those clear, moonlight nights that the cruise lines advertise.

U-132 had been trailing 20 miles astern of the convoy and, when the mast of WALKER was seen approaching, had dived. Two hours later, Kapitänleutnant Ernst Vogelsang surfaced and turned to the eastward. With both Diesels on the line, he rang up full speed, and the U-boat surged ahead in the following sea. Other boats in the pack were also deploying into position, but it took time to swing well out to the side and beyond visual range of the wing escorts, where the U-boats could use their high surface speed to move into position ahead of the convoy. Once ahead, they could either submerge and work in for a daylight attack or preferably, after dark, run in on the surface to launch torpedoes.

After action with the convoy was joined, each captain would be essentially on his own. Close coordination in a convoy melee was next to impossible, and the attack would depend on the individual initiative and training of the various U-boat captains. In such an action, there was always the danger of collision between U-boats, but experience had proved it to be very slight, probably because of the highly effective lookout system maintained by submarines.[3] In the convoys, on the other hand, collision be-

---

[3] Not until December 8, 1942, was the first boat—U-254—lost by a collision with another, U-221, during a convoy attack. Only three crewmembers were rescued in the heavy seas.

tween the less maneuverable merchant vessels was an ever-present danger, and dozens were lost during the war as a result.

During the afternoon, a message was received on GEMINI concerning the attack by U-boats on Convoy HX-212 only three days before in the same area she was now passing. Seven ships had been sunk during one night and another torpedoed. With the possibility that the same wolf pack might sight SC-107, the Battle of the Atlantic began to seem more real, and people wandered up to their abandon-ship stations to check the rigging of the gear and acquaint themselves with the area. Many were assigned to the Navy doughnut-type rafts, which offered some flotation, but little or no protection from the cold water. They were light and easy to stow, but many men died due to their inadequacy. In the warm Pacific, they might be suitable. In the North Atlantic, death was merely postponed an hour or so. Merchant vessels carried a box-type raft, larger and clumsier than the Navy type, but one on which a man could survive clear of the water. During the coming winter, its superiority was to be repeatedly demonstrated.

Late in the afternoon the clouds cleared, and after the sun settled below the horizon, the northern lights flickered and glowed in the sky to port, causing the ships of the convoy to stand out clearly on the moderate seas. It was a beautiful night for cruising, and an ideal one for hunting. With SC-107 in the air gap, and with the heavy volume of U-boat signals which had been heard during the day, the first U-boat attack could come momentarily.

On RESTIGOUCHE, "Debby" Piers knew that SC-107 must shortly be attacked, and COMINCH had sent three more urgent warning messages during the morning in case he should need reminding. They were redundant, for during the day Group *Violet* had been keeping up continual communications with U-boat Command and with each other. More than 25 DF bearings had been obtained on their radio signals. At sunset, both RESTIGOUCHE and the rescue vessel STOCKPORT obtained bearings on a loud clear signal. The bearings were plotted, and crossed only eight miles away, on the port quarter of the convoy. This one was nearly among the sheep, and something had to be done. Piers weighed his dilemma.

Having only five escorts, and with an attack imminent, should he keep all his escorts near the convoy to repel the attack, or should he take the offensive and attempt to forestall the attack by driving down the U-boats before they could close the convoy? Attack is usually the best defense, but such a course assumes that there will be at least some defense; this escort was too weak to do both.

Piers elected to take the aggressive course. HMS CELANDINE was directed to vector to a position eight miles on the port quarters, where the DF fix had been obtained, deal with the shadower, and return two hours after sunset. RESTIGOUCHE, the only fast vessel, would sweep astern of the convoy to discourage the pack from closing in at high speed on the surface, and perhaps to even catch a "trailer" coming up from astern. With departure of the two escorts, only three corvettes were left to defend the convoy, and ARVIDA's radar had given up the ghost.

Months later, Piers was to be criticized for this action. The reviewing command took the position that the convoy was left without sufficient screen. On the other hand, some officers in the convoy complained about the lack of aggressive action. In retrospect, with only 5 escorts to defend 42 ships against eight U-boats, no really suitable action was possible. Within a year, it would be accepted that the best defense against submarine attack was aggressive patrolling by escorts, hitting the U-boats before they could get into the convoy. But it would be over six months before any escort commander had enough vessels or equipment to both adequately defend the convoy and carry out aggressive sweeps around it. On the night of November 1st, there was no solution.

In GEMINI and the other convoy vessels, the captains were fortunately spared the agonizing decisions facing the escort commander. Many of the crew and passengers had already turned in

A corvette in heavy seas. Iron men rode these small ships. Public Archives
Canada

Lieutenant Commander Desmond W. Piers, RCN, the commanding officer of
RESTIGOUCHE and escort commander of the mid-ocean escort of Convoy
SC-107. Public Archives Canada

HMCS RESTIGOUCHE, the escort flagship of SC-107, and until arrival of HMS VANESSA, the only fast escort. Public Archives Canada

Kapitänleutnant Baron Siegfried von Forstner, who commanded U-402. The decoration is the Knight's Cross. Frau Annamaria Rapp

for the night when distant explosions were heard, one after the other. They were obviously depth charges. Hurriedly dressing (it would be the last night for over a year that many would indulge in the luxury of pajamas at sea), they climbed the ladder to the main deck. The darkness astern of the convoy was broken by gun flashes, and starshells hung in the sky, glowing a faint yellow in the night. From two ships in the convoy, snowflakes arched up and exploded, revealing dozens of ships in their reflected light. (Snowflakes were mortar charges, fired from convoy vessels, which exploded at an altitude of 1,000 feet like Fourth of July rockets. The burning embers, which illuminated the area within a convoy, often revealed surfaced submarines running between the columns.) With the depth charges and starshells exploding astern of the convoy, the two ships had gotten buck fever and fired snowflakes prematurely. No submarines were seen, but the pyrotechnic display clearly revealed the convoy's position to the U-boats hovering on its flanks.

The depth charges and starshells astern had been fired by RESTIGOUCHE. Breaking off at sunset, she had swept astern of the convoy for ten miles, then turned and started closing the convoy at 22 knots, sweeping with radar and Asdic.

When six miles astern of the convoy, the Asdic operator on RESTIGOUCHE picked up a doubtful underwater contact at 1,700 yards. The destroyer quickly wheeled and ran down the bearing, sounding general quarters as she closed, but before the crew could reach their battle stations, RESTIGOUCHE was over the contact, and not yet being ready, no depth charges were dropped. Opening out to 1,200 yards, she turned and started a systematic underwater Asdic search.

Asdic would often bounce echoes off whales, schools of fish, water temperature inversions, and wakes of ships, and during the war more depth charges were dropped on false targets and schools of fish than were ever dumped on U-boats. But with the ocean area around SC-107 swarming with U-boats, the chances that this was a legitimate contact were pretty high. RESTIGOUCHE continued the search pattern, while the Asdic operator trained his instrument in five-degree steps. A ping, listen for five seconds, then to the next bearing. Ping, listen again, train again.

Ping——. Ping——. Ping——. Beep!

As the metallic beep bounced back from the target and came in clearly on the loudspeaker, heads jerked around on the bridge.

"Bridge from Asdic. Contact. Two five O degrees. Range one thousand three hundred yards. Good contact."

"Very good, starboard thirty. Half ahead both engines!"

The information began to flow in from the Asdic hut. "Left cut 245. Range one thousand two hundred yards. Right cut 255. Closing doppler."

Ping-Beep. Ping-Beep. Ping-Beep.

From the chemical recorder came the report, "Good Contact. Range seven hundred yards. Range rate seventeen."

On the depth-charge racks and the side K-guns, ratings quickly applied special wrenches and adjusted the depth-setting dials of the depth charges to 150 feet. While lookouts and gun crews scanned the water ahead for any sign of a U-boat, the captain concentrated on the attack.

As the range closed, the bearings began to move rapidly right, and at 400 yards, RESTIGOUCHE lost contact and no attack was possible. Six minutes later, a radar target was picked up at 1,000 yards and the destroyer swung hard left. The range began to close again and the bearing moved rapidly left. Nothing could be seen in the darkness ahead.

"Bridge from Asdic. Screw beats dead ahead bearing 316 degrees."

With both radar and Asdic contact, something was out there, and on the surface at that. Piers, scanning the sea through his glasses, sighted the wake of the submarine, and swung the ship toward the wake to attack. At 300 yards the submarine dived, and RESTIGOUCHE barreled in after it, dropping a ten-charge pattern by eye at the spot where the wake had disappeared.

As the charges exploded, one of RESTIGOUCHE's generators was knocked off the power panel by the force of the explosions, and the steering power as well as the power to the Asdic was lost. For three minutes, with rudder jammed at 20 degrees left, the destroyer circled. When power was restored, and steering and Asdic were back in operation, an expanding search was begun for the U-boat. It was rewarded several minutes later with a faint Asdic contact at 1,300 yards. Six starshells were fired on the bearing to illuminate the water surface, but the U-boat was staying down. Nothing was seen but the glistening reflection of the starshells on the gently rolling swells. These were the same starshells seen by the GEMINI.

The search was resumed. Anti-submarine warfare calls for persistence, and massive amounts of patience. RESTIGOUCHE steamed along her planned search pattern, the Asdic pinging monotonously without any answering echo. Twenty minutes later, contact was regained at 900 yards, then immediately lost. Twice more, echoes were received, but each time RESTIGOUCHE swung to attack, the echoes were lost. The destroyer was dealing with a U-boat skipper who knew all the tricks and probably had a couple in reserve. The third time the contact was lost, the destroyer once again started a systematic box sweep. A persistent hunter is poison to a submerged submarine. Besides forcing it to drain its limited battery power, a destroyer sitting on top prevents the U-boat from getting into position for attack. RESTIGOUCHE intended to squat on this one for as long as it took. But at that moment, five miles away, Kapitänleutnant Baron Siegfried von Forstner in U-402 entered the picture.

Von Forstner had surfaced at sunset and set off in pursuit of the convoy. At 2156, he reached the point at which it had last been reported and dived to listen with his hydrophone. No screwbeats could be heard, but he did hear the noises from a U-boat's Diesels. Surfacing, he saw another U-boat on his starboard quarter, and started off at high speed on the convoy's last reported

course. Forty minutes later, he sighted a destroyer far astern of
the convoy, and turned away to the southeast. It was RESTI-
GOUCHE, fully occupied with her Asdic contact. Wasting little
time in evading the escort, U-402 changed course again toward
the convoy, and soon had shadows in sight ahead and to port.
Forstner continued up the starboard side to get into attack position. Only ARVIDA was on that side of the convoy, and she had
a broken radar. Unseen, the U-boat slipped under her stern, cut
toward the convoy, and shortly after midnight was well past the
corvette and among the sheep. Only 800 yards ahead was the
starboard column of the convoy, broadside on. Two big freighters were in sight, plowing slowly along.

"Hard astarboard. Steady on zero-six-zero.'

The U-boat was close enough, and Forstner swung to slow his
rate of closure. In German and American submarines it was not
necessary to point the boat at the target; the torpedoes, receiving
continually corrected courses into their gyroscopic automatic
steering gear until they left the tubes, would turn immediately
onto the desired course as soon as they were fired.

"Tubes one to five—ready for surface fire!" reported the torpedo officer.

"Bridge control."

A switch was thrown below, and dim white lights in the conning tower showed that the bridge had control of the firing
buttons.

Dropping his binoculars, with which he had been scanning
the convoy, the torpedo officer stepped quickly to the attack
sight, a powerful telescope mounted on the bridge, and trained
it on the first target. It was connected electrically to the main
torpedo attack computer below decks, into which was also being
automatically fed the U-boat's course and speed, as well as target
data cranked in by the computer operators from the torpedo
officer's estimates.

With the attack telescope's cross hairs on the freighter, he
called, "Mark!"

"Lined up," reported the torpedo petty officer, throwing a switch. The computer gears spun round, calculating the information being fed into it. Moments later, two red lights went out, indicating that the solution was complete.

"Follow!" ordered the torpedo officer.

A switch was thrown, and a lamp glowed, indicating that the computer was controlling. At the same time, the constantly changing firing settings were being transmitted automatically to the torpedoes and set on their angling mechanism. The torpedoes could now be fired at any time.

Forstner took one last look through his binoculars.

"Fire when ready!"

The torpedo petty officer at the attack computer chanted, "On-on-on," indicating that the firing data was still being accurately transmitted to the torpedoes.

The torpedo officer checked the cross hairs of the surface attack scope once more and yelled, "Fire!" at the same time pressing the firing button.

Nothing happened. The torpedo had not left the tube, and the firing light had not come on.

"Stand by Tube Two!"

"Fire!"

The boat shivered and a heavy hissing sound was heard as the torpedo was ejected by compressed air. But it was running erratically and missed.

"Damn! Standby Three."

Forstner jumped to the attack scope and took a quick look. They had been easing in toward the freighter and were only 400 yards away. Soon someone on the freighter would have to see them.

"Fire!"

Twenty-three seconds later the torpedo smashed into the ship, sending a bright column of fire and water 90 feet high. Shaken by the concussion, the U-boat crew crouched on the bridge as pieces of debris rained into the water around them.

"Hard aport!"

Out of the corner of his eyes, von Fortsner had seen an escort turning toward him, the bone in her teeth turning whiter as she picked up speed.

"Both ahead full!"

As he cut under the stern of the stricken ship, a last look showed the escort now less than a half-mile away. Escape on the surface was no longer possible.

"Alarm. Dive! Dive! Dive!"

Less than two minutes later, as the U-boat passed through 300 feet, depth charges began exploding, but none were close. The escort passed back and forth over him with the roar of an express train, but without dropping more charges, and von Forstner grinned at his first watch officer. Over the hydrophone could be heard the cracking and breaking noises of a sinking ship.

"Slow ahead together. Keep her at 60 meters." [4]

Picking up a cup of coffee, Forstner added another spoon of sugar, and stirred it slowly. There was no tremor in his hands. The quartermaster handed him an identification book of Allied ships.

"This looks like it, sir."

He took a quick look. "That's it all right. CITY OF BALTIMORE class. Eighty-four hundred tons."

The ship had been the EMPIRE SUNRISE. When the torpedo was still 100 yards away, it had been sighted by the freighter, but too late to attempt evasion. The torpedo hit amidship, blasting a gaping hole in the side, sending the mainmast crashing to the deck and wrecking the starboard lifeboat. Ship control and main engines were disabled.

Immediately, the EMPIRE SUNRISE had fired flares into the air as a signal she had been hit, and turned two red lights at the

---

[4] The Germans measured depth in meters; we used feet. All subsequent figures will be in feet.

truck. For two hours, she settled slowly until the rising water forced the crew to abandon ship. They were quickly picked up by STOCKPORT, the convoy rescue vessel.[5]

In GEMINI, many had stood around on deck for over an hour after the starshell display astern of the convoy, and when nothing else happened, had straggled below to catch a few winks, convinced that the escorts were on top of things. The respite was brief. First came the dull shock as the torpedo hit EMPIRE SUNRISE three miles away, then the shrill clanging of GEMINI's general alarm bell. In the compartment, illuminated only by a dim red light, men piled out of their bunks, attempting simultaneously to don clothing and life jackets.

On the main deck, they were greeted by an unforgettable sight. Every ship in the convoy was firing snowflakes, lighting the scene like daylight, and as they burned, the noise of depth charges was again heard. RESTIGOUCHE, while closing the convoy, had picked up another contact and was dropping a ten-charge pattern. After the firing of snowflakes had gradually died out, leaving the convoy in total darkness, the commodore ordered a course change of 40 degrees to port in an attempt to throw off the U-boats.

Gradually, the chill air forced people below decks, and as the night wore on, several brave souls went below to their bunks to try to sleep only to be quickly roused out by the sound of depth charges. RESTIGOUCHE had made another Asdic contact and dropped a pattern, but was unable to regain contact. GEMINI was getting to be such a nonchalant veteran, that the general alarm was not sounded. Minutes later AMHERST made Asdic contact and dropped a pattern. Sleep was becoming difficult, and

---

[5] Each convoy had a specially trained and equipped merchant vessel assigned as a rescue vessel. Carrying a doctor and sick bay facilities, and necessary equipment to retrieve survivors from the water, they lived a dangerous life while picking up survivors from sunken ships astern of the convoy. Often, no covering escort could be provided, and U-boats would sometimes linger around to insure that their victim went down.

GEMINI's wardroom filled with passengers, drinking coffee and talking in subdued tones. Everyone now had on lifejackets. Three thousand men in 46 ships waited nervously in the darkness.

At midnight, RESTIGOUCHE had moved into position astern of the convoy, patrolling in a zigzag pattern, changing course at intervals of not more than three minutes. It was to save her, for five minutes past midnight, von Pückler in U-381 had a setup on RESTIGOUCHE at 1,800 yards. Taking a last bearing through his periscope, he fired a four-torpedo spread, then dived to 200 feet. Just as his periscope was lowered, RESTIGOUCHE turned away on a new leg of the zigzag, and all four torpedoes missed. The destroyer continued patrolling, unaware that four torpedoes had sped by only yards away.

Three minutes after U-381 missed, the ubiquitous von Forstner in U-402, having surfaced and worked into firing position, fired five fish at the port column at a range of less than 1,000 yards. RINOS and DALCROY in the left column were hit, the former rolling over and sinking in five minutes. The other three torpedoes sped on through the convoy, one exploding four miles away near the seventh column.

The loud crump as the torpedoes slammed into the two adjacent ships shook GEMINI to her ancient keel and in the wardroom, where 30 officers were sleeping on the deck, momentary confusion reigned.

"That's us!" someone shouted, and there was an immediate jam at the single door leading out.

"Get a light on!"

"OK, take it easy. Easy does it!"

Things quieted down, several flashlights were produced, and the crowd filed through the doorway, moving quickly down the passageway to the main deck. As they emerged breathless onto the main deck, GEMINI was still plowing ahead, her engines pounding away. The night was a carnival of lights. On the port quarter, one ship was burning, and the one behind her had sheared out of the column with red lights at her truck. A flare arched into the air from the second ship, triggering snowflake firing throughout the convoy. Finally, the general alarm went off on GEMINI, and while it was ringing, the dull crump of depth charges could be heard off to port. It was a scene of stark unreality, and as the months passed, this feeling would become engraved in the minds of many as one of the prime ingredients of a night combat action at sea. A psychologist might explain the sense of unreality as a defensive mechanism used to avoid the acceptance of such horrors—a mental circuit breaker. A seaman would perhaps shrug it off as the result of being jolted out of an exhausted sleep, and while still half asleep, witnessing a scene too broad to grasp. Whatever the cause, a night action at sea forever after remains clear and unforgettable, but still cloaked in unreality.

The usual reaction to the crash of a torpedo at night is fright, a sudden, natural animal fright, accompanied by the pounding pulse, cold sweat and, as time goes on, by paradoxical yawns. Men forced to wait under extreme stress often tend to yawn, and on the deck of GEMINI, bathed in the flickering light from the snowflakes and the burning DALCROY, the yawning spread contagiously.

No sooner had the snowflakes died out than RESTIGOUCHE picked up another Asdic contact close to the convoy, and fired a nine-charge pattern. The attack was close to the starboard column, and the depth-charge explosions damaged the engines of the HATIMURA, which fired a rocket and turned on red lights. Two other ships, shaken by the depth charges, erroneously reported they had been torpedoed.

The action was now a confused melee. U-84 fired two fish at a freighter, but neither ran true. Five minutes after U-84 missed, U-522 fired four topedoes, hitting the HARTINGTON with two. A 30-ton tank stowed abreast No. 2 hold fell with a tremendous crash through the deck, and fifteen minutes after

being hit, the freighter capsized and sank. All but two of the
crew of 44 managed to get away in two boats.[6]

In the confusion that had now overtaken the convoy, several
ships became dangerously entangled, and two turned on running
lights. Their skippers had acted wisely. The wolf pack certainly
knew where the convoy was; the lights did nothing to give away
its position, and they probably prevented a collision. The snowflake illumination slowly died out, and the convoy was again
left in darkness. Soon, however, snowflakes burst out again on
the starboard quarter and the port beam, and AMHERST made
a six-charge attack on an Asdic target on the port beam. On the
starboard quarter, ARVIDA made an attack on a doubtful
Asdic target, and was rewarded by being made the target of
machine-gun fire by several merchant ships. The gun crews on
the merchantmen had their wind up, and were firing indis-
criminately at any suspected target. One young Armed Guard
officer on an American merchant ship saw several ships shooting
at a spot in the water, and directed his guns to shoot at it "in
case it was a submarine." There were no casualties due to this
intramural firing, but several ships had a bad scare as the streams
of tracers passed overhead.

Man is an amazingly adaptable creature, and within a few
minutes after the torpedoing of HARTINGTON, many drifted
back down to the wardroom of GEMINI; but this time, not
even the bravest ones continued down to the sleeping compartment below the water line. The record player in the wardroom
was blaring out a war-inspired melody entitled "The Fuehrer's
Face."

"Oh, der Fuehrer says, ve is der master race,
Ve go heil, heil, heil, right in der Fuehrer's face—"
"Turn off that Goddamn thing!" someone shouted. The record

---

[6] The two boats stayed together for a day and a night before being separated
by rising winds. The captain's boat, containing 26 men, stayed on the convoy
lanes and was found by a destroyer ten days later. The men had used three
large tubs of lard as food and to coat themselves for protection. Only one man
died in the boat. The other boat containing 21 men was never found.

player was snapped off, and from a corner of the room, a low voice said, "Yeah, let's not get these Krauts any more agitated than they are now."

The tension and the cigarette smoke hung in the room and the smattering of conversation was nervous and forced. The men carefully avoided the subject of what would happen if GEMINI, with her lack of compartmentation and with no watertight bulkheads, was hit. There was no need to discuss it, for everyone knew. By unspoken accord, the white lights had been turned out in the room, and only the dim red emergency light glowed. Going over the side in a raft or boat would be bad enough without being blinded as a result of being in a lighted room. An occasional match flared as cigarettes were lit. With heavy gear and lifejackets on, over 30 men lay on the deck, and there was no longer any thought of sleep, though a few went through the pretense. They were the hunted, and the feeling was not pleasant. The conversation was hushed, as though "They" could hear through the ship's steel sides. It is the waiting that dissolves a man's courage, and brings on cold, clammy fear clutching at his viscera. When you have the means to hit back, it is endurable, but when defenseless, the slow dragging of time becomes an intolerable thing, clocked off by the pounding of your own heart. An escort sailor who has just one time been on the receiving end, with the helpless feeling of waiting to be gigged in the gut, rapidly develops an empathy for his merchant charges.

At 0206, a dull roar was heard in the distance. Everyone jerked up, tense and waiting, but nothing else happened. Two men got up to walk around the deck, but soon returned to report that everything topside was dark. (U-438 had made a submerged approach, and fired at a convoy vessel, but the torpedo had exploded prematurely. The Germans, as well as we, had their share of torpedo troubles.)

An hour later, a similar explosion was heard, caused by a torpedo exploding harmlessly at the end of its run. It was one of a spread fired by U-521, but all three torpedoes missed. The less adventurous U-boat skippers were "browning" the convoy from long range, firing spreads at the convoy with the hope that one or more would hit one of the closely packed ships. It sometimes worked, but it did not have the devastating effectiveness of carefully aimed shots at close range.

During the morning darkness, HMCS MOOSEJAW,[7] a corvette which had sailed late, joined up, raising the badly outnumbered escort force to six ships, of which only four had operative radars. As though to show his contempt for the slight reinforcement, von Forstner took U-402 in on the surface and closed within 1,400 yards of the port column before firing a spread of four torpedoes. EMPIRE LEOPARD was hit and sank in 30 seconds, carrying down all but three of her crew, and EMPIRE ANTELOPE dropped astern in flames. Over an hour later, she sank after her crew had safely abandoned ship.

In probably no other field of combat is a weapon's effectiveness so dependent on the commanding officer as in a submarine. Because of his ability to obtain concealment, a submarine commander concerned only with his own boat's safety is very hard to locate and kill. But a cautious commander does little killing, and his crew, no matter how well trained and eager, can do little about it. The aggressive "tigers," on the other hand, intent on hitting the enemy, take their boats often in harm's way, and as they do, the casualty rates on both sides soar.

Fortunately, the great U-boat commanders were not common, but these few did a lion's share of the sinkings. Total tonnage sunk was not the only measure, however. Many fine skippers came to a violent end before their high rate of killing mounted up. There was also considerable difference in the caliber of their opposition.

Kapitänleutnant Siegfried Paul Gustav Leo Freiherr von

---

[7] MOOSEJAW already had one U-boat to her credit the year before. When she rammed it, the U-boat skipper jumped from the conning tower to the deck of the corvette, while his boat continued the fight. When it was finally sunk, the survivors were somewhat upset with their captain.

Forstner, commanding U-402, was one of the aggressive ones, in the tradition of such aces as Prien, Kretschmer, Schepke, Endrass, and Lueth, even though his tonnage figures, often compiled against tougher opposition, were not as impressive.

The heir of an old Prussian family that had produced a long and distinguished line of professional officers, the young Baron, now on his fifth war patrol, was an experienced U-boat officer and a dangerous one. His menace was all the greater because he was suffering from the frustrations of several quiet and uneventful patrols, during which he had sunk only two ships, while his friends in other boats had been racking up big scores in the slaughter of unprotected ships off the American coast. With his crew trained to a high pitch by months of endless drills, he was willing and eager to take risks in order to score.

On the previous patrol, he had been heavily damaged by a depth-charge attack off Cape Hatteras, but if his nerves had been affected in any way, it wasn't apparent. Cool, daring, and with a killer's tenacious instinct, the 32-year-old Forstner was a thoroughly dedicated professional, the kind it is good to have on your side. Unfortunately, he wasn't, but the uniform he wore did not lessen his excellence.[8]

After sinking DALCROY and RINOS earlier, Forstner had turned at high speed toward the bow of the convoy, hoping to get ahead, reload tubes, and be in a position for another attack. But he had been seen by AMHERST, which opened fire with machine guns, and by a merchant vessel, which fired and hit the conning tower with a three-inch projectile. With the bridge riddled, and the Diesel ventilating trunk shot away, he reluctantly dived. Twice in the next hour, he attempted to surface, only to be driven down by the approach of escorts. Finally, an hour and a half after diving, he was able to surface, run up the port side on the surface, and sink EMPIRE ANTELOPE and EMPIRE LEOPARD. After torpedoing his fourth and fifth ships

[8] See Appendix V, "Profile of an Ace," p. 267.

of the night, he was again forced to dive, but surfacing soon afterwards, he set off in pursuit of the convoy, still eager to do battle.

Von Forstner was not the only man with iron nerves. The rescue vessel STOCKPORT, covered by a corvette, had been busily engaged throughout the night in the dangerous job of picking up survivors, and now had more than 250 aboard. As each ship was hit, her radio operator reported in a steady monotone which never altered or showed emotion, "Number twelve torpedoed. Number thirteen torpedoed. . . ."

Required to drop astern in order to rescue survivors, convoy rescue vessels spent long periods lying motionless in the water while conducting recovery operations. The area aft of the convoys was particularly dangerous, for not only did it contain the trailing U-boats, but a submarine commander often hung around a torpedoed ship to deliver the *coup de grâce* in case it did not sink from the first hit. With no radar or Asdic gear, and often with no covering escort, the merchant seamen of the convoy rescue vessels unhesitatingly carried out their dangerous duties. They were the bravest of the brave.

When the two vessels in the port column were hit, RESTI-GOUCHE had ordered the escorts to execute *Operation Raspberry*—a simultaneous sweep by the screening vessels along the convoy flanks, while illuminating with starshells—in an attempt to sight any U-boats on the surface. Nothing was seen, but minutes after the last starshell faded out, U-522 fired a spread of four torpedoes at the opposite side of the convoy, and quickly dived. Two of the torpedoes hit the MARITIMA, which broke up and sank within three minutes. Snowflakes again broke out over the convoy, and the flashes of the escorts' guns were followed shortly by starshells lighting off high in the air. A ship in the fifth column opened up with machine-gun fire, and the tracers arched over the USS PLEIADES, a nearby Navy transport.

After the snowflakes again died out, the cargo of munitions on the MARITIMA exploded with a terrible impact, rocking the convoy. Five ships were so severely jolted that they reported themselves torpedoed and turned on lights. In PLEIADES, instruments and glass gauges in the engine room were shattered, and the engine-room telegraph operator, thinking the ship was hit, stopped the engines. The master of the OLNEY ordered the crew to abandon ship, but cancelled the order when the vessel was found to be undamaged. Thirty-two of MARITIMA's crew were never found.

There was no letup in the horror of the night. Only minutes after the big explosion, U-522 fired another spread of torpedoes, and two hit the MOUNT PELION, which went down in 20 minutes with seven crewmen. So great was the ensuing confusion that ten minutes passed before the merchantmen received the signal to open up with snowflakes, and only a few responded. A spent torpedo, fired by U-521, exploded in the distance, adding to the turmoil. Twenty minutes later, U-442 "browned" the convoy at long range with a spread of four fish, one of which exploded within the convoy, but did no damage. It was the last attack of the night. With dawn approaching, the U-boats were forced to dive. Even U-boat men needed sleep, and they had for certain not been asleep during the night.

On the escorts, there was no rest. As dawn came, AMHERST, ARVIDA, and STOCKPORT were detached to go back and pick up survivors. Eight ships had been sunk, and STOCKPORT already had over 250 persons aboard, twice her planned capacity. With the poor weather, there was no hope of air coverage, even if four-engine aircraft had been available to reach the air gap. But Piers hoped that he might be able to shake off the pack in the low visibility. The morning passed uneventfully, and the crewmembers not on watch gratefully snatched a few winks of exhausted sleep whenever they were able. Several ships of the convoy were shifted into new positions to fill the gaps left by the eight sunken vessels, two stragglers were coaxed up into the fold, and one "snuggler" was told by a corvette to get the hell back where he belonged. This gentleman had been in the port column, which had been well worked over during the night. Feeling that it was a bit safer further inside the convoy, he had eased up between columns two and three, close up to and inside No. 23.[9] If anyone was going to be hit, he rationalized, let it be 23. But with daylight, and the end of the attacks, he was chased back into position.

At mid-morning, the executive officer of the GEMINI called a meeting of the passenger officers. The ship's officers were mostly green "ninety-day wonders," or Naval reservists called up from the merchant marine with little gunnery training. All passenger officers, said the exec, were to be assigned as battery officers on the two 3"/50 guns or as assistant OOD's. The ship would stand a fully closed-up watch with all guns manned throughout the trip. Everyone nodded, as the setup made good sense. Not only would it increase the ship's readiness, but doing anything would make it easier to endure the attacks. Then, for the second matter: there were not enough life jackets to go around. In fact, they were short quite a few. The exec thought it would be an appropriate gesture if the officers gave up their jackets for the enlisted men.

There was considerable muttering at this oversight on the part of the ship's company in not providing enough life jackets for a wartime crossing, but in the end, the jackets were piled on deck for the troops. There was very little else to do, military *noblesse oblige* being what it is.

On the U. S. Navy transport PLEIADES, thought was also being given to what had become a distinct possibility. Feeling that the escort was ineffective and unable to cope with the situation, her commanding officer ordered all the troops and crew to remain out of the quarters below decks. Officers' country, the passageways, and the wardroom were made available for the en-

[9] The convoy number of a ship indicated its position in the formation. The first one or two digits was the ship's column number, the port column being No. 1. The last digit was the ship's position in its column, the lead ship being No. 1. For example, ship No. 124 was the fourth ship back in the twelfth column.

listed personnel. Many of them slept on the deck of officers' staterooms, and continued to do so for the remainder of the trip.

On GEMINI, some had gone a bit further. A few enlisted men had decided that a heavy coat of grease might prove helpful in protecting the feet in cold water. During the height of the previous night's attack, they had applied heavy lubricating grease on their feet, pulling on socks and shoes over it.

Monday afternoon, November 2nd, brought even more rain and mist, and with it increased hope that the convoy might have shaken off the pack in the reduced visibility. The convoy steamed through patches of fog in which forward visibility was reduced to less than half a mile. Steaming buoys were put over by the convoy vessels. These spar buoys, towed several hundred yards astern of each ship, provided a point of reference for the ship astern to keep station when the ship ahead was blotted out in the fog.

But the weather was not enough to protect SC-107 against a U-boat commander who was tenacious and wanted to make a kill. Kapitänleutnant Herbert Schneider, who had originally located the convoy, and had torpedoed three ships during the night, had surfaced astern of the convoy at dawn and transmitted a report to U-boat Command reporting the sinking of seven ships. It was an exaggeration, but three had been bad enough. After pursuing all morning, he sighted the masts of the convoy at noon, and swung well out to the side before moving ahead of the convoy. As he raced to the northeast, he sighted three U-boats, which had dropped out of the fight due to lack of fuel, and would have to be refueled by a tanker U-boat before they could resume operations. Late in the afternoon, Schneider's U-boat arrived in position ahead of the convoy, and dived to make a submerged daylight attack. It was a tactic that few skippers cared to use against an escorted convoy, but Schneider was one of the aggressive ones. As a watch officer under Hardegan, the highly successful commander of U-123, he had had excellent training,

and had been allowed to handle attacks which sank five ships
before getting his own command. He was another thorough
professional.

Working in at periscope depth, he avoided the starboard bow
escort, and fired two torpedoes. One of them struck the PAR-
THENON, and the other exploded harmlessly between the columns of the convoy. Schneider turned away and went deep, and
ARVIDA and RESTIGOUCHE came after him. Fifty minutes
after the attack, ARVIDA made Asdic contact and delivered an
accurate attack with eight depth charges that shook U-522 badly.
Glass gauges exploded and lights went out. But she had gone
deep "into the cellar," and the depth charges exploded too far
above her to be lethal.

Shortly before dark, the fog thickened, and the U-boats lost
contact. After dark, the commodore wheeled the convoy 50 degrees to starboard, but shortly after the turn a corvette, with her
radar inoperative, became entangled with the merchant ships.
Working within a convoy with good visibility and operating radar
is difficult enough, but being trapped among 35 moving vessels
in pitch dark and fog is nothing less than terrifying. The corvette, staring at the high sides of the merchantmen sliding by
in the dark, turned on its navigation lights, and fired flares. The
merchantmen, alarmed by the fireworks in their midst, began
firing snowflakes and turned on their lights also. Miraculously,
the little Canadian vessel blundered on through the convoy without being hit, and emerged badly shaken on the other side. It had
been a near thing.

Seeing the pyrotechnic display and lights through a break in
the fog, Schneider again closed in and fired at an escort before
diving deep. The torpedo missed. Confused by the fog and the
corvette in their midst, the convoy vessels became badly disori-
ented and spread out. Many ships lost contact with their neigh-
bors. In a five-mile square of ocean, 35 merchantmen, 6 escorts,
and 8 submarines plowed through the night, lookouts straining,
and guns and torpedoes cocked and loaded for bear. As midnight

approached, it was every man for himself, and the devil help anyone who loomed up out of the fog.

Surrounded by the swirling fog, even the bow of the ship was often blotted out, and only an occasional glimpse of the ship ahead was possible. Shortly after 2130, the commodore again altered the course of the convoy in an attempt to elude the wolf pack. Some of the ships received the turn signal, while others plowed through the night unaware of the change.

At this time, GEMINI completely lost sight of the other ships in the convoy. Unbeknownst to the officer of the deck, GEMINI's gyro steering compass had tumbled. The helmsman, following the erratic indication, swung the ship through a wide arc, cutting across the next column, just missing one ship which loomed up in the fog, and continued into the fourth column. The USS PLEIADES, a Navy transport, loomed ahead. GEMINI turned on her red breakdown lights to indicate she was not under control, and PLEIADES turned away under hard rudder, also turning on her lights. Had the situation not been so fraught with tragedy, it would have been comic. Fired at by submarines, shot at by her own forces, and lost, the little freighter blundered through the convoy and the fog with an inoperative compass. All hands strained to catch a glimpse of the other ships hurrying by, hoping to see them in time to prevent being cut in half. As time slipped by, and nothing was seen, the tension began to ease. Somehow, she had slipped through undamaged and was apparently clear of the convoy. Then the realization of their predicament began to close in on GEMINI's people. They were alone, straggling from the convoy, and unable to see more than a few hundred yards ahead. But somewhere in the dark around them were the U-boats, and they didn't have to see. With their sensitive hydrophones, they could hear, and one of them was probably listening to the thump, thump, thump of GEMINI's screw as she plodded eastward in search of the convoy. The lookouts were doubled, and many men quite likely were praying. At midnight, when the relief watch came up, no one went below. All agreed that the more eyes there were, the better were their chances. Furthermore, the flying bridge seemed much safer than being below decks.

GEMINI was not the only one with big troubles. The SS GEISHA, carrying the vice-commodore, lost control during the evasion turn, and sheered off through the convoy, probably at the same time as the GEMINI was blindly feeling her way around. In the foggy night, a corvette and two merchantmen had cruised blindly through the convoy without a collision. The gods of war, seeing the odds against SC-107, must have temporarily called time-out and dropped a protective mantle over the sorely beset ships.

After midnight, RESTIGOUCHE ran astern of the convoy, hoping to catch any trailing U-boats attempting to catch up after the second evasive change of course. While six miles astern in heavy fog, her radar operator picked up a contact at 800 yards. RESTIGOUCHE went to battle stations, and turned to ram, increasing to 15 knots as she closed the contact. At 300 yards, radar contact was lost, and the target passed down the port side, unseen in the fog. Swinging over under hard rudder, RESTIGOUCHE regained contact and began closing slowly in a stern chase. The rate of closure was slow, and it was a fortunate thing. At 200 yards, the target loomed out of the fog; it was no U-boat, but HMS VANESSA, a British destroyer sent from Convoy HX-213 to assist hard-pressed SC-107! RESTIGOUCHE sheered away, flashing a challenge by blinker light, which the startled watch on VANESSA promptly answered. At a combined closing speed of 30 knots, the two destroyers had missed each other by less than 200 yards on the initial contact, and had avoided a second near miss by the narrowest of margins. Both turned back and closed the convoy, now spread out in confusion in the night ahead. CELANDINE, with her radar broken down, had completely lost contact with the convoy, and was far astern, waiting for first light before attempting to rejoin.

The night passed without molestation by the U-boats, which

were themselves having trouble keeping contact. With the confusion existing, a U-boat skipper would have been taking his life in his hands to venture among the merchant ships.

At dawn came a clearing in the fog, and the badly scattered convoy began to regroup. Some of the ships were as much as four miles astern of the convoy, tempting targets to an aggressive U-boat commander. U-438 fired a torpedo at one of them and missed. Sixteen minutes later, he missed again. The tanker plodded along unaware that death had just gone by astern; electric torpedoes leave no wake. AMHERST, on the port bow of the convoy, sighted a surfaced submarine and barreled after it. Before she could close at her slow speed, however, the U-boat dived, and a search by AMHERST and VANESSA failed to make Asdic contact. Fifteen miles astern of the convoy, CELANDINE, hastening to rejoin, sighted a surfaced submarine running after the convoy. The corvette opened fire and the diving U-boat fired a torpedo, which missed astern. Failing to make Asdic contact, CELANDINE rejoined the convoy.

Shortly after dawn, a few men on GEMINI dragged themselves awake, and went to the mess for coffee. It was a morning with special significance. When one treads close to the edge, the mornings are always sweeter and more alive, and the sun dispels some of the terrors of the night. At the same time, it brings the crew the hope of better things to come.

Group *Violet* (it should have been named *Violent*) didn't allow the crew time to finish breakfast. There was a dull shock followed by the sound of an explosion, and the mess quickly emptied. A large tanker, the HAHIRA, in the van of the starboard column, had been hit, and was aflame from end to end. As hundreds of men on other ships watched, a boat shot out from her side. Some of the poor devils had escaped, though the flames had spread throughout the ship almost instantaneously. As she dropped astern, machine gun firing burst out in the convoy, accompanied by the blasting of sirens. A torpedo, one of the salvo fired at HAHIRA, was running on the surface through the convoy. On the emergency signal from the commodore, the convoy made a turn away together from the direction of the torpedo, and no ships were hit.

Back on the HAHIRA, a seeming miracle had occurred. The flames, burning furiously only seconds before, had suddenly died out completely, and only thin smoke rose from the stricken ship. Her fire-extinguishing system must have been unusually effective. Tankers, once on fire, are seldom saved without a massive fire-fighting effort, and such an effort cannot be undertaken in a convoy under attack. HAHIRA dropped further astern. RESTIGOUCHE and a corvette circled her, searching for the attacking submarine.

U-521 had escaped clean after hitting HAHIRA, but Schneider in U-522 was close in approaching for an attack. RESTIGOUCHE, circling HAHIRA, picked up a faint Asdic contact on him and closed to attack. Schneider fired a torpedo at RESTIGOUCHE, then dived deep. RESTIGOUCHE retaliated with an eight depth-charge attack on what she classified as a "doubtful" contact. It was real enough, but despite all the malicious intent, no damage was done by either side.

As RESTIGOUCHE dropped her charges, the concussion was felt throughout the convoy and general quarters sounded again on GEMINI. The weary crew was no sooner on deck than the word was passed to secure. Before the order to secure could be carried out, the bottom fell out again.

A blue smoke column rose from the water ahead of the center of the convoy, and the PLEIADES sheered off and began firing at the spot with machine guns. Nothing else was seen, and PLEIADES resumed her station. Minutes later, several miles astern of the convoy, Klaus Bargsten in U-521,[10] who had torpedoed the HAHIRA earlier, closed in to finish the job, and hit her amid-

---

[10] Bargsten was another well-trained pupil of the famous Otto Kretschmer, under whom he had served as exec in U-99 while that boat sank 243,000 tons of Allied shipping. He had been transferred just before U-99 left on her last patrol.

ships with a shot from 800 yards. Though HAHIRA was protected by a corvette frantically circling her, he coolly waited another four minutes, and fired another fish at the doomed tanker. The third torpedo did the job, and HAHIRA gave up the struggle and slid under, carrying three crewmen with her.[11] There was no time to bemoan her fate. After she went down, a periscope was sighted between the third and fourth columns, and ships all around opened up with machine gun and heavy caliber fire. One merchantman let go with a five-inch projectile which hit short and ricocheted over the commodore's vessel. RESTI-GOUCHE swung around and came down between the columns to investigate, but was unable to make Asdic contact.

During the night of fog and confusion, many of the U-boats had lost contact and were running on the surface attempting to relocate the convoy, which had made several evasive course changes. Reports were made to U-boat Headquarters throughout the day by various boats, with estimates of the number of ships in the convoy varying from 4 to as high as 26. From their low height of eye, the U-boat commanders were having difficulty making out all the ships in the convoy. With intermittent daytime attacks by submerged U-boats, and the heavy radio traffic indicating that many others were closing for a night attack, there was little prospect for rest. The crews of the convoy vessels were showing fatigue, and the naval crews on the escorts, battling vainly to protect the convoy, were reaching the limit of their endurance. The escort commander, on whom rested the ultimate responsibility for the convoy, had had little sleep for two and a half days. It is for good reasons that young men are assigned to such jobs, though their overall experience may be less than more senior officers.

After picking up the survivors from HAHIRA, the gallant little STOCKPORT had 350 survivors aboard, more than three times her normal capacity. The escort commander, realizing that

[11] An amazingly small loss considering the flash fire and three torpedo hits.

she was jampacked, and envisioning the catastrophe that would occur were she hit while rescuing more survivors, requested the commodore to designate the U.S. Navy tugs, UNCAS and PESSACUS, as rescue vessels.

The two tiny tugs, 110 feet long, had been attached to the convoy as an afterthought. They had departed Boston some weeks before enroute via Halifax to Iceland, where they were to be employed assisting shipping in Reykjavik harbor. Both vessels were newly commissioned, as were their skippers, Ensign C. J. Smith, USNR, and Ensign A. J. Guja, USNR. Looking at the two tiny vessels tossing around in the heavy seas, Admiral Watson remarked to the master of the JEYPORE that the Americans were taking a chance to even send them out into the open Atlantic in the fall. Now, they were faced not only with the weather, but the unenviable job of dropping astern of the convoy to rescue survivors if another ship were hit. In the heavy Atlantic swell, only their masts were visible at times, and when they started astern to take up their assigned stations, Admiral Watson ordered them to burn running lights. In the darkness, they could easily be mistaken for a submarine, and a hit from a four-inch shell would be all that was needed to do them in.

After spelling off the two tugs for rescue, the commodore ordered a 20-degree turn to port just before sunset, and arranged for a further 40-degree turn to be made after dark, in hope of throwing off some of the trailing U-boats. Then he went below to the cabin, hoping to get a little rest before the night's activities began. No one in the convoy doubted that they would. Most of the pack were in solid contact and only awaiting darkness before getting down to business again.

As night fell over the cold waters south of Greenland, the lights were burning brightly in Headquarters of U-boat Command in Paris, as the staff examined the plot, and digested the latest progress reports from Group *Violet*. At 1815, the operations officer, Korvettenkapitän Hessler, finished his briefing, and turned to Admiral Doenitz.[12] The Commander in Chief, U-boats, looked at the markers designating Convoy SC-107 and the boats of Group *Violet* around it. Next he looked at the 15 markers, some 500 miles east of SC-107, representing Group *Natter*. On a patrol line to the south and east of Iceland, the group was at present unemployed, was well up on fuel, and had full torpedo loads. Turning to the staff, Doenitz said, "We will commit Group *Natter*. Order them to go in and attack."

Twenty minutes later, the powerful radio command station at Lorient began transmitting the orders, and the boats of the group turned westward, preparing to receive bearings from the stationkeeper now ten miles astern of SC-107. Twenty-five boats would soon be engaged against SC-107 and its seven escorts. Sensing a chance to effect a battle of annihilation, Doenitz had quickly grasped the opportunity.

The implications had also been apparent to Admiral Sir Percy Noble, Commander in Chief, Western Approaches (CINCWA), under whose operational control SC-107 had now passed. In the underground war room at Derby House in Liverpool, Admiral Noble had been following the ordeal of SC-107 with increasing concern as the attacks continued. It had already become painfully clear that this was no attack by one or two U-boats, but a full-blown wolf-pack action. VANESSA had already been pulled off from Convoy HX-213 to aid SC-107. To further weaken HX-213's escort would be inviting disaster should it be attacked. The Admiral's eyes fell on three small magnetic labels high up on the chart, representing three American escorts, the Coast Guard Cutter INGHAM and the destroyers USS SCHENCK and USS LEARY. All three had arrived in Iceland from an escort job the previous day, and were under control of Commander Task Group 24.6. In the entire North Atlantic, they were the only

---

[12] Hessler was Admiral Doenitz's son-in-law, but his position as staff operations officer was not due to nepotism. He had a fine combat record as a U-boat commander and was a topnotch operations type.

three available vessels in a position to reach SC-107 in time to be of help. A message went out from CINCWA, requesting that INGHAM, SCHENCK, and LEARY be sailed to reinforce the escort of SC-107. Commander Task Group 24.6 quickly agreed and the three warships were directed to make ready for sea.

While the few crewmen ashore were rounded up by the Shore Patrol, engineers on the three ships began building up steam, and feverish preparations were made to sortie. At 2200, ING-HAM weighed anchor, and without waiting for the two destroyers, stood out of the fjord and through the submarine nets. From the Task Unit Commander, Commander George McCabe, USCG, went a message to the two destroyers, *Follow and join me at best speed.* Two hours later, the destroyers stood out to sea, working up to speed as their black gangs built up steam. By the following morning, they had joined on INGHAM and the three ships barreled toward SC-107 at 18 knots, shuddering and pounding as they plowed through the 15-foot swells. It was now a race between the reinforcement unit and Group *Natter,* but even if the American unit reached the convoy first, the escort would still be outnumbered. When Group *Natter* arrived, the odds would be even worse than they had been for the first two days.

In the scheme of things, one of the fortunate aspects is the inability of man to see into the future; the present is often difficult enough. As the last light of day faded on the evening of November 3rd, no one in SC-107 was aware of the strength of Group *Violet,* or of the presence of Group *Natter,* or what the night ahead held in store. Ensign George Beemer, the battery officer on GEMINI's aftermount, had been relieved, and after a short conversation with his relief, started below.

"Keep it quiet," he flung back as he started down the ladder.

"Sleep tight," the new battery officer answered, and turned away to examine the convoy.

The visibility was good, and the flickering northern lights lit up the convoy with a ghostly pale light. Turning to the gun cap-

The War Room of Commander-in-Chief, Western Approaches (CINCWA) at Derby House in Liverpool. The CINC is being briefed by an RAF officer attached to his staff, while a Wren on the ladder adjusts markers showing the positions of Allied shipping. One British admiral, noting the Wrens working on the ladder, is reputed to have said, "We must either require the Wrens to wear pants or route the convoys further south." Imperial War Museum

Vice-Admiral B. C. Watson, CB, DSO, RN with the Duchess of Kent at a review. Shortly afterward, he retired and began duty as a convoy commodore. Imperial War Museum

An ammunition ship explodes after being hit by a torpedo while in convoy. Some 580 men, mostly U. S. Air Force personnel, were killed in this explosion. U-132 may have been lost after torpedoing the HOBBEMA under similar circumstances. USCG/National Archives

tain, a bos'n mate who had survived the sinking of the USS LEXINGTON some months before in the Pacific, the battery officer checked to see that he had assigned lookout sectors to the gun crew, and warned him to keep everyone on their toes. With the watch set, he turned his attention again to the convoy.

He had focused his binoculars on the commodore's ship, the JEYPORE, clearly visible in the brilliant northern lights, when suddenly there was a dull flash, and a tall column of water rose up on the starboard side of JEYPORE. Almost simultaneously, the shock wave hit GEMINI like the impact of a blacksmith's hammer on an anvil, solid, metallic, and final, followed seconds later by the muffled boom across a mile of water.

"They've gigged the commodore! Tell conn that the commodore has been hit."

The general alarm was already sounding. The trainer swung the gun around, as the loaders flung open the doors of the ready ammunition box, and the gun captain threw the handle to open the breech block. But there was nothing to shoot at. Noticing all the gun crew looking at the JEYPORE, the gun captain shouted, "Goddammit, keep a lookout all around! The bastard may be anywhere."

JEYPORE, now swinging to the left out of column, had a faint glow forward of her bridge, and sparks were rising from the fo'c's'le. By the time she had passed the third column, forcing PLEIADES out of line, the flames were leaping nearly to the bridge. As everyone on GEMINI stared in horrified fascination, the stricken ship continued her turn toward them, less than 500 yards away. On the starboard wing of the bridge, a small group of men, clearly outlined by the leaping flames, were attempting to take the blazing ship out of the convoy. Others were trying to get a boat swung out on the starboard side, and a few were climbing down the cargo net which had been rigged over the side, or jumping into the sea. The entire fo'c's'le was a mass of flames as she passed 300 yards astern of GEMINI, and the shouts of the crewmen, pierced occasionally by a scream, blended in with the crackling of the flames to form a chilling crescendo of terror in the cold northern night.

The night's ordeal was only beginning. Two flares arched into the night astern, and another ship turned on her red lights and started dropping aft.

The damage had been done by U-89, which had penetrated on the surface between the columns of the convoy. Once inside the convoy, Kapitänleutnant Dietrich Lohmann wasted no time.[13] At a range of 1,800 yards, he had fired two shots at JEYPORE, one of which hit her on the starboard side. Two more shots from the bow tubes at another ship missed. Swinging quickly, he missed a single shot from his stern tubes at TITUS at a range of 1,000 yards, and then escaped through the convoy.

The escort commander called for snowflake illumination, but only one was fired. The constant firing of the past three days had nearly exhausted the convoy's supply of illumination pyrotechnics.

When the torpedo hit JEYPORE, Admiral Watson was standing in the captain's cabin just below the bridge. Glass broke and objects were thrown around, but the Admiral was not sure that they were hit. The explosion, he thought, was not as violent as the one that occurred when HMS ARETHUSA had been mined under him. But as he emerged on deck, the flames and smoke erased any doubts. The phosphate cargo was on fire, and beneath the phosphate and in other holes were munitions. Most of the lascar crew immediately abandoned ship in one boat, and several others jumped overboard. When the staff signalman reported that the secret publications had been jettisoned, the officers, together with several lascars who had remained aboard, began lowering a boat. After it was put into the water, the engine refused to start. To compound the difficulty, the rudder had been

---

[13] Lohman was still another student of Kretschmer in U-99, having sailed as a student commanding officer under the more experienced U-boat ace. Like Bargsten and von Forstner, he was detached just before the last cruise of U-99. SC-107 had the misfortune to be engaged with the "first team." Though Kretschmer was in Canada, a prisoner since U-99 was sunk in 1941, his influence was still being felt.

smashed as the boat was lowered, and the oars were all securely lashed together. The Admiral broke out a knife, cut the lashings, and the 12 men began rowing frantically to get away from the ammunition-laden ship. As the distance widened, Admiral Watson later recalled feeling a sense of relief that the ordeal was finally over. It is a feeling that many other men in combat have experienced when the worst finally happens. Anticipation and waiting can be deadlier than realization.

A small tug was soon sighted, but it went by without stopping in order to rescue survivors further ahead. The second tug, the UNCAS, soon arrived and despite the heavy swell, quickly took the survivors aboard. The little rescue tugs were then joined by a corvette, which led them to other survivors.

Admiral Watson climbed up to the bridge of the tug, and was greeted by Ensign Smith, the commanding officer.

"What can we do for you, Admiral?" asked the young officer.

"A good strong whiskey," replied the Admiral.

"Sorry, sir," was the reply, "but our ships are dry."

Undaunted, the Admiral produced a small bottle, which he had stuck in his greatcoat, and shared it with several of the survivors. Thinking that before the night was over, Smith might have need of reinforcement, he left a little in the bottle on the ensign's bunk. Later, he learned that it had been thrown overboard as something which was not proper on an American ship.

"Smith was," said the Admiral, "a zealous young officer, but still it is extraordinary to send ships to sea in wartime without 'medical' comforts."

The little tugs had completed the pickup of survivors and started after the convoy, when fighting broke out again.

MOOSEJAW had picked up a radar contact ahead of the starboard column, and illuminated with starshells. In the light of the starshells, a trimmed-down U-boat was sighted, and the corvette opened fire with its four-inch gun. The U-boat quickly dived, and at 1,100 yards MOOSEJAW made Asdic contact and dropped a ten-charge pattern. Contact was not regained. Minutes later,

ALGOMA followed with a depth-charge attack near the starboard side of the convoy, also without apparent results.

At 2310, U-132 came in on the surface and slammed a torpedo into the HOBBEMA on the starboard side of the convoy. Minutes later, he fired four torpedoes at EMPIRE LYNX and HATIMURA. Two torpedoes hit each ship, the columns of water rising 60 feet in the air, and both vessels dropped astern, mortally wounded.

"It was," reluctantly admitted the CO of the USS PLEIADES, himself a former submariner, "a beautiful attack."

Thirty minutes later came what was ever afterwards referred to by survivors of SC-107 as the "Big Explosion." After HATIMURA and EMPIRE LYNX were hit, GEMINI had secured from general quarters, and three of the passenger officers went below to the galley, where the cook was baking hot bread. At that stage of the war, and to hungry men, Spam and hot slices of freshly baked bread were considered good eating. They stood around talking, while the cook, who had taken the bread from the oven, tested it to see if it had cooled enough to cut. Suddenly, there was a terrific crash, hurling some men into the air and sprawling others on the deck.

"That's us, boys!"

The cook carefully placed his tray of bread on the galley range, then with one accord the five men in the compartment bolted for the ladder. Dozens of men poured on deck, and headed for abandon-ship stations, before they began to realize that GEMINI was not listing, and that the engines were still running.

The blast had been so violent that the quartermaster on RESTIGOUCHE, astern of the convoy, logged an entry, "This ship hit," and inflated his life jacket to abandon ship. Two miles on the port beam, a corvette recorded, "Heavy explosion close aboard." On GEMINI, the radio operator opened up on the distress frequency and reported a torpedo hit. Several other vessels likewise reported hits, and a number turned on their red lights.[14] Six miles astern of the convoy, the two small tugs were so shaken by the explosion that the engines of UNCAS stopped running, and many of the survivors on board believed her to be hit. It was, said one, "like the crack of doom."

Soon, however, the engines were started again, and the gallant little vessel got underway to where two ships were lying in the water. One was well down by the stern, and the other had been trying to pick up survivors. All around them in the water were lights on rafts and boats. The crew of the rescuing vessel, shaken badly by the explosion and believing her torpedoed, had ceased rescue operations and had themselves abandoned ship. It was the TITUS, which had dropped astern when the JEYPORE was torpedoed earlier. While still astern of the convoy, she had sighted the sinking EMPIRE LYNX and had been picking up survivors when the "Big Explosion" occurred. It lifted her bow out of the water so violently that her crew abandoned ship in two boats. Twenty-two men in one were picked up by one of the tugs and taken to Iceland, where they reported the ship had been sunk. The report of its death, however, was premature, for the master, seeing the ship still afloat, reboarded it with the 16 men in his boat, and got the ship underway again. Survivors of the EMPIRE LYNX were then picked up, as well as several men from the HATIMURA, and the combined crews sailed the ship to England. After arrival, she was dry-docked, and the only damage revealed was a small dent in her port side.

The "Big Explosion" was one of terrific magnitude, and its cause was never determined. Many thought at the time that it was caused by the fire reaching JEYPORE's load of munitions. However, it was later determined that she was 15 miles astern and still burning at the time of the explosion. A more plausible assumption is that the cargo of munitions on HOBBEMA deto-

---

[14] The escort commander suspected that these had only been shaken by the explosion, and were not hit. A check by a corvette proved this to be the case.

nated as a result of fire or a finishing shot by a U-boat. Whatever the cause of the explosion on the night of November 3rd, it must have been one of the more violent before the coming of nuclear weapons. Even U-boats at a depth of 200 feet were heavily jolted, and sent in reports about the severity of the blast.

U-132 never made a report after her attack on EMPIRE LYNX and HATIMURA, and when she failed to return from patrol, U-boat Command, being aware of the big explosion, concluded that she had probably been destroyed by the explosion of a ship she had torpedoed. (Though the idea seems farfetched, U-68 only six months before had been heavily damaged in just such a manner by the explosion of the SS SURREY, which she had torpedoed twice off Panama. The SURREY went down, and at an estimated depth of 2,500 feet, its cargo of 5,000 tons of dynamite exploded, severely shaking the U-boat which was cruising on the surface in the vicinity.)

After the war, however, this assumption was discarded when the British revealed that a U-boat was sunk near Convoy SC-107 on the morning of November 5th by a Liberator of British No. 120 Squadron. As U-132 failed to return from patrol, the British concluded that the boat sunk was U-132, and the fact is carried today in the official records. A recent study of the war diary of U-89, however, disclosed the surprising fact that it, and not U-132, was the boat attacked by the Liberator that morning. U-89 was only damaged and escaped.

What then happened to U-132? Her secret lies 2,000 fathoms beneath the cold gray waters south of Greenland, but U-boat Command's guess that she was destroyed by the explosion of HOBBEMA is as likely a theory as any.

After the big explosion, the people on GEMINI stood by their abandon-ship stations until it became apparent that the ship had not been hit, then slowly dispersed. A few slipped down to the wardroom, drank coffee with shaky hands, and inhaled badly needed cigarettes. In the midst of the speculations as to what had caused the explosion, Lieutenant "Ace" Parker, a Coast Guard officer passenger enroute to join the INGHAM, came in with the news that help was on the way. "The code room says that CIN-CWA has ordered INGHAM and two American destroyers to join us!"

This news caused some animated speculation and boosted morale considerably. Perhaps they were already at sea and much closer than Iceland. As the night wore on, the hot dope re-circulated and built up, and by 2200 came the fantastic story that the support group had already reached the convoy and had attacked a submarine. It was a vivid demonstration of the build-up of rumor, and what is sometimes referred to as "whistling by the cemetery." Actually, INGHAM was nearly 400 miles away, and the rumor mongers were indulging in hopeful self-deceit.

Man almost never admits to his inward self that he won't survive. In the most desperate situation, he will grant that some, perhaps most, of the people around him may not make it, but his faith in his own permanence remains firm. This same rationalization allows men to perform acts of incredible courage, as well as smoke two packs of cigarettes a day. Of Pickett's 15,000 men charging the ridge at Gettysburg, perhaps 14,975 were sure they would survive. And as others dropped around them while they themselves still advanced, their mental dodge was confirmed, right up until the dull thud of the Minie ball.

But at 0100 on November 4, 1942, one officer on GEMINI was not as confident. He recalls:

> I knew with certainty that this was it. The last nagging fear was replaced with the beginning of resentment at having to leave so many things undone. My thoughts, becoming more bitter, were interrupted by a messenger telling me it was 0200 and time to relieve the battery officer on the forward three-incher. I started up the ladder, ready whenever my time came.
>
> Feeling my way along the superstructure, my hand hit an object on the rail. On more careful examination, it turned out to be a cork life ring. Taking out my knife, I cut the line and slung the life ring over my shoulder. At least I now had some means of floating, and as I climbed up to

the forward gun platform, the feel of the life ring was re-
assuring, though the scene of a battery officer wearing a
steel helmet with a life ring over his shoulder will never
make a recruiting poster. After checking over the gun crew,
and giving them instructions, my resignation began to slip
away, and within the hour, I again had hope of seeing the
dawn. With the life ring, I would somehow come through,
and another ship would pick me up. Before I left the gun
platform, the premonition of death had vanished.

Others were not as concerned. In the wardroom, an Army
officer said, "Hell, the only reason this tub is afloat is that it isn't
worth a damn torpedo. They won't waste one on us." He may
have had a point.

The rest of the night was, by comparison, fairly quiet. Three
more attacks, evidenced by torpedoes exploding at the end of
their runs, were made by U-boats, but no more ships were hit.
The wind was rising and the seas were making up rapidly, and
in the pre-dawn darkness, Group *Violet* lost contact with the
badly mauled convoy. At dawn, however, one boat sighted a corvette astern of the convoy and followed it, figuring that it would
eventually close the convoy. For the first time in five days, Convoy
SC-107 was out of contact with the enemy.

Welcome as the respite was, salvation for SC-107 had come in
the pre-dawn darkness three hundred miles to the east. One of
the boats of Group *Natter,* racing westward to attack, sighted
Convoy ON-143, westbound from the United Kingdom to New
York. When the sighting report was received by U-boat Command, Doenitz decided to use Group *Natter* for the attack on
undamaged ON-143 rather than against SC-107. At 0600, the
orders went out, and Group *Natter* began its deployment to attack
the westbound convoy. The change saved SC-107, or what remained of it.

The tiny UNCAS and PESSACUS rejoined the convoy after
dawn. On the two tugs were a total of 240 survivors, literally
jampacked. Men sat or lay in every inch of space, so crowded
that many had to sit in the engine rooms in the small spaces

around the machinery. To compound the misery, the little tugs were rolling and pounding badly in the rising seas. Few people were hungry, and it was fortunate. So busy were the tug crews in merely staying afloat and finding room for their human cargo that the only ration served the first day was dry shredded wheat cereal. An effort to transfer some of the survivors to the various escorts had to be cancelled due to the steadily worsening weather. To make matters worse, water was in extremely short supply, and a first estimate showed less than two days' supply remained on one vessel.

Faced with a situation that could only rapidly deteriorate, the escort commander decided to break off the three rescue vessels, together with the Navy oiler GAUGER, and send them into Iceland under escort of two corvettes. The reduction of the already weak escort by the detachment was a risk, but one that was unavoidable. The two corvettes selected for the mission had inoperative radars, and could best be spared. As the little group, loaded with over 600 survivors, broke off from the convoy at dusk, Debby Piers fervently hoped that the support group would join up before the next attack. RESTIGOUCHE had been in radio contact with INGHAM since morning, periodically transmitting homing signals. In the heavy seas, however, the larger INGHAM had had to slow to 15 knots because of the pounding being taken by the two accompanying destroyers.

The night of November 4th was rough, with high winds, but clear. The northern lights flickered brightly, and with these to silhouette the convoy, any attack was likely to come from the starboard side. U-89, however, which had regained contact with the convoy just before dark, chose to be perverse, and attacked from the port side. Two torpedoes were fired at a range of 2,000 yards at the leading ship of the left column, the DALEBY, and one hit beneath the bridge. The stricken ship sheered out of the column to port, and dropped astern. White flares were fired, and an escort opened up with starshells.

Ten miles ahead of the convoy, INGHAM sighted the flares

and starshells. Correctly deducing that the convoy was again under attack, Commander McCabe ordered INGHAM to general quarters, turned to port to unmask his batteries, and began pumping starshells into the air in an attempt to distract and lure away the attackers.

As the DALEBY dropped astern, there was no rescue vessel to go to her aid, and in the rough seas, her outlook was grim as she began to settle. But the SS BRAUFOSS, an Icelandic freighter, dropped back with her, and recovered 40 of the crew before she went under three hours later. The action by Capt. Erickson of the BRAUFOSS and his crew, all neutrals, was one of great courage and human decency.

After firing the spread of starshells, INGHAM, SCHENCK, and LEARY deployed ahead of the convoy, patrolling for the rest of the night, and the remaining hours of darkness passed quietly. At dawn they took stations assigned in the screen. When INGHAM swung in alongside RESTIGOUCHE, and began receiving instructions by signal light, Piers on RESTIGOUCHE signaled to McCabe on INGHAM, asking if he wished to relieve him of command of the escort. It was a gesture of courtesy to McCabe, considerably his senior, and McCabe declined. Not only should command of the escort in nearly all cases remain with the assigned escort commander, regardless of seniority, but McCabe would be detaching with part of the convoy as it approached Iceland.

Group *Violet* had regained contact just before dawn, and U-boat Command urged that the attack be resumed. But SC-107 had finally emerged on the Iceland side of the Black Pit, and at dawn, a long-range RAF Liberator of No. 120 Squadron arrived from Iceland and reported to RESTIGOUCHE. For several hours, RESTIGOUCHE had been taking DF bearings on submarines around the convoy, and had a plentiful supply of customers lined up. A vector was given the Liberator on the latest bearing, and ten minutes later, she sighted a submarine on the surface in broad daylight and roared in for the attack. The U-boat, operating without worry of air attack for several days, was taken by surprise, and straddled with a stick of depth charges. It was U-89, which had sent JEYPORE and DALEBY to the bottom, and though heavily damaged, she escaped. Within the next two hours, the Liberator, running down HF/DF bearings from RESTI-GOUCHE, had made two more attacks, and exhausted her depth bombs.[15] However, she remained with the convoy for several hours more, and kept the trailing U-boats down. So effective was the presence of the one aircraft that the last boat in contact, U-521, was forced to dive at 1000, and contact with the convoy was never regained. Because of the aircraft threat, U-boat Command ordered that no further attacks be attempted until dark, and further directed that the attack be broken off completely the following morning. The result of lack of any air cover during the previous four days was painfully clear.

As the day drew on, the weather steadily worsened, and by the following morning was blowing a full gale. For the first time in nearly a week, a night passed without a submarine attack or alarm. On November 7th, the Iceland section of eight ships detached under escort of INGHAM, SCHENCK, and LEARY, and the ordeal of SC-107 had come to an end. U-boat Command claimed 23 ships of 136,000 tons sunk, and two escorts damaged.[16] The claim was exaggerated, but the price of 15 ships totalling 81,000 tons was a horrible enough price to pay for an inadequate escort and lack of long-range air cover.

The escort was deficient in both numbers and quality. The fact is undeniable that some of the escorts were manned by green crews, but the low experience level was unavoidable as seasoned sailors were spread thin to man new construction escorts. It is to

---

[15] Piers cautioned the Liberator pilot on his first vector, "Don't use all your bombs on the first one, I've got plenty more."

[16] Karl Doenitz, *Memoirs of Ten Years and Twenty Days* (Bonn: Athenaum-Verlag Junkerund Dunnhaupt, 1958), p. 338. Some of the exaggerated claims were due to the fact that two or more submarines torpedoed one ship. Others were due to the U-boat diving and assuming that a hit had been made when the torpedo explosion was heard. Admiral Doenitz says, "Before the war I had always urged commanders to estimate cautiously and accurately—we are an honest firm!"

the everlasting credit of the Royal Canadian Navy that they did as well as they did. Eventually, the ever increasing numbers of escorts would provide the sea time, the experience, and the resources that would bring victory. But in 1942, not enough escorts were available to defend the convoys, and the constant shuffling to provide them did not permit the formation of permanent escort groups, able to train and operate as a team. Again and again, the necessity for teamwork and group training was to be shown. Even experienced ships, when thrown together in a hastily formed escort group, were to prove inadequate for the job. We were to learn the same lessons during the bitter months of February and March.

Even more glaring was the failure of the Allies to provide long-range four-engine aircraft for air coverage in the mid-Atlantic area. Here, as always, there were conflicting requirements between the bomber people and Coastal Command, which was charged with ASW air cover. The ASW forces came in second best, and not until late spring of 1943 were anything like enough adequate long-range aircraft provided. Like so many other measures, it was "too late" to save hundreds of fine ships that need not have been lost.[17]

On the German side, the immediate outlook was brighter. Fifteen boats had been ordered in against SC-107. Two had been sunk by land-based airplanes before making contact, and one destroyed in a freak explosion. But during the four days of the battle, when no air cover was available, the boats in contact with the convoy had made 29 attacks and sunk 15 ships without other loss or serious damage from attacks by the surface escorts. With the German building program feeding increasing numbers of U-boats into the operational flotillas, and losses at an acceptable level, the U-boat men looked forward with confidence to the coming winter. But there was a vulnerability which was becoming increasingly obvious to the U-boat planners. This was the attrition among the aggressive, experienced U-boat commanders.

[17] See Appendix III, "The Long-Range Aircraft Controversy," p. 256.

These "tiger types" were making most of the kills, but venturing more in harm's way than their more timid brothers, were being killed off at a higher rate.[18] The more conservative commanders, taking fewer chances, were content to "brown off" the convoys from long range, a safer procedure, though producing far fewer results.

During the battle of SC-107, the bold and aggressive von Forstner had made one-third of the kills, while U-522, -521, -132, and U-89 had made the rest. Five of 13 boats had done all the damage. But their day of reckoning was not far off. U-132 had not even had the opportunity to get out an attack report before going down. Schneider and his tough crew in U-522 had only 90 days to live before succumbing under a barrage of depth charges from HMS TOTLAND. U-89 would fall prey to carrier aircraft in May, and less than a month later, U-521 went down with everyone but her skipper. Von Forstner would survive nearly a year, and before he was killed, many of those who witnessed his work against SC-107 were destined to have a grim rendezvous with him on a rough and cold February night near the scene of his November triumphs.

The morale of many of the merchant crews in the convoy was low after the slaughter of SC-107. Although the rescue vessels had done an exceptional job in recovering survivors under extremely adverse circumstances, and the death rate was not as great as it might have been, the ordeal had taken its effect. Some of the hundreds of survivors unloaded at Reykjavik loudly proclaimed that their seagoing career was at an end. One merchant skipper ventured the opinion that "unless something is done to afford better protection to the convoys, we will be unable to find enough men to man the ships." SC-107 was at that time an atypical convoy, the heaviest hit of any in 1942; but unfortunately it

---

[18] That these increasing losses, and the build-up of Allied strength, were apparent to the realistic Doenitz is evidenced by his War Diary entry of August 21, 1942, "These ever-increasing difficulties which confront us in the conduct of the war can only lead, in the normal course of events, to high and, indeed, intolerable losses, to a decrease in the volume of our success and to a diminution, therefore, of our chances of Victory in the U-boat war as a whole."

was to be soon repeated. In the coming winter, the U-boat on-slaught was to intensify and the overall monthly losses within the convoys were to hit even higher totals before the reversal of the battle came with unforeseen suddenness. Before it did, the Battle of the Atlantic was to hang in the balance, and the Allies were to face the grim spectre of defeat.

The day after the Iceland section of SC-107 arrived in Reykjavik Roads, GEMINI was eased alongside the dock to offload. The first passengers ashore walked down the gangplank, and several solemnly got down on their knees and kissed the earth. It was the payoff on a number of fervent promises.

The troops offloaded during the day, and the officer passengers were taken to NOB, Iceland, and housed in Quonset huts to await the return of their various ships to port. The first Saturday afternoon after arrival, several were in the officers' club sipping Scotch at fifteen cents a glass when the air raid alarm went off. Rushing outside, they saw high overhead a speck in the sky—a German recco aircraft out of Norway, taking a look at the harbor area and the fleet anchorage at Hvalfjordur where several major Home Fleet units lay. Five thousand feet over the harbor, three Army P-39 fighters were orbiting in lazy circles, oblivious to the Heinkel high above them. Finally, the Army got the word, and the fighters started climbing, but the Heinkel promptly headed eastward and escaped scot free. It was several weeks before the fighter boys tumbled to the regularity of the schedule maintained by the Luftwaffe, and waited in ambush over the east coast for the Saturday recco flight. Only after three were splashed by the waiting fighters did the Germans decide to amend their schedule.

Other officers took advantage of the wait ashore to ride as observers on PBY's covering an Iceland-bound convoy. The weather was bitter cold, and in the after-gun blisters, they fought a losing battle to keep warm. The sheepskin-lined clothing merely delayed the chilling process. The long flights under miserable and dangerous conditions without even a hostile radar contact were typical of anti-submarine air patrols in that area—hundreds of hours of monotony, interrupted at long intervals by moments of

HMCS ARVIDA enters port loaded with survivors. Public Archives Canada

CGC INGHAM, arriving with destroyers SCHENCK and LEARY, and reenforced the next day by aircraft from Iceland, helped end the ordeal of SC-107. USCG/National Archives

USS SCHENCK fires a starshell spread. USN/National Archives

The Fleet Anchorage at Hvalfjordur, Iceland, known to the escort sailors as "Valley Forge" or "Happy Valley." USN/National Archives

sheer horror, and occasionally a submarine contact. In the existent state of instrument flying, the Iceland-based U. S. Navy aircraft were often unable to provide long-range anti-submarine cover during the coming winter, but they did when they could, and they earned their money when they went out.

On the 17th of November, when INGHAM arrived at Hvalfjordur, her draft of new officers departed on an Icelandic passenger bus for the 25-mile trip over the mountains to go on board. Arriving at "Happy Valley," or "Valley Forge," as the fleet called Hvalfjordur, they were taken by boat out to the INGHAM, swinging to her anchor in the middle of the fjord, with an oiler alongside pumping fuel.

INGHAM was a veteran ship. Based on Lisbon, Portugal, when the U.S. entered the war, she had been quickly recalled, and had been engaged in the Atlantic battle since February. The pre-war crew was nearly intact, only a small portion of the 225 enlisted men being reservists. They were a tough, seasoned lot who, with their bearded faces and junglecloth clothing white with dried salt, would have done Captain Teach proud. Despite their piratical appearance, they were a well-trained crew of regulars on a fine, capable ship.

INGHAM was one of seven sister ships completed only five years before. Of the seven, six were assigned to the North Atlantic run. HAMILTON had been torpedoed and sunk off Iceland in February,[19] and the other five, INGHAM, BIBB, DUANE, CAMPBELL, and SPENCER, were now assigned to the mid-ocean escort groups. Capable of twenty knots, long-legged enough to make an ocean convoy crossing without refueling, and seaworthy enough to maintain speed in seas that forced destroyers to slow down, they proved to be ideal ocean escorts in the rough northern ocean.[20]

In June, Admiral Ernest J. King, Commander-in-Chief, U. S. Fleet, had boarded DUANE in Hvalfjordur for an inspection of

[19] By Ernst Vogelsang in U-132, the same boat which was lost in the "Big Explosion" on the night of November 3rd.

[20] Four of these rugged and well designed ships were still in Coast Guard service in 1983, 46 years after launching! Their mother ship in Iceland, USS VULCAN is the only Navy ship of that era still in service.

fleet units. At a time when Allied shipping was being slaughtered
because of the lack of ocean escorts, Admiral King must have had
some bitter thoughts. In 1939, while serving on the Navy General
Board, he had recommended that this class of cutter be adopted
as the standard convoy escort, and that construction of a large
number begin at once. The Fleet Training Division of the Chief
of Naval Operations bickered for months about details of speed
and armament, however, and the additional ships were never
built. Finally, a new design of destroyer escort was adopted, and
construction began, but it was too late. By the time the first one
was delivered, the crisis of the Atlantic battle had passed, and
hundreds of ships and thousands of merchant sailors had paid
with their lives for the procrastination in this and other anti-
submarine measures. Only six of the HAMILTON-class cutters
were available in the Atlantic, but they produced results out of
proportion to their numbers.[21]

In addition to the remaining five HAMILTON's, a number of
old flushdeck destroyers of World War I vintage were available.
But these flush deckers were short-legged, unable to maintain
speed in heavy seas, and despite their fine personnel, were unsuit-
able as ocean escorts in rough northern waters.[22]

Both the quantity and the quality of American effort in the
crisis of the convoys has been criticized by European observers.
But the dearth of American escorts was not a matter of foot
dragging as much as of pressing priorities in other areas. In 1941,
while the U. S. was still at peace, a sizable number of Atlantic
Fleet destroyers had been committed to anti-submarine patrol
and to help escort British convoys in the North Atlantic, though
the Americans were poorly trained in ASW. In the years between
the wars, little emphasis was given to the unglamorous problem
of protecting merchant convoys in either the American or the
British navies. The U. S. Navy's eyes were on the Pacific and the
Japanese Fleet.

[21] All U-boat sinkings by American surface escorts in the North Atlantic prior
to defeat and withdrawal of the U-boats in May, 1943 were by HAMILTON-class
cutters. "Their performance," said Rear Admiral S. E. Morison, the U. S. Navy
historian, "was glorious; their casualties heavy."

[22] They were suffering badly from old age. One was alongside the destroyer
tender VULCAN when a sailor, chipping away at rust in the shaft alley, punched
a hole through the thin skin.

U. S. Coast Guard Cutter HAMILTON sinking off Iceland after being torpedoed by U-132. USCG/National Archives

An escort sailor. In the early days, these men were mostly tough, seasoned regulars, and the beards marked them as North Atlantic veterans. USCG/National Archives

USS GREER rolls heavily in an Atlantic gale. These ancient and worn World War I destroyers were not suited for the rough northern waters, but their crews sailed them there anyway. USN/National Archives

HAMILTON-class cutter patrolling the flank of an England bound convoy. In the heavy weather of the North Atlantic, there were no finer escorts. They were converted to amphibious command ships later in the war. Following service off Vietnam 30 years later, four are still in Coast Guard service. USCG/National Archives

With the outbreak of the Pacific war, many of the modern U. S. destroyers were hurriedly transferred from the Atlantic to reenforce the hard-pressed Pacific Fleet. Most of the remaining modern destroyers were assigned to protect major Atlantic Fleet units or to duty with the fast troop convoys, where speed was essential, but which by virtue of that speed rarely encountered U-boats or combat action.[23] The few remaining fleet destroyers were withdrawn from the North Atlantic in the early fall of 1942 for the North African invasion, and afterwards remained in the Mediterranean or with the Central Atlantic convoys running between the States and Gibraltar. During the coming crisis, there would therefore be no modern U. S. destroyers available for northern waters, and the crucial battle of the North Atlantic convoys would be fought by the Royal Navy, the Royal Canadian Navy, and a handful of Polish, Norwegian, and Free French escorts, old American flush-deck destroyers, and the modern HAMILTON-class Coast Guard cutters.

The paltry U. S. contribution at this stage was also due, to a lesser degree, to Admiral E. J. King's aversion to multi-national forces and to most things British. An acknowledged Anglophobe, COMINCH had little taste for mixing British and American forces, and resisted it on most occasions.[24] While the absence of more modern American surface units may not have proven the difference, the U. S. failure to provide long range air cover for the convoys was a near fatal omission, and could not be excused on the pretext of priority demands in other theatres. (See Appendix III/The Long Range Aircraft Controversy.)

The performance of the U. S. Navy in the crisis has been compared unfavorably with the stellar performance of the U. S. Coast Guard contingent. The old Navy flush-deck destroyers of 1918 vintage were in poor repair. In addition, while neither service entered the war with much ASW training or experience, most of the Coast Guard skippers and many crewmen had served

---

[23] A number of American heavy units with their escorting destroyers did see action with the British Home Fleet on the Arctic convoys to Russia in 1942–43.

[24] The new title of COMINCH (Commander-in-Chief) was coined when King took the post. He had no liking for the old title of CINCUS, which was pronounced, "Sink us."

during the long Rum War of the twenties and thirties, and some of their experience chasing the elusive smugglers may have had applicability to the U-boat problem. By the fall of 1942, moreover, seasoned Navy crews were being diluted to provide crews for new construction, which the Coast Guard did not experience for another six months. Finally, the HAMILTON's, being the Coast Guard's newest and best units, had a priority call on the service's best personnel; the old destroyers were in line only after the needs of the Navy's first line combatants were met. Given all these factors, the difference in results were to be expected, but it does not detract from the courage and the stamina of the U. S. Navy men who sailed those ancient and worn destroyers into stormy seas and conditions for which they were never intended.

The draft of Coast Guard officers reporting to the new and modern cutters operating out of Iceland were more fortunate. Five of them reporting to INGHAM were received with open arms, for they were long overdue, and some officers being relieved were going back to the States for assignment to new construction vessels. The skipper of INGHAM was Commander George McCabe, a veteran seaman and a pugnacious Irishman, with a lust for action. He had been aboard only two months, but his aggressiveness had the crew of INGHAM jumping, and their tails were well up. The officers were an experienced lot, nearly evenly divided between regulars and some highly competent and seasoned reservists.[25] With experienced officers and petty officers in demand to form the cadres for new construction vessels, INGHAM's experienced crew would eventually be broken up, but for the coming winter they were to remain untouched, only because the Stateside manning detail officers were unable to locate or get their hands on them.

Lieutenant Commander Sid Porter was the executive officer, a gentlemanly and thoughtful man, somewhat the antithesis of the usual whip-cracking exec, but one who nevertheless got things done. In three months he would be dead, the victim of a sub-

---

[25] Within three years, over half of the officer complement would be commanding their own ships.

marine torpedo on a cold, raging night.[26] The navigator was Lieutenant Commander James D. Criak, with a mind like a computer, and a superb professional seaman. The rest of the officers were topnotch, as experienced as any group of Americans in the U-boat war, but nevertheless handicapped to some extent by the Navy's lack of basic doctrine and ASW training that nine months of combat action had not completely overcome. The U. S. Navy, including the Coast Guard, had simply not been prepared for this kind of war, and but for the hard-earned experience of the Royal Navy, freely passed on, would have likely been run off the Atlantic in 1942 by the mounting U-boat offensive.

Anti-submarine war is an unglamorous type of drudgery for which there is no simple or single approach. Few officers in the peacetime years took an interest in it, and those who did were often penalized for their efforts. Captain F. J. Walker, the Royal Navy's top expert on ASW, was twice passed over for promotion. Only with the coming of war and the submarine threat was he belatedly promoted to captain as a result of his brilliant combat record. The same type of discrimination was not unknown in the U. S. Navy.[27]

Not only is ASW a relentless and often monotonous type of effort, but it is appallingly costly in terms of the effort in manpower and matériel required to meet the threat posed by a few hundred submarines and several thousand submarine combat personnel. Winston Churchill admitted that, "The only thing that ever really frightened me during the war was the U-boat peril." [25]

With his brilliant strategic insight, he more than any other Allied leader realized that the Battle of the Atlantic was the one campaign whose loss would inevitably prove fatal.

In his masterful *The Second World War,* he related:

Amid the torrent of violent events one anxiety reigned

---

[26] LCDR Porter, after being detached from INGHAM, was returning to the United States on a merchant vessel, which went down with all hands.

[27] There were probably other factors also. Many of the most successful U-boat killers and combat leaders were rugged individualists, and as such not likely to advance rapidly in the peacetime Navy. Only with the coming of war, and the acid test of combat, did they come into their own. One admiral, himself a rugged and salty type, was reputed to have said, when ordered to a top command, "When the country gets into trouble, they always call for the sons-of-bitches."

supreme. Battles might be won or lost, enterprises might
succeed or miscarry, territories might be gained or quitted,
but dominating all our power to carry on the war, or even
keep ourselves alive, lay our mastery of the ocean routes
and the free approach and entry to our ports.[28]

As the winter of 1942-1943 approached, we were perilously
close to losing them.

But to accuse those responsible for Navy policy of neglect is
an oversimplification. An escort can be built in less than six
months, while a major fleet unit takes two years or more. With
only limited funds available, a choice had to be made as to what
ships to build, and the decision was made to build the heavy
units. But there is, in retrospect, little excuse for the failure to
develop prototypes, and even less for the failure to develop
equipment and tactics. The warning was ample, for World War
II repeated a pattern in the Atlantic surprisingly similar to that
of World War I, and the first war's nearly successful U-boat campaign should have provided ample incentive to avoid another
such debacle. But little was done and the Navy entered World
War II woefully unprepared to deal with the most serious threat,
and only after 18 months of war was the situation remedied by
hard-learned and dearly-bought experience. So in INGHAM in
November, 1942, many lessons were still to be learned, and she
was one of the most experienced American units.

On the 22nd of November, she stood out of Happy Valley to
escort the tanker SS CULPEPPER to Seydisfjordur on the East
coast of Iceland, where she would refuel major units of the British Home Fleet returning from a Murmansk convoy. The trip
was uneventful, and after dropping anchor in the fjord, liberty
was granted to one section. As the first boatload of bluejackets
hit the beach for a long-overdue liberty, they passed two officers
standing on the dock and saluted smartly. War hadn't dimmed
their sense of military courtesy. The last two men out of the
boat were on shore patrol assignment; they took a long look and
didn't salute. The two officers on the pier were very militarily
and impeccably dressed, but in German Luftwaffe uniforms! The

[28] *Ibid.*, Vol. III, p. 111.

SP's promptly pulled out their pistols, and stood the two officers against a building. They turned out to be U. S. Army Intelligence officers, dressed as Germans in order to test the port security measures in Seydisfjordur, and were released; they were lucky not to have been shot. Their treatment was not as rough as that given three of the ship's officers who went hiking in the mountains. Returning near dark, they were challenged by a now alert Army sentry, and found themselves looking into the cold barrel of a Garand. Ordered to produce credentials, they discovered to their chagrin that they had failed to bring any along in their hiking gear; so with hands clasped behind their heads, they were marched to the provost marshal, urged on at frequent intervals by the sharp point of a bayonet. After some uncomfortable moments, they were identified by other officers and released to return to the ship and get identification papers and proper uniforms.

The North Atlantic is where the seaman takes his graduate course in weather, and the curriculum is tough. In late fall, a semi-permanent storm center, called the Icelandic Low, forms in the vicinity of Iceland, and for the next few months brews one howling storm after another. The combination of low temperatures and high winds makes it seem far colder than the thermometer indicates.[29] The second night in Seydisfjordur was devoted to a lesson on Foehn winds.

A British task group returning from Archangel entered the harbor during the afternoon, and an anti-aircraft cruiser came along INGHAM's port side. As the fjord was deep, and the cutter had an anchor down, the cruiser tied up alongside with one anchor under foot. The British had a wine mess, and most of INGHAM's officers not in the duty section were soon aboard the cruiser. The night was cold, with a light 10-knot breeze blowing. Shortly before midnight, the wind began to rise and, within five minutes, was blowing 30 knots. The OOD, worried about dragging anchor, took station on the bridge. After checking the navigation bearings, he ordered steam at the throttles, and called

[29] A 30-knot wind blowing with an air temperature of 30° F. is in terms of discomfort equal to a still-air temperature of minus 10° F. With wet clothing, the effect is even greater.

the executive officer. The exec was taking a shower but said he would be up right away. The CO was ashore.

The OOD checked the bearings again, and saw that the ship was dragging. The wind had reached 50 knots, with frequent higher gusts. It was too late to hoist a motor launch which had been streamed astern, and it soon carried away. When the quartermaster turned a searchlight on the nearby cliff, the OOD was startled by its closeness, and realizing that the ship was dragging faster than he had thought, rang up slow ahead with 30 rpm's on each shaft. The senior duty officer, arriving on the bridge, called the anchor and special sea detail and sent the messenger below to request the exec on the bridge as rapidly as possible. With a cruiser alongside, it was, he felt, nothing for junior officers to be handling on their own.

When the exec and the navigator reached the bridge, the wind was howling at 70 knots, making it difficult to see anything for the spray. Porter took over. He was going to have a job on his hands working out from between the cliff and the cruiser.

The storm, one of the dread Foehn winds, increased quickly to its full fury of nearly 100 knots. INGHAM's officers had been hurriedly recalled, and the cruiser was requested to cast off and get underway. With that studied nonchalance which is both admirable and exasperating in the Royal Navy, they went about it as though preparing for a leisurely peacetime summer training cruise. Only one officer could be seen on the cruiser's bridge, and no activity was evident on her fo'c's'le. INGHAM was by now going ahead with considerable power trying to hold herself and the cruiser off the cliff. From the cutter's bridge came the order to drop the port anchor underfoot, but it had little effect, and she was pushed closer to the cliff. Anchors and power combined were not going to hold with the drag of the cruiser on her. It had become a matter of save ship!

With a warning to the British that they were casting off, the crew of the cutter started to throw off the wire cables holding the two ships together. Some of the ties couldn't be loosened due to the strain. "Cut them!" ordered the bridge, so with fire axes one after the other was cut. Before the last could be cut, it snapped with a crack, and the cruiser drifted off into the darkness. She rode out the night and was anchored safely in the middle of the fjord the following morning.

With the cruiser off their back, the exec and navigator gradually worked the ship off the cliff and into deeper water. With the same suddenness with which it had come, the storm died out, and the fjord was soon calm. It had been a convincing demonstration of the fury of the sudden storms which sweep down from the high plateaus and through the narrow fjords.

After the anchor chain was paid out in deeper water, the exec walked up to the fo'c's'le and looked over the proceedings. Lighting up a cigar, he shook his head and said, "I'm going to get a cup of coffee. Then I think I'll get a change of skivvy drawers."

The following night, when the "happy hour" resumed on the cruiser, among the hosts were two RAF pilots, returning from a stay of several months in Archangel, and they made a living the hard way.

The British had for some time been suffering heavy losses from air attacks on the North Russian convoy runs. A cold-blooded planner in the Admiralty dreamed up a partial answer. One or two merchant vessels in each convoy were fitted with catapults, and an aging Hurricane fighter was provided for each of them. Only old and worn out planes were used, for they weren't coming back, and new fighters couldn't be spared. Pilots apparently could. When the incoming wave of Luftwaffe bombers was sighted, one or two fighters were catapulted and climbed up to attack them at odds of 1 to 10. If the fighter pilots were lucky, and survived the aerial melee, they circled overhead until their fuel was exhausted, then bailed out over the rough icy water, hoping to survive long enough for one of the convoy vessels to stop and pick them up. Yet both of the returnees professed eagerness to have another go at it, their only reservation being the long layover at Archangel, which they described as a "bloody awful spot."

Leaving the ship that night, the Americans carried a small puppy as a gift from the cruiser. His mother, said the cruiser's gunnery officer, was a thoroughbred Russian wolfhound and his father was a British admiral, and as a result, he had no pedigree.

He was to serve in INGHAM as Ship's Dog, First Class, for many months. Had he abstained from beer, and refrained from biting officers, he could have made Chief.

The trip back to Hvalfjordur, screening the CULPEPPER and the USS PLEIADES, was uneventful until radar made contact at night on an unidentified object at 2,500 yards. INGHAM went to battle stations and increased to full speed to ram should it prove to be a submarine. At 800 yards, a lookout sighted a small iceberg ahead, and the OOD executed a smart turn away, convinced that at times it doesn't pay to be too aggressive.

In Hvalfjordur, the ships had a week to catch up on repairs and liberty, and many of the escort officers went into Reykjavik to celebrate. The center of such night life as existed in the city was the Hotel Borg, where a dance was already underway. Oddly enough, all of the girls sat at tables on one side of the room, and the numerous Allied officers on the other. The only fraternization was on the dance floor. Having been occupied by the Americans, following a British-induced invitation, the Icelanders were making the best of the situation, but they were not liking it. Besides the occupation question, the attention paid to the Icelandic girls by the sailors and airmen was resented by the local swains, and an American walking along a street with a girl was likely to hear muttered remarks from men bystanders, the context of which could only be guessed by the rising color of the girl's face. But few of the local girls would at that time consort openly with Americans, and almost none would extend a walk into an invitation home, where the attitude was likely to be hostile and even pro-German. If the Kriegsmarine in northern Norway received anything approaching like treatment from the Norwegian girls, then it was a frigid war all over.

Young men being ever hopeful, a junior officer, urged on by his friends, crossed the ballroom at the Borg, and politely asked a girl to dance. When none of the four at the table even acknowledged his presence, the J.O. beat a confused retreat to his table.

"Oh hell, don't be bashful," said one of the old Iceland hands, "just go back and ask another one. They're all pretty cold, but you'll find one that's tired of sitting."

On the next try, one of the girls consented to dance. After ten minutes of carrying on what he deemed a sparkling line of chatter without any response, the young officer said, "Don't you understand English?"

"Yes."

"Well, why don't you say anything?"

Looking coolly at him for the first time, she said, "I come to dance, not talk."

The conversation was ended, as were any lingering illusions that "the natives are friendly."

With little future prospects at the Borg, the group drifted out to NOB, where good Scotch was cheap, and the patrons were reasonably sociable. After midnight, one of the ensigns stepped outside the officers' club for a breath of air. Looking down the street at the row of Quonset Huts which served as quarters for the PBY pilots, his mouth dropped open as a naked girl ran squealing around the corner of a hut, under the dim street light, and into another hut. Following close behind was an "airedale" with a pair of skivvies and a bottle as his only adornments. Pausing under the street light to check the tracks in the snow, he let out a whoop, and followed the girl into the hut.

The frustrated ensign walked back into the club shaking his head. The "black shoes," [30] he loudly proclaimed, didn't have a chance. Being in port only a few days each month, they had no continuity of operations. The airmen, on the other hand, not only had flight pay, but according to the escort people's biased version, never flew in the winter time, saving their energy for creative rather than destructive pursuits.

The seagoing types at the bar ordered another round and brooded on the injustice of it all. To a man, they could picture that *Stulka* in the hut 100 yards away saying, "I didn't come to talk. . . ."

---

[30] Seagoing officers usually wore blue uniforms ashore and were referred to by aviators as "black shoes" or "rope chokers." The aviators were "brown shoes," "airedales," or "zoomies."

IV

DECEMBER / SCRATCH
ONE HEARSE

On December 13th, INGHAM, with destroyers BABBITT and LEARY, was again at sea 400 miles south of Iceland screening the 12 merchantmen of Convoy ONSJ-142 in typically cold, foggy, and rough weather. Commander George McCabe, the skipper of INGHAM and escort commander, chewed on his cigar and scanned the seas ahead, then for the third time in an hour, walked back into the chart house and looked at the chart with Jimmy Craik, the navigator. The convoy continued steaming south at seven knots.

Convoy ONSJ-142 had departed Iceland two days before to rendezvous with the main westbound convoy, ON-142, for the trip across to the States. The small Iceland group had reached ICOMP,[1] but found no sign of the main convoy, and McCabe didn't know where they were. He was not alone; neither did CINCWA, under whose control they were operating.

The main convoy had taken departure from Oversay, a small outcropping of rock off the British Isles, a week before, and had been observing radio silence since. Naval control authorities knew what route and speed they were *supposed* to be making good, but the convoy had probably been slowed by the westerly gales and head seas. Furthermore, the escort commander could have ordered a course diversion to avoid a U-boat patrol line

[1] Iceland Convoy Ocean Meeting Point.

lying in the eastern Atlantic.[2] A convoy at sea could receive radio messages freely, but except in a dire emergency, it did not transmit, for the German HF/DF's could obtain its approximate position if radio silence was broken.

Convoy ON-142 had last been seen two days before by a patrolling Sunderland, and there had been no further reports. McCabe did not know for sure what they had been doing since. As darkness approached, he wheeled the Iceland section to the southwest. He would hold on the course of the main convoy during the night to prevent it passing in the darkness, and would again attempt to locate it the following day. INGHAM moved from the van to the danger spot astern of the merchantmen, where a trailing U-boat might attempt to overhaul a slow convoy.

At noon the following day, there was still no sign of air coverage or of the main convoy. Thinking himself perhaps too far south, McCabe changed course to the northwest and continued the search. Three days had gone by without a sighting, and the probability of error was steadily increasing. Not only was the position of the main convoy in doubt, but INGHAM itself had not had a star or sun fix since leaving Iceland. Running on dead reckoning navigation, her own position could be in error by many miles. Craik was up early, hoping for a break in the clouds to shoot a star or sun line by sextant, but the day dawned gray and rainy. Just after noon, however, the sun suddenly broke through the clouds. A messenger piled down the ladder to call the navigator, and a quartermaster brought the chronometer and sextant to the bridge wing. Running up to the bridge and grabbing the sextant, the navigator braced against the bridge combing to steady himself against the ship's motion. The sun hung low over the southern horizon.

"Stand by, mark!"

The quartermaster jotted down the time from the chronometer

---

[2] An escort commander could divert 50 miles to either side of the track without obtaining permission or breaking radio silence to report it.

and the navigator read the sun altitude from the sextant arm.

"Nine degrees, forty-two point seven minutes."

The quartermaster jotted the reading down. The sun line had been taken none too soon; as the navigator started into the wheelhouse, the sun disappeared behind the clouds. Entering the wheelhouse door, he reached back for the slip of paper on which the convoy's future actions heavily depended. At that moment, the ship rolled heavily to port, the quartermaster grabbed for a handhold, and the paper was whisked over the side and far astern in the forty-knot wind. The navigator stood biting his mustache, his countenance getting several shades darker.

"Do you remember the time, Ingersoll?"

The quartermaster looked blank, while Craik visibly controlled his emotions. Without that paper, INGHAM was still on DR navigation, and in the prevailing weather, no navigator could swear to its accuracy, no matter how skillful he might be.

Unless contact was established soon, the two short-legged destroyers would have a fuel problem. Throughout the afternoon, they plowed on, and at dark McCabe ordered the convoy swung again to the southwest to parallel the estimated main convoy track.

As aggravating as the situation was, it was nothing new. Unless the two convoys broke radio silence to home in, or an aircraft report was available, there was no alternative for the joiners but to crisscross the scheduled track. Fortunately, there were no indications of U-boats nearby. If the small convoy, with only three escorts to defend it, was picked up by a wolf pack, the situation could quickly turn to worms.

The following day brought a break in the weather and the welcome news that a PBY was coming out from Iceland. This boy would be at extreme range from his base, but he might be able to locate the two convoys and help them get together. During the morning, the navigator was able to get several good sun lines. Now, at least, he knew with some certainty where he was.

During the noon meal came the first Asdic contact. The sound of the engines increasing speed was followed in rapid sequence by the deeper roll of the ship as she altered course, the clanging of the general alarm, and loudspeakers blaring throughout the vessel, "Now hear this. All hands to submarine general quarters!" [3]

Almost as one man, the dozen officers at the table scrambled to their feet, and headed for the quick-opening watertight door, but even before the wardroom emptied, the first depth charge went off astern of the ship. This one was set shallow, and lifted the dishes off the table. The ship opened out and started a turn to port in an effort to regain Asdic contact.

The OOD was setting up an expanding search. Flipping the intercom switch, he directed Asdic, "Sweep bearings 315 to 045."

For half an hour the search continued without success. If there was a U-boat down there, it had gone deep. The initial contact had been a good one only 3,500 yards ahead of the convoy. Knowing that the U-boat was nearly in position to shoot, the OOD had barreled straight in and dropped a depth charge to distract it, then opened out to regain contact for a deliberate attack with a full pattern. The merchantmen had made a 45-degree emergency turn away from the spot, leaving INGHAM to sit on the contact, while BABBITT and LEARY dashed around the convoy, trying to screen as much of it as possible.

Failing to re-establish contact, McCabe ordered a resumption of base course, and again took up the three-day hunt for the main convoy. The noon fuel reports from the two destroyers were bad news. If the main body wasn't sighted by dark, he would have to break radio silence.

---

[3] "Submarine general quarters" differed from "general quarters" in that the bridge watch was not relieved by the general quarters bridge personnel. Once an attack had begun, the bridge personnel making the original contact carried it through to avoid disruption.

As the Old Man stood on the wing of the bridge glumly chewing his cigar, a lookout yelled, "Aircraft bearing three four zero, five miles, angle five."

Half a dozen pairs of glasses swung to the bearing.

"It's a PBY," announced the JOOD.

"Good old VP-73," said someone. "This guy's a long way from home."

The slow, awkward flying boat passed low overhead and began to circle. There was no radio contact, and the signalman began the laborious task of exchanging messages with it by blinker light, running from one side of the bridge to the other as the plane circled us. Finally he had copied the vital information, *Convoy 30 miles north.*

McCabe signaled the commodore to alter course to the northwest, then took INGHAM around the convoy and up to the north at 19 knots. Soon smoke could be seen over the horizon, and shortly afterwards signals were exchanged with HMCS AGGASIZ. By nightfall, the Iceland section was tucked safely into the main convoy. Three days of countermarching and worry had been required to rendezvous with a convoy one day behind schedule. Escort men maintained — not always in jest — that the U-boats must often know the convoy positions better than the joining escorts. There was a ditty sung in bars from Halifax to Liverpool to the tune of "Daisy, Daisy" that went:

> CINCWA CINCWA, give us your answer do,
> We're half crazy trying to comply with you,
> You've given us three directives,
> For reaching one objective,
> Now one's enough, it's quite tough,
> Not to mention the other two.
>
> EASTOMP, WESTOMP, what's the difference where,[4]
> They're never where you tell us,

[4] EASTOMP, WESTOMP—The Eastern Ocean Meeting Point and Western Ocean Meeting Point. Geographical locations, changed each trip, where the local escort groups and the mid-ocean escort group met to relieve each other.

But you'll always find us there,
This is a ten-knot convoy, barely making five,
But we'll take 'em where they're going,
And we'll bring 'em in alive,
At least two-thirds.

After the last merchantmen had eased into place in the west-bound convoy, INGHAM broke off with LEARY and BABBITT and headed into the night at 17 knots to reinforce the escort of Convoy SC-112, over 500 miles to the southwest, and reportedly being trailed by several U-boats.

During the previous week, Convoy HX-217 had been picked up in the same area by U-boats, and 22 of the pack had been ordered against it. But the German attack was not well co-ordinated, the air and surface escorts were alert and aggressive, and only two ships were lost from the convoy. The Germans were plagued with bad weather, poor communications, and navigation problems; two boats collided in the darkness, the first collision of the war between U-boats during a convoy attack, and one went down with heavy loss of life. Another U-boat was sunk by an escorting aircraft. All things considered, both sides were fortunate to get away with so little bloodshed.

On the night of December 16th, the three American escorts intercepted SC-112 and swung into position in the screen. There was little activity at the moment, but U-boats had been nibbling at the big eastbound convoy for the past three days. Several depth-charge attacks had been made by the escorts against U-boats attempting to get at the merchantmen, and U-663 had been so heavily damaged that she was forced to give up the chase and return to port. Unbeknownst to the escort commander, the nine boats of Group *Ungestum* had been approaching from the east to attack, and on the 15th had almost contacted the convoy. However, the wolf pack was too far north, and the convoy had slipped by to the south of the patrol line, thanks to aircraft which kept the U-boats down so well that none were able to sight the merchantmen. When, on the following day, the pack discovered that the convoy had slipped past them, they reversed course and set off to the east in pursuit. But the weather had worsened, and in the snow, hail, and mountainous seas, contact was not made. In the 50 merchantmen and 10 escorts, the routine of life at sea continued, free for the moment of harassment by U-boats.

For most of the crew, life at sea in a man-of-war is divided into watches, four hours on and eight hours off, with a third of the ship's company on watch at all times. In this respect, a ship is like a factory on three shifts. But there the similarity ends, for at sea there is no eight-hour day, nor are Saturdays and Sundays free. In addition to standing two four-hour watches, the watchstander must turn to for several more hours of departmental work and the endless maintenance required on a ship. Furthermore, all hands are always subject to the demanding clamor of the general alarm, calling them to battle stations.

The primary watches are the ship control (bridge) watch; the engineering watch; gunnery watches; and the damage-control detail.

The nerve center of the ship is the bridge watch, consisting of an officer of the deck (OOD), one or two junior officers of the deck (JOOD), and the enlisted members of the team—the helmsman, messenger, radarmen, Asdic operators, quartermaster, and lookouts.

Below, in the noise and heat of the engineering spaces, are the members of the "black gang." The boiler room is manned by several boiler tenders and firemen, under the supervision of a chief petty officer, whose job is to mind the boilers. He varies the boiler fires, steam pressure, and steam output as the demand fluctuates with changes in the ship's speed. In the engine room, the main steam propulsion turbines and auxiliary machinery are tended by an engineering watch officer, a chief petty officer, and several machinist mates and firemen. At the main engine control panel, petty officers man the throttles controlling the turbines, keeping an alert eye on the engine-room telegraphs by which speed changes are ordered from the bridge.

One or two "ready" guns are manned continually at sea in wartime. On the HAMILTON-class cutters, one 3-inch gun forward and a 20-millimeter machine gun on either side were always manned and ready. Though the main battery armament consisted of four 3-inch and two 5-inch guns, the two heavier guns required a larger crew and were more exposed to the weather. For quicker action, reliance was placed on the rapid-firing 3-inch ready gun. Though it had only a fraction of the hitting power of the 5-inch, it could handle any surprise target until the other gun crews could reach their battle stations. On the long wet nights, often on ice-coated decks, the ready gun crews huddled soaked and cold throughout their four-hour watches, maintaining a lookout, and attempting to keep some circulation going. In heavy weather, every third or fourth sea would break over the bow, throwing cold green water over gun and gunners. Under such conditions, the ready crew was usually allowed to retreat to the ready crew shelter, just below the gun platform. It was a miserable, cold, and thankless watch, and gun targets were infrequent during convoy escort.

While the black gang sweated in the 110-degree heat of the boiler and engine rooms, and the gun crews huddled in frozen groups, the bridge watch inhabited the temperate zone, but it was comfortable in only a relative way; the wheelhouse and wings of the bridge were wet and cold.

In a special compartment aft of the bridge, the radarman, Asdic operator, and quartermaster had things fairly soft. They were warm, they had comfortable seats, and they were able to smoke and drink gallons of hot coffee, but the demand for alertness never ceased, for theirs was the responsibility to give the first warning if a submarine attempted to penetrate the screen either submerged or surfaced.

INGHAM had the early SC-1 radar, the first production model issued to the fleet, and it was only a year old. Though it was to escort work what the first antibiotics were to medicine, it was a crude instrument compared to the latest high-powered equipment that would be installed when she again reached the States. A merchant vessel, under good conditions, could be picked up no further than five miles, and a surfaced U-boat at perhaps two. But it was a boon to the OOD in maintaining station on the convoy, and throughout the watch, the radar operator fed range and bearings on the ships in the convoy to the conning officer,[5] who adjusted his patrol pattern to stay within the assigned sector and proper distance from the merchant ships. Later, there would be a radar PPI scope on the bridge, in which the OOD could see small white dots representing all the ships for several miles around. It made station keeping simple, and gave a clear picture of the convoy disposition on the darkest nights or in heavy fog. But with the SC-1, there was no composite picture, and the conning officer was reliant on ranges and bearings fed him by the radar operator. Mentally absorbing the information and using the old Mk.I human brain as a computer, he calculated the course changes to maintain or adjust his position with relation to the convoy.

With a typical force, an escort was stationed on each bow, on each quarter, and ahead and astern. Depending on the visibility, a distance of between one and three miles from the merchantmen was maintained.

Within the broad limits of their stations, the escorts patrolled or zigzagged at all times. Course changes were made every few minutes, and sometimes as often as every 30 seconds. The frequent heading changes not only helped confuse a U-boat attempting to get a good torpedo set-up to fire at the escort, but also made it difficult for him to predict where the escort would be so that he could slip by to get at the merchantmen.

Throughout the watch, there was a constant flow of conver-

---

[5] The conning officer gave orders to the helmsman, and was responsible for maneuvering the ship. The duty rotated between the OOD and the JOOD's, usually at hourly intervals.

sation, leaving little opportunity for any member of the team to dope off.

"Come right to zero zero seven."

"Come right to zero zero seven, sir."

"Radar, range and bearing to the corner ship?"

"Corner ship bearing two two three, sir, range four five double oh."

"Very well."

Superimposed on everything was the constant ping, ping, ping from the Asdic, as it probed the water beneath the surface, usually through an arch of 90 degrees. Ping—wait several seconds for any answering echo, then train five degrees. Ping—wait again, then train five more degrees.

Every half-hour, a petty officer from the damage control detail, charged with security throughout the ship, reported to the OOD, "All secure topside, sir. No lights about the deck."

Every hour, the crucial radar and Asdic positions were relieved and the alternate operators took over, while the offcoming operators rested in the shack or went below for a quick snack. The hourly rotations continued throughout the four-hour watch.

Midway through the watch, the helmsman was relieved by the lee helmsman, who had stood the first two-hour watch as a lookout on the wing of the bridge. Coming in from the wing, cold and soaked, the lee helmsman saluted the conning officer, "Permission to relieve the helm, sir, steering 040 gyro, 028 steering compass?"

"Permission granted."

"Radar, range and bearing on the corner ship?"

"Bearing 217, range four eight five oh, sir."

"Very well. Right 15 degrees rudder."

"Right 15 degrees rudder, sir. Rudders 15 right."

"Very well."

"Passing 050."

"Passing 060."

"Passing 070."

"Steady on 115," ordered the conning officer.

When the ship had steadied on the new course, there came the confirming report, "Steady 115, sir."

"Very well."

The precise, formalized exchange between the conning officer and helmsman has been evolved over the years to prevent misunderstanding. At sea, especially when working close-in to other ships, there is no room for error.

With time, a conning officer becomes adept at solving the relative motion problem in his head. The more experienced conning officers, required to make 20 or 30 course changes an hour, develop a mental clock, and seldom exceed the allowable few minutes maximum on any course. The next course is selected after the order to the helm is given, and while the ship is swinging. But in so doing, the conning officer has to remember to give a course on which to steady, or the helmsman will continue the turn. To insure that the officer does not forget, the helmsman is required to call out every 10 degrees of heading until given a course to steer. On one memorable night, the OOD on INGHAM goofed.

The ship was patrolling a mile ahead of the convoy, when time came to zigzag.

"Right 15 degrees rudder."

The helmsman acknowledged, and as the ship began swinging, the OOD stepped to the wing of the bridge to take a quick look at the convoy, barely visible in the distance. As he did, he was momentarily distracted by the quartermaster, who had a routine report to make, and completely forgot that the ship was still turning; the howling wind completely drowned out the helmsman's voice as he was calling out the headings. Leaning against the bridge combing, the OOD was scanning the night ahead with his binoculars when suddenly he saw a dark object ahead. There was supposed to be nothing ahead of the convoy.

"Gun crews, action stations!"

A Foehn wind howls down through a fjord, bringing winds in excess of 100 knots, and creating steep seas even in the protected waters. USN/National Archives

Bridge gang on a Coast Guard escort exchange signals with another escort. USCG/National Archives

Members of a ready gun crew on an old destroyer maintain a lookout while attempting to keep warm in the cold winds. In the bitter winter, few American ships had adequate protective clothing. USN/National Archives

Depth charge projector fires, hurling a 300-pound depth charge 150 feet abeam during a night depth charge attack. USCG/National Archives

"Both engines ahead flank. Steady as you go!"

"Standby depth charges. Setting 50 feet."

"Call the captain."

The essential steps taken, he threw his glasses again on the object ahead and prepared to barrel in. But the shadow in the night was now much larger. There were also other objects there. They were merchantmen! He had let the ship swing through half a circle, and was bearing down on the convoy.

"Right full rudder!"

Slowly the ship swung while the oncoming merchantmen came ever closer. Finally it had swung through a complete circle and, only 800 yards from the convoy, steadied on course and began opening out. It had been a close shave. There was a bit of sticky explaining to do for an irritated skipper who had been unceremoniously aroused from a sound sleep, but it could have been worse. The OOD had almost sounded general quarters, and there would have been a couple of hundred angry men rather than one.

But exacting as station keeping was, radar made it duck soup compared with the year before when it had to be done by eye, even on a dark night or in fog. In the days before radar, if contact with the convoy was lost, there was nothing to do but ease back in until the merchantmen could be seen again visually. The close shaves were legion.

While the bridge, gunnery and engineering watches got on with the war, other men carried out more prosaic, but equally essential, functions. Among the most indispensable were the cooks, bakers, and commissary personnel, for the morale of a ship is closely related to the quality of the chow. It is usually topnotch. Unfortunately, rough weather diminishes the appetite and pleasure in even the best food. Special boards were placed on the tables to prevent the plates from sliding, but even with these, eating soup when the ship is rolling 40 degrees makes eating with chopsticks seem like child's play. In extremely rough weather, even the saltiest seamen were content to subsist on cold sandwiches.

Even sleeping was a problem. The preferred method was to wedge into a bunk, face down, with a lifejacket wedged under an arm to keep from being thrown out onto the deck. If such a position was uncomfortable, it was at least secure. At sea in a combat zone, only a greenhorn would undress to sleep; donning several layers of damp clothes took too long when the general alarm rang.

Coming off watch, soaked to the skin and miserably cold, the experienced watchstander removed only his coat, cap, and boots. The heat in the cabin would be turned up full, and dressed in wet clothes he would turn in for a few hours of exhausted sleep. Awaking for the next watch, the coarse blue junglecloth clothes would be dry, stiff, and covered with a white layer of salt; they would not be removed from the time the ship left port until it returned.

In 1942, most American escorts had woefully inadequate clothing for the cold northern ocean. At one time, INGHAM had only three sheepskin coats. One was shared by the three senior OOD's, being handed, dripping wet, to the oncoming watchstander. The other two were shared by the captain, exec, and navigator. Everyone else got by with junglecloth suits, supplemented with wool knitted goods handed out by the Red Cross. The knit helmets, gloves, and scarves proved to be a godsend in that awful winter. But while the escort sailors were freezing, the clerks and storekeepers sitting around heated Quonset huts at the shore bases were outfitted with new sheepskin coats. Not until February did they filter down to the fleet, probably as a result of overly full storehouses ashore.

High up in the hierarchy of the non-watchstanders were the ship's surgeon and his pharmacist's mates. Despite days in cold wet clothing, irregular hours, and food gulped down as opportunity existed, colds and respiratory ailments among the 230 officers and men of INGHAM were almost non-existent. No one got ashore long enough to be exposed to any contagious illness. (If there were any lingering theories that the common cold was caused by wet feet or a draft, the large-scale clinical experience above latitude 60 degrees north should have disproved it.) The ship had not experienced even a case of VD for months. It wasn't altogether by choice; in that barren part of the world, a simple case would have probably been somewhat of a distinction, but the Icelandic girls simply weren't approachable in the time frame available to the escort sailors.

As a result, the sick bay crew daily polished their tools and inventoried their pills with no takers other than an occasional accident victim. The surgeon was utilized as a code room watch-stander, operating the decoding machine to break the incoming coded radio messages. With radio silence in effect, there were rarely any outgoing ones. When not required in the code room, he reposed in his bunk, sleeping and occasionally browsing through a book or magazine. He also censored the crew's outgoing mail, which would be posted when we again arrived in port.[6] The good doctor became the butt of constant jibes from the weary deck watch officers concerning the amount of sack time he was accumulating. Tired of defending his medical inactivity, he resolved to do something about it and undertake elective surgery.

The somewhat clandestine clinic was discovered by the executive officer while making his morning rounds. Three patients were in the sick bay, all looking uncomfortable.

"What's the trouble, Perkins?" asked the exec.

"Circumcision, sir," replied the gunner's mate.

"How about you, Pawloski?"

"Same thing, sir."

His eyebrows lifting, the exec turned to the last man.

---

[6] Censoring was done by clipping out the offending parts of a letter with scissors. One enterprising young officer, carrying on a voluminous correspondence with a number of ladies, solved the problem of time by clipping out most of the pages before starting to write. He would then fill in the remainder in jig time. After arrival back in the States, all of his feminine companions were agog with curiosity as to what had been clipped out. He replied, assuming an air of secrecy, "Well, if it was censored, I don't think I'd better say, but it was rough out there, etc."

"Not you, Weissman!"

"No, sir," replied the seaman. "We Jews are a lot more fore-sighted. I slipped on the bridge ladder."

The word quickly spread. Some humorist posted a sign that read:

> FREE PLASTIC SURGERY. SATISFACTION
> GUARANTEED. OPTION OF KNIFE OR PINK-
> ING SHEARS. CHOOSE FROM SIX DIFFERENT
> PATTERNS.

Business picked up, and on the next week's Sick Report, two more men had gone under the knife.

"That," said the exec to the Doc, "is enough. At this rate, we won't be able to man our battle stations. From now on, not more than two men at a time can be on sick report for optional surgery."

Business at the "clinic" returned to a more normal level, and Doc resumed his code room stint and sleeping, interrupted only by a light surgical schedule as patients were discharged and others called in from the waiting list.

But if the recently discharged patients looked forward eagerly to promises of increased sexual prowess, one small group had developed considerable anxiety in this respect. In December, the Navy Bureau of Medicine and Surgery issued a message warning of possible dangers in overexposure to radar waves. There was some evidence that a man standing in close proximity to the antenna could absorb enough radiation to suffer physical damage. The radar operators, of course, were far removed from the mast-top radar antenna and in no danger. However, a rumor spread throughout the fleet that radarmen could absorb enough radiation to render them sterile. To many, this was synonymous with impotency.

The matter came to a head when one of the OOD's discovered a radar operator sitting with his back to the scope, peering at it over his shoulder.

"What kind of watch do you call that?" asked the OOD.

"Just trying to protect the family jewels, sir," said the radar operator, reluctantly swinging around to face the "deadly" machine.

The radarmen wanted to stand a good watch, but what was the good of winning the war if there was nothing to go home for. The matter was referred to Doc, and with his reassurance, the radarmen were soon facing the enemy again.

Commander George McCabe of INGHAM was a firm believer in radar as an offensive weapon, and he had a pet theory of "one upmanship" that was shared by a number of other escort commanders. If the U-boats were staying on the surface at night, he said, then they would be picked up by radar long before Asdic contact was made. But with their sensitive hydrophones, he believed the U-boats were picking up the sound of our Asdic pinging before we could get into radar range, and diving deep to avoid detection. If the other side was depending on our pinging to alert them, and we didn't ping, they would have to rely on visual sighting. Pitting their naked eyes against our radar, they would be at a disadvantage, and we could likely catch one cold and clobber him.

"That's fine, sir," argued one bright young man. "But if they come in submerged for an attack, we've bought the farm."

"You have a point," agreed the Old Man, "but these guys are not going to be diving five or ten miles out from the convoy at night. They are going to stay up as long as possible. We'll use Asdic when we are in the close screen where they might be submerged; but when we are out on a sweep away from the convoy, we may come up on a mighty surprised Kraut if we strangle the Asdic."

The theory had its pros and cons. What we did not know at the time was that the Germans had developed a radar search receiver, the FuMB, or "METOX," which would detect the waves emitting from a warship's radar.[7] The device gave no range, and

[7] See Appendix I, page 244.

only a rough bearing, but it did alert the U-boats that an escort with radar was somewhere in the vicinity. Installation in the U-boats had begun only three months before, and many did not yet have it, but once installed, it was to prove highly effective until the Allies introduced the new ten-centimeter wave length radar, which the METOX was unable to detect. Obviously, eliminating the Asdic pinging would offer no advantage if the U-boat was able to detect the radar emissions at an even greater distance than the Asdic pings. If McCabe's ploy was to succeed, it would have to be against a boat without a radar warning receiver.

As December 17th faded into night, McCabe had yet to put his theory to a test.

No one knows what pet theories of operation Reserve Leutnant zur See Hans Botho Bade entertained.[8] There are no war diaries, no former shipmates on U-626, no post-patrol reports. U-626 had finished her shakedown training in the Baltic in early November, was passed out by the training and shakedown people, and on the last day of the month arrived at Bergen, Norway, to top off with fuel and supplies before sailing on her first war patrol. On December 8th she departed Bergen and moved toward the North Atlantic operation area. No sightings were made by her, and only occasional weather reports were made to U-boat Command. During the time INGHAM and her cohorts were searching for Convoy ON-142 for three frustrating days, U-626 had moved westward, passing north of the Shetlands and to the south of Iceland along the route known to escort sailors as "Reich No. 1," so heavily was it used by outbound U-boats.

At 2130 on the night of December 17th, Bade was some miles ahead of a convoy and apparently broke radio silence to send off a message to U-boat Command. It was not copied by the German radio station at Lorient, but a signal was received by an HF/DF-

---

[8] Bade before the war had been a merchant marine officer with a master's license. Called into the naval reserve in October, 1939, he served a year as second officer of U-69 before taking command of the new U-626 in June, 1942. Though an experienced seaman, the 33-year-old Bade was obviously short on submarine experience. His combat command totaled only nine days before his first and only contact—with INGHAM.

equipped escort in Convoy SC-112, and a quick bearing showed the U-boat to be ahead of the convoy. INGHAM, in the van, moved out farther ahead as an outrider.

McCabe decided to implement his theory; the Asdic was placed on listening mode rather than pinging, and INGHAM moved out ahead, sweeping with radar. When five miles ahead of the convoy, she slowed to 12 knots, where her screw cavitations were far less detectable than at higher speeds.

While INGHAM was opening out ahead of the convoy, U-626 probably submerged. What Bade had in mind is a mystery. He may have wished to listen with his hydrophone in order to pick up the convoy's screwbeats, or perhaps he intended to make a night submerged approach for an attack. Though the usual procedure was to come in on the surface for a night attack, a new skipper may have seen more security submerged. There is also the possibility that he had heard INGHAM's propellers, or had picked up her radar emissions on his radar search receiver and gone down, though no one knows if he was even operating a METOX. Whatever may have been his motive, he gave his position away. A more experienced skipper, hearing an escort approaching, would have gone deep, rigged for silent running, and crept away at slow speed. Bade, however, was going ahead at high speed on both motors. At 2315, the alert Asdic operator on INGHAM yelled, "Loud hydrophone effect, bearing 030. Fast screwbeat. This is a submarine!"

Lieutenant (j.g.) Lou Sudnik, the OOD, quickly checked the bearing with radar and binoculars. Nothing on the surface.

"Asdic from Conn, are you sure that isn't our own screws?"

"Yes, sir. This is much faster than ours, and it is real narrow, between 015 and 035."

"Both engines ahead standard. Steer 025."

"Sound submarine general quarters! Set depth charges to 150 feet."

INGHAM surged ahead and the crew raced to their stations. On the depth-charge racks and K-guns, the watch standers set the depth-setting mechanisms to go off at 150 feet. Two minutes later, the huge 600-pound depth charges began dropping, shaking the ship as they went off, and producing huge mounds of water astern of the ship a few seconds after the concussions were felt. When the last charge went off, INGHAM opened out for nearly two minutes, then began turning to go back in for another attack.

"Commence echo ranging. Search 170 through 240."

There was no further need for stealth. Now they could ping for range.

"Contact, bearing one eight five. Range one one double oh. No doppler."

"Steady one eight five. Both engines ahead full!"

"Left cut, one seven five."

"Right cut, one niner oh. Range niner five oh. Up doppler."

"No recorder trace."

"Nine-charge pattern. Setting 150 feet."

Trembling from the thrust of her turbines, INGHAM drove toward the submerged target ahead. On the port bow a carbide float light, dropped to mark the center of the first pattern, was bobbling on the waves. This boy was moving rapidly away from the scene and making a lot of noise doing it.

"Screwbeats have slowed. Right cut two oh oh."

"Poor trace!"

"Steady two one zero. Use range rate 19 knots. Fire on recorder."

"Left cut, one niner eight."

The target was moving right, and at 400 yards the conning officer made his move, taking a final lead angle to place the depth charges ahead of the U-boat, where hopefully it would run into them as they sank to detonating depth.

"Come right to two two five."

"Right cut two one zero. Range three double oh."

"Instantaneous echoes."

The cutter and U-boat were so close that the outgoing ping had merged with the returning echoes, and for agonizing seconds there was no more information. Everything now depended on the accuracy with which the officer on the attack recorder fired the pattern. The special chemically treated paper moved slowly upward, and as the few faint marks moved under the firing arm index, he called out, "Fire one!"

The talker relayed the order by phone, and to insure that the word got back, a short blast on the whistle was sounded. The quartermaster started his stopwatch with the first charge, timing the pattern.

"Standby. Fire two!"

Another 600-pounder rolled over the stern, and Lieutenant "Emo" Osborn, the attack recorder officer, pressed two red plungers in front of him. K-guns on each side roared, hurling 300-pound depth charges 50 yards to either side.

"Fire three."

Another charge went out over the stern, and two more to the sides.

The ship jumped and quivered as the massive charges exploded. When the last one had gone off, INGHAM began opening out. Suddenly there was a heavy explosion, and people on the bridge ran out to the wing to see what had happened. The Skipper straightened up as he returned the bridge depth-charge release lever [9] to neutral position.

"I dropped one more on the bastard myself. This war is too impersonal."

Opening out to 1,200 yards, INGHAM began an expanding square search pattern, probing the depths with Asdic. The gun crews stood ready, barrels pointed outboard, breech blocks open, and the loaders with shells cradled in their arms. Reaching the end of the first leg, she came to the next course, moving around the last float light that had been dropped. On each leg she opened out further. After a half-hour, there had been no further contact. The radar operator was becoming more insistent in his warnings: the convoy would soon be overrunning the position of the attack.

---

[9] The stern depth charges were usually released by a lever at the racks. The release lever on the bridge was for use in case communications failed.

One of the van escorts was already in sight to the south. Reluctantly, McCabe broke off the search, and resumed station ahead of the convoy. There was no evidence of damage, but on a dark night, it would have been impossible to see small objects in the water. Even if they were there, the convoy's passage soon erased any evidence. But the contact had been a good one, and there was little doubt among the crew that it was a U-boat. Commander McCabe, in his report of the action, said, "Though there was no evidence of damage, I believe we got him. I request that when German records become available after the war, they be checked for a sinking here."

The British were not as optimistic. Always on the conservative side, they classified the action as "Possible submarine. No evidence of damage." [10] Over three years later, the captured German records were checked. On December 17, 1942, at that location, U-626 had simply disappeared without trace. Her first and only war patrol had lasted just eight days. What went on in those last minutes aboard the doomed U-boat is forever buried in 2,000 fathoms of water at position 350 miles south-southeast of the southern tip of Greenland. As Commander McCabe said, it was very "impersonal."

Convoy SC-112 was not molested further, and other North Atlantic convoys for most of the month of December escaped with little or no losses, but the respite was to prove only temporary. The invasion of North Africa had caught the German High Command flat-footed, with their heaviest concentration of U-boats on the North Atlantic. With many Allied escorts pulled from the northern ocean to screen the invasion fleet, the U-boats had reaped a record harvest in November. In all areas, 117 ships of over 700,000 tons were sent to the bottom, most of them in the first two weeks. After the African landings, Hitler demanded that additional U-boats be shifted to the North African and Mediter-

[10] The British insisted on positive material evidence or bodies. One escort, after a depth-charge attack, noted sea gulls swarming in the area. A boat was put over and brought back a bucketful of human entrails. The Admiralty granted a "kill" assessment.

ranean theatres. Doenitz objected vigorously. The prime strategic effect of the U-boat war, he insisted, lay almost entirely in the quickest possible sinking of the most tonnage, and where it was sunk was of secondary importance. The area of greatest traffic, and one in which the convoys were compressed into a relatively narrow shipping lane, was the North Atlantic. Hitler and the Naval High Command, however, equated the U-boats' effectiveness to their immediate effect on the threatened African theatre, and insisted that direct action should be taken to interdict the flow of supplies to the Allied landing forces in North Africa.

The views of High Command prevailed, and Doenitz was forced to transfer a large number of boats from the northern ocean to the Gibraltar and Mediterranean approaches. After some initial successes against the invasion fleet, conditions became exceedingly difficult for the U-boats. Allied convoys were heavily escorted in that area, and almost continuous air coverage was given them from Gibraltar and North African bases. U-boat losses on the African approaches mounted without compensatory sinkings of Allied shipping. Finally, on November 26th, Doenitz was allowed to pull out the remainder of his boats from the dangerous Gibraltar area and move them to safer waters further out on the America-Gibraltar route. But due to the wide area of ocean in which convoys could take evasive routing, the U-boats could not locate them, and little success was obtained. A few independents were sunk, but the returns were meager for the large number of U-boats involved. Doenitz had been right, and the overriding decision of Naval High Command to concentrate on the Gibraltar approaches had created a U-boat vacuum between Newfoundland and England. Not until December was U-boat Command able to dispatch replacement groups onto the North Atlantic routes, and during the respite, hundreds of Allied merchantmen were delivered safely to British ports.

Even after new boats arrived on station, they were unable to resume the tempo of killing that had been reached in November. One reason was the Allies' resumption of evasive routing, sending their convoys on routes far off the short Great Circle course, and around the U-boat patrol lines.[11] After failing to intercept several expected convoys, U-boat Command correctly deduced what the Allies were doing. The obvious countermove was to lengthen the U-boat patrol lines in order to determine where the new routes lay, but in so doing, there was the risk that the convoys would slip undetected through the larger gaps between boats. Even if detected, concentrating the scattered boats onto a convoy would prove extremely difficult. There were simply not enough U-boats to detect all the convoys moving over ever-changing and widely spaced tracks. More boats were fed in from French and German bases. But by the time they could be deployed, the Allies had recovered from their weaknesses of November, escorts had returned from the African invasion operation, and the protective screens around the convoys were again up to strength. The Germans were further hindered by a series of violent storms moving eastward across the Atlantic. In the howling gales, mountainous seas, and reduced visibility, the U-boats could not find the convoys. As a result, the Iceland-based escorts were able to take a quick and badly needed breather during the last week of December.

INGHAM, BABBITT, and LEARY arrived in Happy Valley on the night of December 23rd, and were greeted by a signal from CAMPBELL, which had just arrived from the States, advising that she had mail aboard. Despite high winds and a blizzard, a boat was put over after midnight and soon returned with the precious bags. Each mail call was Christmas all over again, and little else was done until the incoming letters were well digested. It was nearly dawn before most of the crew had finished reading their mail and had turned in.

After arrival in port from a long stretch on escort duty, only a brief period of rest was allowed before the never-ending routine of maintenance and training was resumed. Ships that under nor-

---

[11] When the U-boats moved to the American coast in early 1942, losses on the trans-Atlantic route dropped so drastically that the British ceased evasive routing, and sent convoys on the short Great Circle course to save time. When the U-boats returned to the northern route, the Admiralty was slow to resume evasive routing.

mal peacetime conditions would have spent less than half their time at sea were now being driven relentlessly three weeks out of four, with routine maintenance worked in whenever time permitted. Only the more serious material casualties were remedied by the destroyer tender VULCAN's work force; the other repairs were accomplished by the ship's company.

Daily, the maintenance work had to be interrupted for drills and training: gunnery drills, depth-charge handling practice, damage control training, and above all, anti-submarine attack training. Each day in port, one of the ship's three attack teams would catch a boat across the fjord to the HMS BLENHEIM, which had an Attack Teacher, and for two hours, run after run would be made against the "U-boat," represented by a small, moving, lighted "bug" on the attack table.

The boredom and doping off sometimes seen in peacetime drills or in rear areas were conspicuously absent. Men in daily contact with the enemy have an intense and personal interest in anything that helps them stay alive, and training was taken in dead earnest. While there is always a certain amount of loud and lusty bitching, a healthy custom dating back at least as far as Caesar's legions, the real malcontents and screw-offs among good combat crews are not common. In a situation stripped of the niceties and reduced to the basic elements of kill or be killed, the most highly esteemed shipmate is the one who knows his business, and who will stand up in a crisis. The ones who don't measure up are either jacked up by their shipmates or disposed of by the stress of combat.

Contrary to much of the propaganda that is put out back home, the great majority of combat men do not fight for Mother's apple pie, to build a brave new world, or to defend wives, sweethearts, and children, one reason being that there often seems to be no immediate and compelling threat to any of these institutions. In combat, a man's greatest loyalty is to his own unit, and his prime motivation is the preservation of his fellow soldiers and himself, and to insure this he must kill the enemy before the enemy can kill him. Though the love of country and inspiration of ideological ideas as subconscious motivation should not be discounted, they are seldom as immediate or as compelling as unit loyalty.

To the trained and well-indoctrinated professional fighting man, the history, customs, and traditions of his service and unit, and the *esprit de corps* which pervades it, constitute a challenging standard. To the long line of fighting men who have preceded him, as well as to his present shipmates, the professional feels an obligation not to fail. While few would openly admit it in those words, so strong is this imbued spirit that men will subordinate the instinct for self-preservation rather than be found wanting.

In warfare, a man relying on patriotism rather than training can quickly lose his enthusiasm with the first cold shock of combat. The disillusionment is often accompanied by panic and collapse. Professionals seldom fold with the first setback, but fall back on discipline and training until the situation can be stabilized.

For this reason, and because wars are fought for the most part by civilians and reservists functioning around a small hard core of regulars, the purpose of training is to convert civilians into "professionals" for the duration of their stay in the military service. With training comes not only the professional outlook, but the discipline which allows a man to function as an efficient fighting machine when all of his senses may be urging him to absent himself from the scene at the first opportunity. At sea there is no getting away from the danger; from admiral to seaman, everyone is "in the same boat." But to act and think clearly while experiencing basic and natural animal fear comes only with training and experience.

So day after day, at every opportunity, the constant training went on. From captain to the lowest steward's mate, each man knew that beyond the fjord, the cold angry sea and a skilled and relentless enemy lay. Whatever was to be encountered there, they dared not be found wanting.

V

NATURE'S FURY

As the New Year arrived to the accompaniment of howling gales and horizontally-driven snow, there was little to celebrate; the ships in the fleet anchorage at Hvalfjordur were fully occupied maintaining position and avoiding each other and the rocky shores. All vessels had steam at the throttle, with the ship control watches manned, and many were using their engines to relieve the strain on taut anchor cables. But the view of the snow-covered landscape and desolation of "Valley Forge" was not as bleak as the outlook in London and Liverpool, where the staffs were confronted with the dismal graphs of shipping losses, dropping imports, and gloomy situation reports.

At the end of December, having finally persuaded the High Command to release large numbers of U-boats being employed with little success off the Azores and Gibraltar, Doenitz had succeeded in bringing a number of them into contact with west-bound Convoy ON-154. The hastily formed wolf pack, which had been trailing the convoy in a heavy fog, found itself inside the convoy screen when the fog suddenly lifted and, before the escorts could regain control, sank 13 ships. The savage onslaught, after several relatively quiet weeks, was a depressing finale to a black year for the Allies.

The year 1942 had seen 8,000,000 tons of merchant shipping destroyed, increasing the shipping deficit by another million tons, and imports into the United Kingdom had fallen to two-thirds of the tonnage received in 1939, the last year of peace. The U-boat fleet during the same period had been receiving new boats from the builders' yards at a rate that allowed them to easily replace losses as well as add to the growing number of boats at sea.[1] The most critical Allied shortage, moreover, was fuel oil, and at the end of the year, less than three months' commercial fuel supplies were on hand in the United Kingdom. As the fuel situation of the armies in North Africa was even more critical, a decision was made by the Admiralty to sail tanker convoys direct from the oil port of Trinidad to North Africa. Escorts were pulled from the northern ocean groups for the task, and the first convoy, TM-1, sailed early in January. It was set upon off the Azores by U-boat Group *Delphin,* and seven of the nine tankers were sunk. At the turn of the year, 20 ships from two convoys had been destroyed without any blows struck in return.

In the face of this grim situation, INGHAM sailed from Iceland the second week of January, accompanied by destroyers LEARY and BABBITT, to escort Convoy ONSJ-160 to a rendezvous with westbound Convoy ON-160. Although the escort was already numerically too weak for the job, when they were barely out of sight of Skagi Point, BABBITT was detached by CINCWA, leaving only two escorts for the 14 ships.[2] If any U-boats were to make contact, the stage was ripe for a disaster.

The situation was alleviated to some extent by a nearly continual air cover of Hudsons and a rapidly worsening weather picture, which promised to hinder the U-boats more than the convoy. We now know that, in early January, many of the boats which

---

[1] In January, 1942, Doenitz had 249 U-boats, of which only 91 were operational. At the end of the year, he had 212 operational boats out of 393 in commission.

[2] The number of escorts required for a proper screen was not proportional to the size of the convoy, but was more affected by the number of U-boats operating against it. Assuming an escort of five ships was required to defend against a single U-boat attack, perhaps nine might be required to defend against a three-boat attack. Within limits, this force could do as effective a job for a 60-ship convoy as for one of 45 ships. On the other hand, if the convoy was reduced to 20 ships, the number of escorts could not be safely reduced in the face of the same number of U-boats.

had attacked ON-154 were running short of fuel and torpedoes and had to be recalled, leaving only 13 boats on station in the North Atlantic. The deep, low-pressure storm center located off the Newfoundland Banks, and moving toward the northeast, was being followed by several other storm centers, and the sweep of these storms across the Atlantic was to establish the month of January, 1943, as one that meteorologists and historians would reference in future textbooks. But January was not to claim all the "honors." In that terrible winter, the weather would break records of fifty-years standing, and 116 days out of 140 would see storms of gale force or greater on the northern ocean. Many years and dozens of storms later, veteran seamen would still hark back to the storms of that winter to define the superlatives of weather at sea.

Three days out of Iceland, the merchantmen were tucked into the main westbound convoy and, for the next four days, ING-HAM and LEARY worked as part of its escort.

As far as anyone knew at the time, no U-boats were in contact with the convoy. INGHAM ran out 15 miles to investigate a U-boat chased down by a Hudson; but no contact could be made, and she soon hustled back to the convoy. Action-wise, the night passed quietly, and in the absence of any close-by radio transmissions, there was no evidence that the U-boat had sighted the convoy. But we now know that a great deal almost took place during the night. At 2050, according to the U-boat Command War Diary, U-632 missed two shots at an escort. The diary of the U-632 itself reveals that she made contact with an escort in the rough seas, rain, and darkness and fired two torpedoes. In the storm, both missed, and the U-boat went deep, never catching sight of the merchant ships. Which escort was the intended target is not known, but the commander of U-632 described it as a 3,000-tonner. As the other port-side escorts were small corvettes, it is likely that INGHAM was the intended victim; if at times the men were inclined to curse the foul weather, that night was one instance where "it is an ill wind that blows no good."

The weather held at or near gale force, but worse was yet to come. On January 21st, with the barometer dropping steadily, INGHAM broke off from ON-160 and headed north to join east-bound Convoy HX-223. LEARY, unable to refuel from a tanker in the heavy seas, had to be detached to return to Iceland.[3] The longer-legged INGHAM was urgently needed with the eastbound convoy, for the Admiralty's U-boat Tracking Room was showing an alarming increase in U-boat activity. Newly arriving U-boats were pouring into the operating area, and when the cutter sighted the smoke of the HX convoy at 20 miles, escorted by American Escort Group A3 under Captain Paul Heineman in Coast Guard Cutter SPENCER,[4] U-boat Command had succeeded in establishing groups of 7, 17, and 18 boats in three patrol areas, and the convoy was steering straight for one of them. CINCWA warned that within 24 hours, the wolves could be among the sheep.

The week before, Doenitz had noted in his War Diary that no convoy contacts had been made on the North Atlantic during the first half of January and, with chilling prescience, had concluded that the reason was the diversion of the convoys from the short Great Circle route which they had been following for the previous six months. The move was not unexpected; U-boat Command was puzzled as to why the Allies had waited so long to do so. The German C-in-C promptly moved nine U-boats into a patrol area centered 150 miles southeast of Cape Farewell, Greenland, where —from intercepted radio messages and knowledge of the regularity of convoy sailings—he estimated the convoy should be on January 23rd.

At noon on January 22nd, Convoy HX-223 was, in fact, only 24 hours from the western edge of the U-boat patrol area and steering almost exactly for the center. Both the estimates of the Admiralty Tracking Room and that of U-boat Command were all too accurate.

[3] It was the last view of an old friend. LEARY was detached from Task Group 24.6 shortly after she arrived back in Iceland and, on Christmas Eve of that year, was torpedoed and sunk with the loss of nearly a hundred of her crew.

[4] Escort Group A3 also included the Coast Guard Cutter CAMPBELL and four British and Canadian corvettes. It was a "melting pot" group of various national and service origins but a well-trained team, nevertheless, and one that was to see some of the bitterest fighting of the Atlantic war.

The Fleet Anchorage at Hvalfjordur, Iceland, during a gale. In such conditions, there was little rest for the weary. USN/National Archives

A Convoy forms up off Iceland after clearing the harbor. From Iceland, the ships were escorted to a rendezvous with a main westbound convoy. USN/National Archives

U-442 in front of a burning tanker during the slaughter of Convoy TM-1 in January, 1943, in which seven of nine tankers were sunk. U-442 also participated in the attack against SC-107 during its previous patrol. USN

USS LEARY, known affectionately as the "Weary Leary." Torpedoed and sunk on Christmas Eve, 1943, with the loss of 97 officers and men. USN/National Archives

The Tracking Room's daily estimate of the position of U-boats —at sea—derived during 1942 mostly from HF/DF fixes on U-boat radio transmissions and actual sighting reports, had now been augmented by Ultra information as the result of British penetration of the German Triton cipher in December after 10 months of effort. The Ultra input was straight from the "horse's mouth," consisting of decodes of actual U-boat position reports between boats at sea and U-boat Command. Transmitted each afternoon on a regular radio schedule to Allied ships at sea, the daily estimate of U-boat dispositions always found an attentive audience in the code rooms of underway vessels. None guessed how very accurate the information was, for the source was the most highly classified war secret. Unknown to the Allies, the daily estimate was also copied by the Germans, who had long since also broken the Allied code and were able to quickly decipher it. Only a short time after CINCWA, Admiral Sir Max Horton,[5] had seen the estimate, it was also in the hands of the enemy, and the continuing grim battle of wits between the opposing commanders resumed.

It was the age-old game of war—if I knew what he knows and I were in his place, what would I do? If he does what I would do in his place, what should I do to counter the move?

On January 23rd, the box score—in essence—stood as follows:

Horton, January 1: We have followed the short Great Circle route for six months, and they have been concentrating along that route. I will therefore divert the convoys to more northerly routes and bypass their patrol lines.

Doenitz, January 15: We have made no contacts for two weeks. They are probably diverting their convoys further north. I wonder why they didn't do it before. I will move the patrol line further north to a position just south of Greenland.

[5] Admiral Sir Max Kennedy Horton, G.C.B., D.S.C., Royal Navy, had relieved Admiral Sir Percy Noble as C-in-C, Western Approaches, on November 17, 1942. A famous submariner of the First World War, he had been Flag Officer commanding British submarines before taking over Western Approaches. Taking over a command which had been vastly improved under Admiral Noble, Horton was to prove the right checkmate for Doenitz.

Horton, January 22: There is a concentration of U-boats forming ahead of the convoy. Before it penetrates the concentration, I will divert it further to the north, bypassing the danger area.

Doenitz, January 23: From the Allied U-boat situation report, he knows there is a U-boat concentration ahead of the convoy. If I were Horton, I would divert the convoy further north. There has been no contact with them, yet, to the south of Greenland. I think he has already diverted further north. On this assumption, I will move some of the boats from the area southeast of Greenland and form a new patrol line, lying north and south, off the east coast of Greenland.

Implementing his estimate on January 23rd, Doenitz ordered the boats southeast of Greenland—plus others—to take up station, by 1100 on the 24th, on a 450-mile-long patrol line off the east coast of Greenland. The convoy would, he calculated, reach the patrol line by noon that day.

Except for one factor, the German Admiral's reasoning had been faultless. His concentration south of Greenland had been well-placed, and the convoy at noon of the 22nd had been heading directly for the center of the wolf pack, which should have made contact on the 23rd. But allowances had not been made for the mighty storm which was moving into the area, bringing the convoy almost to a standstill.

As a result, at noon on that day, the convoy was still 150 miles west of the wolf pack's center, and the U-boats, escorts, and merchantmen had little time to think of each other; they were all engaged in a common fight for survival against a killer hurricane, the likes of which even the saltiest seaman had seldom encountered before. Great seas, 60 feet from crest to trough, rolled in endless procession across the tortured ocean, whose surface was beat to a white froth by winds of over 100 knots. The tops of the towering seas were torn off by the howling winds, carrying spray hundreds of feet into the air and reducing visibility to near zero.

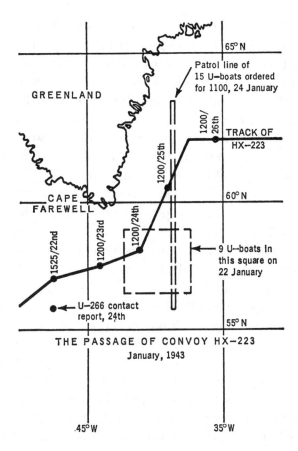

GREENLAND

Patrol line of
15 U—boats ordered
for 1100, 24 January

65° N

1200/ 26th

TRACK OF
HX—223

1200/25th

CAPE
FAREWELL

60° N

1200/24th

1200/23rd

1525/22nd

9 U—boats in
this square on
22 January

U—266 contact
report, 24th

55° N

THE PASSAGE OF CONVOY HX—223
January, 1943

.45° W

35° W

To add to the misery of the cold and battered sailors, the air temperature dropped to freezing, and the water, being near freezing, began forming coats of ice on the plunging, rolling ships.

As bad as things were on the surface vessels, the U-boats were suffering more. Less than half the size of a destroyer, and with the conning tower only a few feet above the water, a U-boat offered little protection to the men forced to stand watch on the open bridge, soaked to the skin and freezing in their oilskins. Tossed around like chips of wood in the great seas, the U-boats were repeatedly submerged completely by passing waves, the conning tower finally breaking the surface with the half-drowned watch standers gasping for breath. Not infrequently, a watch officer would turn to check his lookouts and find only a broken safety belt where a seaman had been moments before. Water poured in torrents down the open conning tower hatch, adding to the ever-present cold dampness below decks, and frequently short-circuiting the electrical circuits with an accompanying shower of sparks, smoke, and fire. The off-duty men, clinging to their bunks as the boat rolled on its beam end, endured the pounding in cold, sodden misery until their time came to go topside again. When the limit of endurance was reached, the boat would be forced to dive, losing its mobility and searching ability as it did.

On INGHAM, it was evident, even to those off watch below, that things were getting steadily worse topside. The ship was rolling up to 50 degrees, and the bow time after time plowed into the oncoming mountains of water, bringing the ship to a momentary shuddering halt from which it would rise steeply to meet the sea before again plunging ahead.

Sleep was impossible, and shortly before midnight, the arrival of the messenger of the watch was not unwelcome.

"Time to go on watch, sir. It's a real lulu. Winds over a hundred knots and cold as a witch's tit. The OOD says watch your step coming up. We're taking them clean over the bridge."

The oncoming watch stander climbed out of his bunk, holding on tight as the ship rolled to port, and the messenger, soaked and frozen, eased out the doorway, working himself along the passageway as he continued his rounds.

After getting on boots and additional clothing, the watch standers felt their way up to the hatchway leading on to the main deck and waited, judging when they might make the short five-step dash to the ladder leading to the comparative safety of the superstructure deck. A misjudgment, and a man could be over the side and that would be it. A big sea broke, burying the quarterdeck. As the ship emerged, with the water pouring off, a man would see his chance and leap through the hatch, grab a handrail, and clamber up, reaching the next deck as the ship rolled sickeningly to starboard, burying her side under green water. The wind and sleet would hit him full force, cutting at his face and nearly taking his breath. Inching along the deck, leaning into the wind and holding tight with both hands to the lifeline, he would finally reach the bridge and step into the wheelhouse, already soaked and miserably cold.

The sight was one never to be forgotten. Though the night was pitch black, and thick low clouds hurled by overhead, the ocean surface, beaten to a nearly solid white by the fury of the storm, was clearly visible. The ship was heading directly into the storm, and ahead of it loomed the great rolling mountains of water, each threatening to come down and break the ship. Though the bridge was 35 feet above the waterline, the seas towered up at a 45-degree angle above that. As a new wave loomed up, INGHAM rose to meet it, climbing steeply up the front; as the sea slid past, her bow was left momentarily hanging in the air before dropping sickeningly into the next trough, where it buried with a resounding impact, sending shock waves throughout the ship to add to the vibrations of the screws racing madly as they came out of the water.

When it seemed that she must continue on down, with the fo'c's'le under water up to the No. 2 gun, the bow slowly rose and then with increasing speed climbed to meet the next swell, throwing tons of green water up into the howling storm and back over the bridge. Even the flying bridge, 45 feet above the surface, was knee-deep in water, which poured down on the wings of the bridge and the men huddled there as the ship rolled to either side. The night dragged slowly on, and it seemed impossible that the ship could avoid being overwhelmed, but each time, she emerged shaking and trembling to meet the next one. She was literally "going over two and under one."

INGHAM, a fine sea boat, was fighting for life, and conditions on the little corvettes and destroyers were far worse. By 0300, she had slowed to five knots, barely maintaining steerageway, and had long since ceased patrolling station. In the storm, the radar was useless, and the OOD had no idea where the convoy was. He could only maintain base course and hope. In the driving snow, spray, and nature gone mad, the lookouts would be lucky to see another ship at 500 yards. There was little chance that a U-boat could see even that far, if any were rash enough to still be on the surface.

As bad as things were, they could have been worse, but there was no assurance that the situation would hold. A few degrees' drop in the air temperature could bring on increased icing of the ship's structure. Because of the amount of water and spray smashing over the ship, once icing started, a ship could eventually become top heavy enough to capsize unless the ice could be cleared. With the decks continually awash, there was little chance of getting working parties on deck. Throughout the night, constant checks were made on the temperature, which was only three degrees above the temperature at which salt water freezes. The convoy was 150 miles south of Cape Farewell, the southern tip of Greenland, and the wind was still out of the east-northeast. If it backed to the northwest, bringing down the colder air from the icecap, they were in trouble.

Although badly beaten—and faced with the threat of icing up —INGHAM was not yet in real trouble; others were. Two merchantmen, losing control in the storm, had collided and one was limping back through the storm to St. John's, two holds and her forepeak flooded, and steering by a jury rig. CAMPBELL had dropped aft to stand by the other cripple, but in the howling storm there would be little she could do to help if the situation worsened.

By daylight the wind had dropped to 50 knots, and the visibility improved in the intervals between snow squalls. The convoy had scattered, and less than a dozen ships were sighted during the morning. In mid-afternoon, INGHAM started back to locate the others. The first one sighted was a British freighter, with a mast leaning at a crazy angle and all boats on one side carried away. Other ships showed varying degrees of damage. By night, she had accounted for 20 ships out of the convoy of 51, as well as three of the corvettes, and began getting them into some semblance of a

In heavy seas south of Greenland, a Coast Guard cutter plows into mountainous seas. USCG/National Archives

CGC INGHAM in heavy seas rounding up convoy stragglers. USCG/National Archives

formation. But as darkness fell, the wind, which had suddenly shifted to the south, was again blowing at hurricane force; during the night, it was, once again, every man for himself.

Sunday morning, January 24th, was—if anything—worse than the previous day. The low had stopped and deepened, and the battered ships, unable to make headway, were caught in its grasp. CAMPBELL reported that she was unable to maintain station and was being set to the westward. SPENCER, herding a small group of seven ships, was unable to rejoin and, late in the afternoon, ordered INGHAM to take over as escort commander. Throughout the night and the following day, INGHAM worked around the scattered ships, urging them to close up. Three corvettes, ROSTHERN, DIANTHUS, and NAPANEE, assisted, and by noon, 25 ships had formed up under the protection of the four escorts. Despite the weather, the remnants of the convoy swung through a difficult turn to the north-northeast and began clawing up the east coast of Greenland, which now lay only 75 miles to port. The wind soon shifted to the northwest, coming down off the frozen icecap, but luck was with them, and as the temperature dropped, the wind and seas also diminished and icing did not become a serious threat.

That things were improving could be guessed by looking at the color of two aviation officers from Patrol Squadron 73 who had come on the trip as passengers to see what the war at sea was like on board ship. Both had been miserably sick throughout the trip and spent much of the time in their staterooms, retching miserably. Even so, they occasionally managed to hold down some food. As the storm began to abate, the Airedales perked up, and their color and will to live returned, but both swore that it would be the last physical contact they would have with the "black shoe" Navy. It was approximately the same reaction that some of the "black shoes" had registered about flying after plodding around in a PBY with them.

But the seasick Airedales were not the only personnel casualties of the storm. A messenger, leaving the galley with a pitcher of steaming coffee for the bridge watch, was upended and dumped most of the coffee over his chest, neck, and arm, suffering second-degree burns. Later in the day, the OOD stepped out to the wing of the bridge to take a look around the horizon. With both hands jammed into the deep pockets of his parka, he turned to give a course change to the helmsman, facing inboard as he did so. Suddenly, the ship rolled steeply to starboard; his feet went out from under him, and as the wet deck came up, he was unable to get his hands out of his pockets to catch himself. He made a beautiful one-point landing on his chin, resulting in a painless entry into blackness. Minutes later, he came to while being picked up off the deck, only to again pass out cold when he attempted to stand. The second return to consciousness was some twenty minutes later, after he had been carried below to the captain's cabin just below the bridge. Other than a headache and a sore jaw, he was soon little the worse for the experience, and had the chance to sleep off the rest of the watch in the relatively palatial surroundings of the Old Man's cabin.

As the weather improved, INGHAM began sweeps ahead and astern of the convoy, looking for strays. Nearly 20 ships were unaccounted for. From SPENCER came word that the KOLL-BJORG had broken in half in the storm, and no one held much hope for the crew in the raging, icy waters. As night again fell over the convoy, course was altered to the eastward. The convoy was then at latitude 62 degrees North, in the Denmark Strait, and far above the latitudes where the U-boat patrol lines were likely to be. It was just as well, for during the height of the storm, INGHAM had come down heavily in the sea, rupturing her Asdic dome and putting the underwater detection gear out of commission.

The following day, the weather moderated further, and shortly after noon, the two sections of the convoy were rejoined as SPENCER and CAMPBELL came into sight with nine merchantmen. Eleven ships were still missing and would have to proceed to port on their own.

While the two sections were separated, they had passed through the patrol line that the U-boats had established to the east of Greenland without being detected. Many of the U-boats had been unable to reach their assigned stations due to the heavy seas and navigation problems, and those that had were able to see little in the towering seas and driving snow. At just that time, with U-boat Command in Berlin [6] baffled by the inability of their boats to contact a convoy that they were sure must be passing through the area, U-266, in a position 250 miles southwest of Greenland, and hundreds of miles removed from HX-223, heard on his hydrophone loud noises which he felt positive must be a convoy. Grasping at any clue, U-boat Command ordered boats to that area, pulling many of them from the area to the east of Greenland. Nothing was found to the south, and the staff finally concluded that inexperienced hydrophone operators on the U-266 were chasing phantoms. But this erroneous contact report, and the premature reaction by U-boat Command in shifting forces, helped clear the way for HX-223 through what could have been a dangerous ambush.

On the 27th of January, INGHAM and NAPANEE broke off to escort three tankers to Iceland, opening out with them zigzagging at 11 knots in the still heavy swells. At nightfall, the weather was good enough for a movie to be shown on the mess deck. A supply of five movies was usually taken to sea, and near the end of a voyage, each movie would have been shown several times. By the third or fourth run, many of the crew had memorized much of the dialogue, and a variation that seldom failed to produce entertainment was to lower the sound level, while the crew supplied their own ad libbed commentary. While much of it would have never passed the movie censors, in some instances it was an improvement on the script of the Grade B movies that seemed to find a home in the Fleet Film Libraries.

It was during the "intermission" of this movie, while the reels

---

[6] When Doenitz became C-in-C, Navy, in early 1943, he still retained control of U-boat operations. To enable him to hold both jobs, U-boat Command Headquarters was moved from Paris to Berlin.

were being changed, that the mystery of the evaporating alcohol was solved. The sick bay had a sizeable supply of alcohol for medical purposes, and despite the strictest precautions, it had been mysteriously diminishing at an untimely rate. Repeated investigations, and even a change in the lock securing the supply, had proved of no avail.

The chief pharmacist's mate, taking advantage of the break in the movie to run up to his shop for a fresh pack of cigarettes, opened the door, flipped on the light, and caught a boatswain's mate red-handed, drinking alcohol out of a tray containing surgical instruments! Subsequent questioning revealed that the culprit had, for many weeks, been entering the sick bay and having a private, nightly cocktail party, using the alcohol in the various instrument and syringe trays. Though it required a strong stomach, it may have been tastier than the hair tonic, torpedo juice, compass alcohol, and boiler room ferment clandestinely consumed by thirsty sailors from Anzio to Okinawa throughout the war. Months on end with no relaxation or grog are likely to make Jack an enterprising fellow at finding alcoholic substitutes.

The errant boatswain's mate had barely been put on report and logged when, at 2345, radar picked up a target at 4,000 yards on the starboard bow, and the sleeping crew was aroused by the demanding clanging of the General Alarm. Heeling far over in a tight turn, INGHAM headed for the target. At a little over one mile, the target dived and faded from the scope. INGHAM continued in and dropped a pattern of depth charges at the estimated position. For three hours, an expanding search was carried out, but with the damaged Asdic cluttered with water noise, no further contact was made. Had the U-boat skipper been an aggressive one, he could have added a large escort to his bag with little personal danger, for the cutter was unable to detect a submerged target. Fortunately, the U-boat followed the usual procedure and went deep rather than chance a two-way fight with an escort, so with dawn approaching, INGHAM broke off and headed back again for her charges. The following night, she eased alongside the tanker in Reykjavik Harbor and began taking on fuel.

There were many repairs to be made and provisions to be taken aboard, and from Commander Task Group 24.6 came the word to expedite preparations and be ready for sea within 48 hours. The in-port period would be brief, and there would be little rest.

Regardless of the length of time in port, there was little recreation in Happy Valley. The nearest females were the nurses at the Army Hospital, many miles away over the mountains, and due to the nomadic wanderings of their ships, there was small chance that any seagoing officers could advance far enough on the waiting list to get a date. With several thousand men eager to compete for the attention of a dozen females, the nurses could afford to be choosy, and there was for them little percentage in wasting their time on seagoing types who appeared only at long intervals. This left only the long hikes on the icy shores of the fjord, never very popular, and the "officers' club" at Camp Falcon, on the shores of the anchorage.

The "club" consisted of two Quonset huts set end to end, a bar running the length of the building, and a battered old piano. It was open for only two hours daily; but the liquor was cheap at fifteen cents per glass, the customers were loud, and the camaraderie was high. The gatherings were truly international, consisting of Englishmen, Canadians, Poles, Free French, and U. S. Navy and Coast Guard officers. With a British battleship, three cruisers, and the destroyer tender VULCAN represented continually [7]— and swelled by the escort groups when they were in port—the club was always crowded, and the liquor flowed freely. To avoid a long wait at the packed bar, the accepted procedure was to order

[7] The VULCAN remained permanently in the fjord to service the escorts, while the battleship and cruisers, stationed there to bottle the Denmark Straits to the Germany heavy units, seldom moved. The escort sailors loudly averred that when the big ships swung around their anchors with a change in wind, their hulls could be heard scraping on the piles of empty cans and coffee grounds beneath them.

two doubles, down them quickly, and plunk the glass down for a refill while in position facing the bartender. As a result, the parties got underway with amazing rapidity, for with only two to four hours each month to drink and forget business, time was precious. Within 15 minutes of the opening each day, the piano was going, and the singing groups were in full swing. From these gatherings came many original barroom ballads, which an enterprising junior officer on a destroyer finally mimeographed under the title of "North Atlantic Lyrics—The Embryonic Beginning of a Great New Musical Literature."

A copy was sent to Admiral Sir Max Horton, the Commander in Chief, Western Approaches, and it contained the lament entitled "CINCWA, CINCWA." [8] The Commander in Chief and his staff apparently had a keen sense of humor, for several weeks later came a tongue-in-cheek song for the collection, composed by the staff, that went:

> The staff of CINCWA must regret, that Twenty-Four point Six,
>> Should think we get the 'arf pence, while all they get is kicks;
> We always think of Iceland as a very pleasant place,
>> And wish that we could have it as our operations' base;
> Through wintry days and longer months, we've got into the habit,
>> Of seeing Iceland convoys led by INGHAM and the BABBITT;
> You trot down to the ICOMP just to say you've been to sea,
>> Then hurry back to Iceland, reaching home in time for tea;
> In winter when it's cold, we hear you go to bed,
>> As soon as dinner's over, say at sixteen hundred Zed;
> And in the summer when its warm, the weather's very fine,
>> The sun shines the whole clock'round, so why should you repine;
> Now if you're inclined to grumble, will you kindly make a rule,
>> To think of your poor comrades at their desks in Liverpool;

[8] See Page 96.

For what you have to grumble at, we really cannot see,
If North Atlantic escort life is all it seems to be.

The singing was fine relaxation and, at the end of two hours, the crowd weaved toward the landing for the long, cold boat ride out to the anchored ships, a little steam blown off and a few bad memories washed away.

The enlisted men also had a club but, by some quirk of the Establishment, were allowed only beer, and that was rationed. As a result, some resorted to buying bootleg whiskey smuggled in by merchant seamen, and selling for thirty-two dollars per bottle. But not many merchant seamen had whiskey, either for sale or their own use, and they were not allowed to use the Navy enlisted beer mess ashore. One unfortunate merchant ship had been lying in the fjord for many months, her back broken by a mine explosion, and her crew had no outlets or recreation of any kind. The tension quite naturally built up and one afternoon came a report of a "mutiny" on board. Marines were ordered over from the VULCAN, and INGHAM was alerted to ready a boarding party. It proved to be a minor tempest of frustration rather than a mutiny, and orders were quickly issued cancelling the boarding party.

That men engaged in a bitter battle for survival should be forbidden the solace of an occasional cup of cheer and forgetfulness is a thing peculiarly American, stemming from the days of Josephus Daniels, a hard-shell prohibitionist who served as Secretary of the Navy in the First World War. While most responsible men will agree that alcohol and machinery do not mix, a supervised small ration of grog while in port—if not at sea—is hard to rationally condemn. For most of its existence, the Royal Navy has issued a daily grog ration to its men, and if it has affected their fighting qualities, we might do well to copy the results. But during the long, dreary months of war, the ship crews were forbidden liquor even on shore in the anchorage, and their recreation was almost non-existent. That their morale remained high was one more proof that it is built on a man's sense of accomplishment and values, and not on creature comforts.

Uncomfortable as January had been to the crews on the storm-battered and tossing ships, their ordeal was not without compensations. The combination of diversive routing made possible by the December Ultra breakthrough into Triton and heavy storms had prevented the patrolling U-boats from finding the convoys, and tanker Convoy TM-1 was to be the only one heavily hit during the month. In the entire Atlantic area, only 15 ships were lost from all causes; this light casualty rate, following a relatively easy December, considerably brightened the Allies' outlook. But few officers in the know imagined the lull was anything but temporary, or that Admiral Doenitz, continually probing for weak spots in the Allies' defenses, would long tolerate such meager results from his ever-increasing U-boat fleet.

VI

FEBRUARY 1-15 / THE HARDEST BATTLE

Disappointed by the failure to locate the convoys during the stormy month of January, Doenitz ordered a maximum effort as February arrived with more storms. The number of operational boats available in the Atlantic area had risen to over 175, of which 100 were at sea, and two strong groups were deployed off Newfoundland in a patrol line extending for several hundred miles. The Allies were now sending most convoys over longer and diversified routes in an effort to avoid detections, even though such diversions were costly in ship time at sea. This, in turn, forced the U-boats to extend their patrol line to cover a greater area, and in the prevailing weather, with greater distances between U-boats, some avoidance from detection was being achieved by the convoys.

Late in January, B-Service intercepted and broke another encyphered Allied routing message, this one concerning Convoy SC-118, scheduled from New York to the North Channel, with valuable cargoes for Russia. U-boat Command had its first clue.

The second soon followed. At the end of the month, U-456 had sighted eastbound Convoy HX-224 in a heavy westerly gale, and set out in pursuit. Five other boats were available, but all were astern of the convoy, and would require several days to catch up. U-456 went in alone and attacked, sinking three ships on February 2nd. It was not a heavy kill from a large convoy, but the sinking of one tanker was to have far-reaching implications. Two days later, U-632 picked up a survivor from this tanker, and he gratuitously informed the U-boat commander that another slow convoy was following on the same route two days behind HX-224. This incredible act of carelessness or treason was to cost the lives of hundreds of seamen and soldiers.

When Doenitz received the information, it erased the last doubts from his mind. He had the proposed routing of SC-118 from the intercepted message, but had been doubtful that the slow convoy would adhere to the route because of the attacks on HX-224. With the latest confirming information from U-632, he decided that they would and acted accordingly. Concentrating all available boats into a group, designated *Pfeil* (Arrow), he ordered them on to the estimated track of the oncoming convoy, to patrol to the westward. His reasoning was faultless, and the following night SC-118 ran into the middle of Group *Pfeil*, then passed on to the east—undetected! No one on either side was the wiser.

The convoy, consisting of 44 merchant ships and tankers, had departed New York on January 24th. Off Newfoundland on the last day of January, British Escort Group B2 under acting Commander F. B. Proudfoot, Royal Navy, in HMS VANESSA, had taken over the escort from the Western Local Escort, and the convoy was joined by 19 more merchantmen from Halifax and St. John's. B2 was an unusually strong force numerically for that stage of the war, and consisted of three British destroyers, three British corvettes, the Free French corvette LOBELIA, and the Coast Guard Cutter BIBB, which was assigned temporarily. However, the group had not worked together as a team, and three different Allied services were represented. The regularly assigned senior officer of Group B2, Commander Donald MacIntyre, RN, was absent from the Group while his flagship, HMS HESPERUS, was undergoing repairs after ramming and sinking U-357 several weeks before. The services of MacIntyre, next to Walker the leading U-boat killer of the Royal Navy, were to be sorely missed in the coming days. Proudfoot, as senior officer present, assumed acting command of the Group, to which he was a relative stranger, having himself just assumed command of VANESSA.

The first three days had passed uneventfully. On the fourth day, however, one of the merchant vessels fired a snowflake rocket by mistake, and even in daylight it was seen 20 miles away by an escort. VANESSA closed the commodore and asked him to warn the merchantmen to be more careful.

The night of February 3-4 dragged on routinely after the convoy had slipped unknowingly through Group *Pfeil,* until early in the morning darkness, despite the specific warnings that had been passed, a careless merchant seaman on the SS ANNIK, tinkering with a snowflake projector, fired it! The brilliant pyrotechnic display burst in the sky over the convoy. Startled men on 71 ships stared as the burning embers fell, and 20 miles away, the alert watch on U-187 also saw it. U-187 was a new boat, and this was her first contact after 22 days on an uneventful maiden patrol. She closed the convoy, determined its course and speed, and in the early dawn darkness began transmitting a sighting report.

The message was copied by U-boat Command. It was also intercepted by the Rescue Vessel TOWARD, at the rear of SC-118. TOWARD had HF/DF gear, and obtained a bearing on the U-boat signal, which was promptly transmitted to HMS VANESSA. HMS BEVERLY was ahead of the convoy at the time, and with commendable alertness changed course and started out the bearing without awaiting orders from VANESSA. She would, she informed VANESSA, search out 20 miles.

Less than an hour later, she sighted U-187 on the surface and went after it at 22 knots. When the range had closed to 5,000 yards, orders were given to commence firing. BEVERLY, however, was an old ex-American flush decker, and her fire control equipment was antiquated. The gun pointer, unable to see the U-boat in the troughs of the heavy swell, could not fire, and when the range had closed to 4,000 yards, U-187 dived.

BEVERLY was soon joined by HMS VIMY, and the two destroyers set up a systematic search around the area. VIMY made Asdic contact, and delivered three depth-charge attacks in rapid succession. After the last attack, the U-boat broke surface near BEVERLY, and as the destroyer dashed in firing, slid slowly under by the stern, while the crew abandoned ship. BEVERLY picked up 40 officers and men before VIMY signalled over, "Leave some for me!" The captain and the last three men were obligingly left to VIMY.

It had been a classic reaction by the escorts. The contact boat had been quickly pounced as soon as it transmitted a sighting report and silenced for keeps. In the escort business, a little prevention is worth tons of cure.

But U-boat Command had copied the contact report on the first transmission, and relayed it to the sixteen boats of Group *Pfeil*. Five from Group *Haudegen* were also ordered to the attack.

SC-118 was seemingly ill-starred. A broken cypher had given away its routing, a merchant seaman survivor had further betrayed it, and despite warnings against such an unlikely event, the accidental firing of the snowflakes had given its position away when it was almost away scot free. Though the escort had taken care of the boat making the sighting with dispatch and finality, the U-boats had already begun gathering around the convoy.

Group B2 was itching for a fight, despite the many breaks that had gone against them, and they struck back sharply and aggressively. As the U-boats moved toward the convoy, chattering freely, TOWARD and BIBB, the two vessels with HF/DF, were obtaining bearings on their radio signals. When a loud signal or plot of cross bearings indicated a U-boat was close by, it was reported to VANESSA, who would promptly order an escort to "cast out" on the bearing to locate and attack it. Throughout the afternoon and night, escorts were time and again thrown out as far as 20 miles. On one cast out, VIMY sighted a surfaced U-boat and gave chase. Twenty minutes later it dived, and VIMY asked for help in hunting it down. But Proudfoot, with four escorts already away from the convoy on sweeps, did not wish to further deplete his close screen. While VIMY was chasing, BEVERLY, on the other flank, sighted a U-boat close aboard and tried to ram. The boat got inside her turning circle, and a mad circling chase ensued, with the destroyer firing charges to the side from her K-guns whenever she could get the U-boat close abeam. Finally the U-boat managed to dive, and BEVERLY rejoined, reporting that she had given her opponent a "good plastering." During the next three hours, CAMPANULA, BIBB, BEVERLY, VIMY, LOBELIA, and MIGNONETTE made depth-charge attacks on U-boats attempting to close the convoy. There were targets aplenty for all. Though no U-boats were sunk in these attacks, several were damaged and badly shaken up. The hard-nosed escorts not only prevented any from getting inside the screen, but during the night so badly harassed the U-boats that they lost contact with the convoy entirely. Escort Group B2 had things well under control.

Then another fluke occurrence loosened their grip. The convoy commodore executed a course change in an effort to shake off the enemy. Unfortunately, his radio transmitter failed at the crucial moment, and the escorts were not advised. To make matters worse, the left three columns of merchantmen failed to receive the course change signal, and continued on their way. While the other 11 columns turned to starboard, the port section went on its own way for 15 miles before the escorts could straighten things out and turn it toward the main body. The split had confused the escorts, but it had confused the Germans even more. Most of Group *Pfeil* followed the smaller section. No one was molested during the night, and LOBELIA caught a U-boat on the surface, illuminated with her searchlight, and shook it up thoroughly as it dived.

After LOBELIA abandoned the search for the U-boat, she ran across the American transport HENRY MALLORY, straggling well astern of the convoy. Closing the big vessel, LOBELIA tried to signal her with a light, but could get no reply. The MALLORY was a fast vessel capable of 14 knots, and there was no excuse for her to be so far astern, heavily loaded with troops as she was.

When dawn came on the 5th, the two sections of the convoy were rejoined, but the weather became increasingly bad during the morning, and by noon, the seas were heavy, with snow, rain, and hail. The U-boats had completely lost contact and were unable to regain it in the prevailing weather. The weather, however, with fine impartiality, prevented any aircraft from providing cover for the convoy.

During the previous night, the steamer WEST PORTAL had straggled from the convoy, and at 1300 paid the usual price for such an act when U-413 overtook and sent her to the bottom. Before she slid under, her desperate calls for help were received by VANESSA, but her position was not known, and with U-boats again closing the convoy, no escorts could be spared to search. During the afternoon, BEVERLY made two attacks, and VIMY made one. The convoy was still secure, but WEST PORTAL died with all hands—a victim of her own wandering.

The lesson of the WEST PORTAL should have been taken to heart by the MALLORY, but by 1500, she was again straggling well astern of the convoy. Three other stragglers were 10 miles astern, and at 1915, the SS POLYKTOR also dropped aft with a steering casualty. After two days of unceasing and successful effort, Commander Proudfoot still had a heavy cross to bear, and several messages to the laggards by the escorts were curt and to the point.[1]

It was at this juncture that INGHAM joined the weary escorts after driving at high speed from Iceland. After arriving in Hvaljordur from the battering two weeks with HX-223, a diver had been sent down to examine the damaged Asdic dome. He had found a two-foot hole torn in the underwater Asdic dome by the heavy seas, but there was no opportunity to repair it. On February 3rd, she was ordered to proceed at best speed and reinforce

---

[1] The British were very clever at the use of Biblical references in their signals, and a short Biblical citation often conveyed the thought better than several paragraphs of text. One British destroyer, sent astern for the third consecutive day after the same straggler, was informed as usual by the straggler, "Am making best possible speed." The thoroughly fed-up destroyer skipper signalled "Hebrews 13:8." The merchant skipper, opening his Bible to the chapter and verse, read, "Jesus Christ, the same yesterday, and today, and forever."

Escort Group B2.[1a] The urgency had been generated by the ominous appearance of the many symbols on the U-boat tracking room plot.

When U-boat Command had moved Group *Pfeil* to intercept SC-118, numerous radio signals were exchanged with the U-boats concerned. As the U-boats transmitted, Allied shore HF/DF stations took bearings, and when they were plotted, more and more intersected in a small area of the Atlantic some 600 miles south of Greenland. To the submarine tracking room people, it was clear that a submarine concentration was building up in that area, and less than 250 miles away, SC-118 was steaming toward it. Warnings were sent to VANESSA, and additional escorts were requested by CINCWA from CTG 24.6. First INGHAM, then BABBITT and SCHENCK, were ordered to proceed from Iceland.

As the cutter approached SC-118 on the night of February 5th, a radar target was picked up, and general quarters sounded. Two minutes later, all guns were manned and ready as INGHAM plowed through the heavy seas at 17 knots, keeping the radar target 20 degrees to starboard, where the forward battery could bear. At little more than a mile, the signalman aimed the small red-lens Aldis lamp at the target and flashed the challenge of the day. Back came the correct response. It was HMS MIGNON-ETTE. INGHAM swung around in a wide circle and paralleled her, while the signalmen talked back and forth with their dim hooded lights. The convoy was 20 miles to the northeast. The cutter had come in astern of it without making radar contact. Leaving the little corvette in the darkness, she headed off in pursuit, and before midnight was on station two miles astern of the convoy. If trailers attempted to overhaul the convoy during the night, it was a good hunting stand. There was only one thing wrong—water rushed through the two-foot tear in her sonar dome, making the Asdic useless at speeds over eight knots. If she were to find a U-boat, it would have to be on the surface. Astern

[1a] The Iceland-based escorts, being close to the main battle area, were heavily utilized to re-enforce threatened convoys. But the necessity to move in at short notice and work with an unfamiliar group and escort commander in the thick of action was not conducive to optimum performance.

was the best place for her to be, where any U-boat was not likely
to be submerged. But the night passed quietly around SC-118,
and the escort crews caught up on badly needed sleep.

Early in the morning, the weather improved and the first RAF
Liberator arrived from Iceland, firing a green identification flare
before venturing within gun range of the convoy. The "Airedales" promptly got about their business, and within 20 minutes
had chased the first U-boat down astern of the convoy. BIBB and
INGHAM, the only two long-legged escorts, were ordered astern
of the convoy to work with the Liberators and sit on the contacts.

Numerous U-boat sightings were made, and four attacks
carried out. U-465 was badly damaged, and broke off to limp
homeward. Eleven U-boats sighted aircraft and were forced to
dive, losing their freedom of movement as they did so. As a
result, no U-boats were in contact after mid-afternoon.

But the ocean was literally alive with U-boats, and the escorts
could not be everywhere. At 1820, the radio silence was broken
by an SSS SSS SSS, followed by POLYKTOR's call sign. The
unfortunate vessel, which had broken down the previous day,
was trying to overtake the convoy when it ran onto U-266. Her
hull ripped apart by a torpedo, she was sinking alone. Soon the
transmissions ceased. POLYKTOR died, carrying most of her
crew with her.[2]

Shortly after dark, three boats regained contact, and broadcast
the convoy's course and speed. It would be only a matter of time
before others joined them for the attack.

But Proudfoot and pugnacious Group B2 were having no part
of waiting like lambs for the slaughter. When BIBB got a strong
radio HF/DF signal to the south, VIMY was ordered out on
the bearing. Leaving her station on the port beam, the destroyer
slipped ahead of the convoy and went boiling out to starboard.
Fifteen miles from the convoy, Asdic contact was made. Slowing
to 15 knots, she began a deliberate attack.

---

[2] The captain and chief engineer were picked up by a U-boat and carried to
Germany as prisoners-of-war.

U-267 had surfaced soon after dark, only to be driven down again within one minute by a Liberator which got in to two miles before being sighted. Now, 20 minutes later, she was listening with her hydrophones, attempting to pick up the convoy. A slight sound was heard to the north, where the convoy was estimated to be. Turning to the northeast, she eased up to periscope depth. Suddenly, the hydrophone operator yelled, "Loud screw beats. Destroyer!"

"Take her down. 450 feet!"

Before the startled control room crew could react, depth charges began exploding around her. The lights went out, and the U-boat became bow heavy, nosing down at a 50-degree angle. Men fell and slid against the vertical bulkheads.

"Both back full!"

The dive was stopped, and with full up plane, engines were thrown ahead. But the boat again started down. Finally at 720 feet, periously close to the depth at which water pressure would crush the boat's hull, the descent was stopped by blowing all ballast. At half speed on one engine, the other being disabled, U-267 leveled off at 400 feet and crept slowly away from the convoy. Severely damaged, and trailing a wide oil slick, she turned for home on one noisy engine. The crew waited shaken and pale for the next attack. It never came. VIMY was unable to regain Asdic contact, and returned to the convoy. Her people were not overly optimistic about their attack.

In the convoy, no sooner had the last far-distant reverberations of VIMY's depth charges died out than others began exploding much closer.

The Free French Corvette LOBELIA, on the port quarter of the convoy, had picked up a radar target at two miles and gone to general quarters. For the courageous Frenchmen, it was the start of three days of continuous action that would be equaled by few ships in this or any other war. As LOBELIA swung toward the target, the U-boat dived. LOBELIA followed and dropped a five-charge pattern. Twelve minutes later, the U-boat surfaced, and started off at high speed. Following at full speed, the corvette opened fire with starshells. The U-boat promptly pulled the plug and went deep, followed again by LOBELIA's depth charges. Asdic contact was soon regained, and another full pattern was dropped. MIGNONETTE joined up, and the two corvettes resumed searching, but the U-boat was having no part of any more surface action, and crept silently away "in the cellar." MIGNONETTE departed, but LOBELIA searched for another hour before giving up.

While the two corvettes were searching for the intruder on the port quarter, ABELIA picked up a U-boat coming in on the bow, and gave chase, firing starshells and machine guns. After ten minutes, the slow corvette had closed the range only slightly, but her gunfire was getting too close for the U-boat. Down it went, and a ten-charge pattern was laid in the swirl of its dive.

The escorts were putting on a textbook performance that had seldom been equaled in an action against a U-boat group of such strength. But too many boats were around, and something had to give. With VIMY, MIGNONETTE, and LOBELIA away from the convoy, and ABELIA engaged, the port side and quarter of the convoy had been left bare. An area of 12 miles was left without an escort, and so rapidly had the situation developed that the escort commander had no time to deploy ships from other sectors to cover the gap. Up through the opening came U-262.

Without interference, she moved up between the port columns, which were so close together that her commander was worried by the lack of maneuvering room. Finally, he found himself between two large tankers, and ahead, out of position between columns, was a third ship. Unable to proceed further in the cozy situation, U-262 reluctantly fired at the starboard quarter of a tanker. Both torpedoes failed to explode. The tanker turned sharply away. Dropping back, the U-boat unloosed two torpedoes at the ship to starboard, and though no hit was seen, both of them exploded.[3] Turning again to port, he fired at a tanker, and missed. It was his last torpedo. Bitterly, he transmitted a contact report, and turned toward the stern of the convoy. SC-118 was using up luck in great gulps.

But much of the luck was being manufactured by Group B2. At 0100, the USS BABBITT, which had just joined, picked up a contact 4,000 yards ahead of the convoy and closed it. At the last minute, the U-boat turned sharply, getting inside BABBITT's turning circle. Around and around they went, and whenever the U-boat passed abeam, BABBITT let fly with depth charges from her K-guns. Seizing the first opening, the U-boat dived, unharmed but shaken.

U-262, after the frustrating experience with its last five torpedoes, was now cruising astern, where U-boat Command had directed it to take over the trailing duty and keep the convoy in sight. It was a welcome respite for the crew to unwind from their recent experience, and five miles astern at night seemed nearly as safe as the U-boat pen at Lorient.

"Target one nine zero!"

The commander and watch officer threw their glasses on the bearing at which the lookout was excitedly pointing. It was only a shadow, but better to check it. The U-boat started a leisurely turn to port. As the distance closed, the moon emerged briefly from behind the clouds.

"Destroyer! Alarm! Dive! Dive! Dive!"

As the U-boat crash-dived, the vessel was coming straight at it, a bone in her teeth. It was no destroyer, but LOBELIA, which had been heading back for the convoy after her four-hour encounter with a U-boat. The swirl where the U-boat dived was

---

[3] U-262 may have hit the Polish ZAGLOBA, whose fate has remained a mystery for over 20 years. The attack was near ZAGLOBA's position in the convoy, the description of the ship attacked fitted the Polish ship, and she was missing from the convoy next morning, and assumed to be a straggler. When she never arrived in port, she was declared missing at sea. There was no alarm or report of an attack in the convoy at the time U-262 fired, but the failure to raise an alarm may be the reason that all hands perished.

plainly visible, and the little French corvette began dropping depth charges.

The first exploded as U-262 passed through 250 feet. They were well-placed, and the U-boat shuddered and jumped in her agony. Lights went out, the air supply trunk and ventilation extract trunk were torn away, and men were thrown to the deck. The stern settled heavily, and was only held up by going ahead at full speed. The boat finally leveled off at 575 feet, and crept away. LOBELIA was unable to regain contact, but one more boat was out of the fight, and headed for a long stay in the repair yard.

It is unfortunate that at that instant the curtain could not have been dropped on what had been a great escort performance. For nearly three days, surrounded by over 20 U-boats, SC-118 had battled on, and only one ship within the convoy had been hit. Two stragglers, it is true, had been lost, but with the convoy threatened, there was little anyone could have done to prevent their demise. The wolf pack, on the other hand, had been given a thorough working over. One boat had been sunk, and several damaged. As February 7th arrived, U-boat Command, thoroughly discouraged, recorded in the War Diary that only 11 boats were left fit to operate, and the pack had lost contact. The staff was mystified. Why weren't the boats able to get in and attack? At the very least, why weren't they able to keep contact?

Had the choice been theirs, it is doubtful if Group B2 would have wished to end the scrap then. They were heavy winners, and like poker players with good hands, and most of the chips stacked in front of them, there was a strong desire to see it through. Then a new player entered the game.

At 0213, his conning tower broke the water four miles to the starboard side of the convoy, then the hull shook itself clear of water and rose on the long swells. He climbed quickly to the bridge, followed by the watch officer and lookouts. After scanning the horizon quickly, and being satisfied that it was clear, he turned his attention to the convoy which could be dimly seen as dark shadows to the north.

Turning to the watch officer, he said, "Get out the contact report now."

The message went out to U-boat Command:

Convoy AK6668,[4] 60 degrees, 7 knots.

It was signed FORSTNER!

He had been driving his boat hard for two days attempting to locate SC-118, and despite slow progress due to numerous aircraft, had finally made contact during the night. Three weeks out of La Pallice, France, and with a full load of torpedoes, he was on his sixth patrol as skipper of U-402, and the first since his murderous assault on SC-107 on the morning of November 2nd.

As U-402 turned toward the starboard side of the convoy, and rang up flank speed, he was not dealing with the weak escort he had run through in November, but a fired-up group eager to kill Germans, and who had already proven that they could do just that. Yet, even had he known, it is highly unlikely that Siegfried von Forstner would have slowed one knot, for up ahead, the convoy vessels could now be seen clearly. Of escorts, there were no signs.

Less than two hours before midnight, BIBB had reported a strong HF/DF signal to the south of the convoy, and was promptly told to run it down. The cutter had cast out and was now 15 miles south of the convoy. After she had departed the screen, Proudfoot had failed to fill her vacated station on the starboard side with another vessel. As Forstner began his approach, MIG-NONETTE picked up a contact astern of the convoy, and CAMPANULA moved over from the starboard quarter to help. The entire starboard side and quarter of the convoy was uncovered and Forstner moved in swiftly.

---

[4] U-boats reported geographical positions in grid coordinates rather than latitude and longitude.

From 1,500 yards, he hit a small freighter, which caught fire and sank quickly. Quickly shifting targets, he fired two fish at a large tanker, but both missed.

Swinging with hard rudder, he fired from his stern tube, and was rewarded with a loud concussion two minutes later. The tanker turned on a red light and fired flares.

The man was a thorough workman. Entertaining some doubts whether or not the tanker would sink, he closed it again after ten minutes and put an "eel" in the engine room. Twenty minutes later, the American tanker R. E. HOPKINS went down with the loss of 15 men. The small freighter had been the convoy rescue vessel TOWARD, and her sinking was to have a consequence out of all proportion to her size.

After firing the fifth torpedo, Forstner cut astern of the convoy, and slowed down to trail while his crew worked feverishly to reload the torpedo tubes. Snowflakes and starshells lit up the night, and lights, survivors, rafts, and boats marked his trail of destruction.

The tight rein that B2 had been holding on the U-boats began to unravel. Eight minutes after U-402 put the second torpedo in HOPKINS, U-614, taking advantage of the confusion on the starboard side, slipped in from port and sent the straggling freighter HARMALA to the bottom with two torpedoes.

HARMALA had contributed to her own destruction. When U-402 started the fireworks on the starboard side with her attack, HARMALA, desiring no part of the activity, hauled out of column, and headed across the stern of the convoy for a quieter spot on the port side. When she finally resumed the course of the convoy, she was three miles astern of the port column, and was torpedoed several minutes later.

Three ships had been torpedoed in 20 minutes, and there was no rescue vessel to pick up survivors; the rescue crew were themselves the first victims. MIGNONETTE was sent off to rescue survivors, with LOBELIA to cover her. Only two escorts, CAM-

PANULA and SCHENCK, were left to cover the stern of the convoy.

The newly arrived SCHENCK had been an irritant to Proudfoot all night. Earlier, he had told the American destroyer to take station on the port quarter to fill in the gap left by LOBELIA's departure. But for some reason, she appeared to have lingered in the van between VANESSA and ABELIA, where according to Proudfoot, "She was a nuisance." Now, with three ships torpedoed, SCHENCK was, he thought, up on the starboard bow, diagonally across the convoy from where she should have been.[5]

At just this moment, CAMPANULA reported an Asdic contact astern. The escort commander decided to "dispose of" SCHENCK by sending her to help CAMPANULA.

In actual fact, the much maligned SCHENCK was on her proper station on the port quarter. But when the orders came through to assist on the starboard quarter, she dutifully started out.

As she cut across the stern of the convoy, a brilliant display of pyrotechnics marked the spot where U-614 had got in her licks. At 0323, the destroyer sighted life rafts, and using them as the starting point, began an anti-submarine sweep. Seven minutes later, radar contact was made at two miles, and a starshell was fired. When it proved ineffective due to the low clouds, another was fired, and by its dim light, a black shape was seen ahead. Receiving no reply to her challenge, SCHENCK barrelled in to ram. At the last minute, the target was identified as CAMPANULA. Both engines were backed full, rudder put hard over, and a collision narrowly averted.

With SCHENCK and CAMPANULA tangled up with each other, MIGNONETTE and LOBELIA picking up survivors, and BIBB running down an HF/DF bearing, the stern was devoid of

---

[5] The vessel which Proudfoot saw on the starboard bow was probably BABBITT, a sister ship of SCHENCK, which had dropped back into the inner screen earlier while making a depth-charge attack.

escorts. Except for the escorts ahead, the convoy was completely unprotected. The weary ships had been pushed too hard for too long. With the rescue ship lost, the job of rescuing survivors had devolved on the escorts. Some had promptly broken off to help when directed by the escort commander, while others were rescuing survivors on their own initiative. Proudfoot had lost touch with what was happening astern and, with it, control of the situation.

That it had occurred is no reflection on an able escort commander. Communications were so jammed, due to the intensity of the action, that he was unaware of the exact whereabouts of his units, and VANESSA's radar had no PPI scope [6] to provide an overall view of their disposition. Also, like other British escort commanders, he had the burden of handling his own ship as well as directing the escort and the convoy. In a night melee, the American system of having an escort commander riding on another captain's ship has obvious advantages.

Faced with a rapidly worsening situation, he still might have restored control by taking VANESSA astern of the convoy to see what was happening. But he remained ahead—a good position for a cavalry leader, but not for the escort commander of a slow convoy at night.

Quick to take advantage of the vast gap left in the screen astern of the convoy, Forstner overhauled the convoy and at 0340 hit the big tanker DAGHILD, leaving her sinking.

Confused and hurt though they were by Forstner's deadly foray, Group B2 refused to fold, and struck back hard.

After her last depth-charge attack had sent U-262 limping off, little LOBELIA had been ordered to close MIGNONETTE and screen her while she picked up survivors of TOWARD. Enroute she ran upon survivors of the HARMALA. They were pitifully few. The ship, laden with iron ore, had been hit with two torpedoes and had gone down so rapidly that no boats could be launched. Those who escaped had dived into the water or man-

---

[6] See Appendix I concerning radar and PPI, p. 242.

aged to scramble on rafts that were hurriedly thrown over, and as LOBELIA came up on the lights in the water, the cold, exhausted men could do little to help themselves. LOBELIA picked up one man, and maneuvered to drift down on a raft. As she stopped 12 miles astern of the convoy and rigged boarding nets, a radar contact was picked up three miles away. It was U-609, coming in to see what was going on. The U-boat had picked the wrong man. Lieutenant Pierre Morsier, a Fighting Frenchman in every sense of the word, turned toward the radar target and rang up full speed.

The U-boat heard the corvette's screws as they speeded up, and promptly took off down wind. At 3,500 yards, LOBELIA, unable to close the range, illuminated with starshells, and the fleeing U-boat was lit up plainly. For 20 minutes the wild chase continued, LOBELIA alternately firing starshells to illuminate, and high-explosive projectiles to hit when the U-boat was visible. The range closed slowly and at one mile the escort opened fire with 20-millimeter machine guns. It was too much for Kapitän-leutnant Rudloff, the commander of U-609, and he dived. LO-BELIA picked up Asdic contact at 1,200 yards and closed in. The U-boat turned off to the right, but LOBELIA detected the move and took a 15-degree lead ahead of it. Ten charges were dropped, and the corvette began opening out for another run. Thirty seconds after the last charge had exploded, a long rumbling noise was heard, followed by a loud explosion. A large air bubble broke water near the depth-charge pattern. The Asdic echo became wooly and faded. Soon nothing at all was heard. The shattered hulk of U-609 sank slowly to the bottom, 2,000 fathoms down. She had finished her fourth and last war patrol.

The bridge watch of ABELIA, on the port bow of the convoy, had been watching the running fight between LOBELIA and U-609 when their attention was suddenly diverted by the radar operator's report, "Contact, Green ninety, range three thousand five hundred yards. Small target."

Quickly checking the bearing, ABELIA heeled over in a tight

turn and rang up flank speed. This one was only a half-mile ahead of the convoy, and within a couple of minutes would be among the merchantmen. At 400 yards, the submarine was sighted fine on the port bow, and ABELIA swerved left to ram. The surprised U-boat started down, sliding below the surface when the corvette was only three ship-lengths away. The range was too close to make Asdic contact, nor was it needed. A swirl of white water marked the diving spot, and ABELIA plastered it with a full ten-charge pattern set shallow. Contact was not regained, but one more badly shaken U-boat was out of the fight.

Fighting B2 had regained the initiative. Only the bolder U-boat men were attempting to penetrate the screen, and they were being badly mauled.

But the fatal void of escorts astern of the convoy had still not been filled, and SC-118 was vulnerable to any U-boat commander making a thrust from astern. One ship was even more exposed than the rest, and in the cold darkness before dawn, the American troopship HENRY MALLORY, straggling several thousand yards astern of the convoy and jampacked with troops, was struck by a torpedo.

The sinking of the HENRY MALLORY was a grim spectacle, and as the story unfolded, it became uglier. Questionable planning by naval authorities, poor station keeping, an inadequately trained crew, lack of leadership, and panic contributed to the disaster. The story is not made prettier by the knowledge that, even after she was hit, the loss of life need not have been heavy. The only bright spots were the isolated cases of individual sacrifice and heroism, and the rescue efforts by the escorts, led by the Coast Guard Cutter BIBB.

The MALLORY was a 6,000-ton cargo-passenger vessel chartered by the Navy from the Clyde Mallory Line as a troop transport. The crew consisted of 76 Americans, 1 Canadian, 2 Puerto Ricans, 1 Russian, and 1 Filipino. Many of them were inexperienced, but this was not an uncommon situation at a time when we were straining to find personnel to man a rapidly increasing

The Fighting French Corvette LOBELIA. After its epic fights around SC-118, the gallant little vessel entered port at the end of a tow line. Musee de la Marine

Siegfried von Forstner on the bridge of U-402. His entry into the fight around SC-118 changed the entire tide of the battle. Wolfgang-Friedrich Frhr. von Forstner

Capitaine de Corvette Pierre de Morsier, captain of the Fighting French Corvette LOBELIA. His accomplishments during the bitter week-long fight around SC-118 have seldom been equaled in antisubmarine warfare. Musee de la Marine

The SS HENRY R. MALLORY. Newport News Shipbuilding

merchant fleet. In addition to the merchant marine personnel, a Navy Armed Guard crew of 34 men was aboard, for the MAL-LORY was well armed. The passenger list included 136 Army officers and men, 72 Marines, 173 Navy personnel and 2 civilians, all destined for Iceland. The captain was on his first trip as master, having served on previous trips as chief mate.

Though capable of 14 knots, unusually fast compared to most merchant vessels running the North Atlantic, MALLORY had been assigned to a slow seven-knot convoy. On noting her in the convoy, the escort commander expressed surprise at her presence in this slow group of vessels. Why had she not been assigned to a faster HX convoy, or even routed independently, where her speed would have given a greater guarantee of safety than it did in the slow SC convoy?

It is likely that the Convoy and Routing Section of COMINCH considered that her speed, though high enough to justify independent routing with cargo, was not great enough to justify the risk with troops aboard. The decision to place her in a slow SC convoy, rather than with the faster HX-224 which preceded it, was undoubtedly due to the fact that no Iceland section was being detached from the fast convoy. In retrospect, the safer course would have been to sail her with the faster convoy, allowing her to break off and proceed independently into Iceland as the convoy passed south of that island.

Even her position within the convoy was ill chosen. She was easily the most valuable ship, and should have been well up in the middle of the convoy. Instead, she was well to the left side and aft, where she was subject to attacks from port or astern.

Her assignment within the convoy is somewhat academic, for during the trip, she repeatedly dropped astern and straggled, an inexcusable thing for a ship of her speed. The temptation for an inexperienced master to leave a convoy under attack and seek a cooler spot is understandable, though such a course of action often proves fatal. Regardless of the fireworks, the safest place is always within the protection of the escort screen. The MALLORY, however, had straggled on the 4th and 5th when the convoy was not under attack and the escorts had the U-boats firmly under their thumbs. To add to the damning indictment of poor judgment, MALLORY did not zigzag while straggling. With her speed she could have made a radical zigzag pattern and still kept up with the convoy. Had she done so, she would have proven a more difficult target.

Some survivors blamed MALLORY's straggling on the action of the ships ahead and astern of her. The ship ahead, the SS DAY-LIGHT, was constantly surging ahead, then dropping back, forcing MALLORY to make like changes. This would have been both irritating and tiring for MALLORY's bridge watch, and may have increased the temptation to drop further astern where there was more maneuvering room. The ship astern, it was alleged, was continually crowding in ahead, and on several occasions forced MALLORY to drop aft. On the night of the attack, when the escorts astern were engaged in numerous scraps with the U-boats, this "snuggler," wishing to get as far away from such proceedings as possible, bent on extra turns and crept up alongside MAL-LORY, then slowly ahead where greater safety lay. Though he might be accused of a certain amount of cravenness, the snuggler must be credited with a more developed sense of self-preservation than the master of the MALLORY.

Whatever his reason, sometime during the early morning hours after the attacks on the convoy had begun, the MALLORY's master reduced speed and slowly dropped astern, where he maintained a steady course at seven knots, a perfect target for any U-boat which happened along.

Within the ship, the crew and Armed Guard were at battle stations, where they had been since the HOPKINS was torpedoed. All guns were fully manned and 16 lookouts were posted to keep watch in all sectors. The passengers, however, were allowed to turn in, and many were asleep. Some were undressed. Others, however, were up and fully clothed, and some were apprehensive. A young Army officer spent the early morning hours writing a letter to his bride of a few weeks, ending with the statement, "There have been a lot of explosions and firing tonight, and we don't know what is going on. We are all pretty frightened." The letter was neither completed nor signed when it was taken from his corpse 12 hours later.

MALLORY's officers had taken some steps to deal with an emergency. Boat drills had been held twice daily, but only two had been conducted at night, and these were not carried far enough. When a practice alarm was sounded, all hands would proceed to the boats, a muster would be held, then the drill secured. The boats were never swung out, nor were the passengers acquainted with the contents of the boat. It was assumed that they had no need to know, for the ship's crew would be with them, and would handle the boats. Unfortunately, most of the crew were not well-qualified small-boat men, and only a few had their lifeboat certificates. When the reckoning came, many would not be at their stations, and some boats would have to be launched by the passengers themselves.

At 0600 Greenwich time, the lookouts were relieved, and some of the gun crews were allowed to secure. The weather was cloudy with snow squalls, winds were rising, and the seas were rough. The oncoming watch and lookouts were not yet dark-adapted, and in the reduced visibility, could see little. It would be a good while before most of them could see well in the darkness. Even those who had taken the precaution of wearing red goggles and avoiding bright light before coming on watch would require a little time before their eyes adjusted.

A number of eyes were well accustomed to the night, however. Less than a mile away, four pairs of excellent Zeiss binoculars were trained on the dark shape of the MALLORY. The captain of the U-boat called down the hatch, describing what he saw:

"This is a very large freighter of about 9,000 tons with five hatches and a high funnel. Looks like a MATHURA type. Range, one thousand, bow right, angle one oh oh, speed eight. Standby to fire!"

The U-boat was U-402, with Forstner and his deadly crew. Four scalps were on his belt for the night, but with four torpedoes left, he was again on the hunt. After torpedoing DAG-HILD earlier, he had lost contact with the convoy, and while attempting to regain contact, had witnessed the firing by LOBE-LIA as she ran down U-609 several miles away, and heard the distant crump of depth charges as the corvette finished the job. There was nothing that Forstner could do to assist, and he continued after the convoy. At 0536, he had overhauled and torpedoed the freighter AFRIKA. Leaving only after she had settled to her rail in the water, he set off again after the convoy.

While still well astern of the convoy, the rampaging U-boat sighted a smudge in the night to port. Forstner wasted no time, and promptly cut toward the target, which was cruising slowly alone on a straight course, with no escorts anywhere around. It was a setup where even a green Leutnant zur See couldn't miss. Perhaps he should let the first watch officer make this attack. But he quickly dismissed the notion. The range had closed to 900 yards, and there wasn't time. Everything was ready. One "eel" would be enough on a cold turkey setup like this.[7] He took a last look through his binoculars.

"Fire!"

Aboard the MALLORY, there was no warning, no torpedo track, no submarine sighted. The torpedo crashed into No. 3 hold on the starboard side, wrecked the sick bay, destroyed one lifeboat, and blew off No. 4 hatch. Damage was heavy in the Marines' compartment. The concussion lifted the bunks out of their supports, dropping them onto the ones below. Many Marines were injured and dazed in the pileup. The refrigerating plant was wrecked, and the nauseous ammonia mixed with the smoke of explosives spread through many compartments.

No general alarm was sounded. Most of the passengers and

---

[7] It is fortunate that Forstner did not realize that his target was a loaded troopship, in which case he would have likely fired more than one torpedo. Had he done so, the loss would have been even greater.

crew were jarred awake by the explosion and rushed on deck, many only partially clothed. But in some compartments, men slept through the explosion, being unable to distinguish the shock from those caused by the ship pounding in the heavy seas.

The extent of panic may never be known, for the testimony of survivors is conflicting. That there was confusion and fright is certain, and understandable. In such circumstances, it can occur on the best disciplined man-of-war. In the minutes immediately after the explosion, men were trapped in one compartment by a jammed door. In another, the ladder leading topside was blown away. When men are trapped and their accustomed exits blocked, the classic ingredients for panic are there, and it is likely that it momentarily took over. But cooler heads prevailed, and the door was forced open. Lines were thrown down into the other compartment, and men began to help others out. But some were not as steady, and one survivor related, "We were all helping each other, then I saw a bayonet come out. I grabbed a rope and climbed out hand over hand."

The best panic preventer is leadership, and it was not forthcoming from the ship's company. No commands came from the bridge after the attack. No flares were sent up. No radio distress message went out. No orders were given to abandon ship. As the ship settled slowly, individual boats and rafts were put over, apparently at the initiative of the men gathered around each boat.

Though the seas were rough, the boats and rafts should have been able to get away safely, for there was ample time, and the ship was settling on an even keel. But the crew was not up to the task. Only five of the nine undamaged boats got away from the ship. One of these was partially swamped with water, and another was badly overloaded. A third was only partially loaded, and capsized soon afterwards. A fourth was launched with the seacock open, and began flooding. The pumps did not work, and the desperate men bailed with hands and caps in a futile attempt to keep the water down. Three boats had capsized as they were lowered, one of them being loaded with injured men. No. 4 boat hung up while being lowered, and was cut from the falls, falling into the water where dozens of men were swimming.

The absence of supervision turned the abandon ship into a riot, and the soldier and sailor passengers were left to fend for themselves.

But as in any such disaster, some men stand tall. One was a Filipino steward, who went from compartment to compartment making sure that everyone was alerted. In one compartment, he aroused several Army officers who were still asleep. He was not heard from again, and is believed to have gone down with the ship. A number of Army officers bravely worked to the end, looking after their men, and attempting to get them into rafts. Two Navy officers, Lieutenant Hartman, a paymaster, and Lieutenant Joseph Dowd, were last seen aiding men to enter the boats by flashlights.

Only 175 persons got away in boats, while some more got off on rafts. No swimmers survived in the icy waters. The rafts, which are relatively easy for even inexperienced men to launch, fared little better than the boats. No. 4 raft was frozen to its supports, and several of the Navy gun crew spent 20 minutes trying to free it before giving up and taking to a balsa doughnut-type raft, which afforded far less protection. Those rafts that were launched were secured alongside by one-inch manila lines, and there were no knives or axes to cut them loose. When the ship went down, many were drawn down with the ship or capsized. No passengers had been instructed on how to cut the lashings, and lower the floor of the rafts for greater stability, and as a result, the rafts repeatedly turned over in the heavy seas.

An hour after the torpedo hit, the MALLORY took a heavy list to port, and went down steeply by the stern. Many survivors were crowded on the bow, and as it rose higher, they began jumping. One Army officer leaped to the water far below, and was seized by panic as he went below the icy surface.

"I drank great gulps of water before I finally broke out on the surface," he said. "Then I was sick and vomited. When I did, a warm glow spread over me, and the panic subsided. I swam to a piece of wreckage, and climbed onto it."

After the ship had gone down, the sea was littered with wreckage, boats, rafts, swimmers, and bodies. Many died within a few minutes. Those who were fully clothed lasted longer. But many had on little clothing, and suffered terribly before dying. Those in the water or clinging to the doughnut-type Navy rafts with their bodies mostly submerged went first. The ones clear of the water on the box-type merchant marine rafts fared better. Many boats had swamped, and the occupants sat in the icy water, and attempted to bail with their hands. Within a half-hour, the cries of the men swimming in lifejackets had mostly ceased and silence settled on the dreadful scene.

An Army lieutenant, on his hands and knees on a hatch cover, stared around him at the floating bodies, rocking slowly and silently in their lifejackets, and resigned himself.

"I knew I was dying," he said, "and that they wouldn't come back to get us with the fight going on. I thought what my wife would do when they told her. It was all I thought about."

If there were those with more hope, it was well that they didn't know the true situation. No one in SC-118 or Group B2 even knew MALLORY had been hit. Ships were often sunk within a convoy without anyone knowing, and a straggler stood even less chance of its predicament being known. The convoy, now 15 miles away in the night, was steadily opening out to the eastward, and the escort commander was holding his remaining vessels close.

Yet we now know that most of MALLORY's people could have been saved had it not been for a terrible quirk of fate. Only 20 minutes after she was hit, an escort vessel was seen, less than two miles away, by people in the sinking ship. It was probably the destroyer SCHENCK.

Approximately ten minutes after MALLORY was hit, SCHENCK had been ordered to sweep astern and search for the survivors of the TOWARD. She promptly set out, only to have the orders cancelled by VANESSA before she had even worked up to speed. As the American destroyer started swinging to return to the convoy, numerous lights were seen in the distance. They probably, thought the skipper, marked survivors, so he started toward them, at the same time requesting permission of VAN-ESSA to proceed and pick them up. But the request was denied by the escort commander, who added in explanation that LOBE-LIA would recover them.

But the escort commander, not knowing that MALLORY had been hit, was also not aware that LOBELIA was 30 miles astern of the convoy and fully occupied. As things turned out, it would be over 20 hours before she would rejoin. As SCHENCK reluctantly turned away, unaware of the survivors' identity, the last chance of life for scores of them went with her, for the lights almost certainly marked the sinking MALLORY.

Tragic as were the results, Proudfoot's decision, in the light of the information available to him, was not an unreasonable one. The loss of the TOWARD, the convoy rescue vessel, had been a heavy blow, for without her, only the escorts were left to pick up survivors and they could ill be spared. Six vessels had gone down, and the hundreds of survivors, the dying, and the dead were scattered over 30 miles of ocean. An escort commander has a duty to rescue survivors, but he also has an overriding duty to protect those who are still with the convoy. If a choice must be made, cold logic points to protection of the undamaged vessels. So not until daylight did VANESSA plan to detach more escorts for rescue work. Unknown to VANESSA, individual escorts had encountered survivors during the night and rescued some, but, other than SCHENCK, none were in the vicinity of the MALLORY survivors. Daylight would be too late for most of them.

After the sinking of TOWARD, BIBB was the only vessel left with HF/DF, and her DF operators were busy. At 0645, she cast out on a strong DF bearing, but the U-boat dived. At 0854, she ran out again to the southwest on another DF signal. An hour later, a red flare burst in the air on her starboard bow. BIBB went to general quarters and closed the area. At 1000, a boat was sighted loaded with survivors, and lights were seen scattered over a large area of water. Dawn at that far northern latitude was still nearly an hour away. BIBB picked up the first survivors, learned they were from the HENRY MALLORY, and notified VAN-ESSA. Another message followed, requesting help. Not only were survivors everywhere around him, but Commander Roy Raney, the commanding officer of BIBB, knew full well the risk involved in a warship stopping at night in a submarine-infested area to pick up survivors. Should BIBB also be hit while lying alone and vulnerable, 240 more men would be in the water. Nevertheless, while awaiting VANESSA's reply, he commenced rescue operations.

Shortly after, VANESSA answered, "Rejoin at best speed!"

When the message was shown Raney, he cursed softly under his breath, and looked out at the water covered with hundreds of American troops. He was aware of Commander Proudfoot's need for the only HF/DF-equipped ship but he felt equally certain that the escort commander was not aware of the magnitude of the disaster. He crumpled the message in his fist, stepped out to the wing of the bridge, and said to his executive officer, who had the conn, "Stand down on the next boat. We are going to pick up these men."

Though temporarily attached to Group B2 for the passage of SC-118, Raney, being several years senior to Proudfoot, was not strictly subject to the Englishman's orders. The British officer could request, but he could not order BIBB to carry out tasks. The situation often occurs when a warship with a captain senior to the escort commander is attached temporarily to a group. But the escort commander in such a case, if he wishes to be diplomatic, will "request" a senior to do thus and so, and the senior will almost invariably comply. Failure to do so would undoubtedly subject the senior to severe criticism from upper echelons, regardless of the niceties of seniority. Raney knew this, if he thought about it at all, but despite the fact, and also knowing full

well the risk to his own ship, he continued picking up the survivors. The loss of a loaded troopship was fortunately a rare casualty,[8] and unusual measures were required. In the short time remaining to them, Raney intended to save as many survivors as
possible. He would take the responsibility for his actions.

Had the survivors been able to select their rescuer, it is doubtful if they could have done better. A veteran aviator and seaman,
Roy Raney had spent much of his 18-years' service engaged in
rescue work at sea and in the air. A hard-muscled man with an
inexhaustible supply of nervous energy, he paced the bridge rest-
lessly, befitting his servicewide reputation as a driver. But he
drove himself hardest of all, and his crew swore by him. He had
been executive officer on the USS WAKEFIELD when the big
transport burned at sea, and had taken command of BIBB only
a few weeks before. But he knew his business, as did his seasoned
crew. Moving among the rafts and boats, BIBB's crew began a
frantic race against time. In the 50-degree water, four hours after
the sinking, nearly all the swimmers were dead, and many of the
men on rafts were dead or dying. Crew members of the cutter
went over the side on the cargo nets or into the water to help survivors too weak to help themselves. It soon became evident that
excessive time was being used to get dying or badly injured men
aboard, and that the delays would deprive other uninjured men in
the water of a chance for survival. When Raney learned that two
men had died after being brought on board, he ordered that
rescue efforts be concentrated on men who were at least able to
pass a line under their own arms to be hoisted. It was a harsh
choice, but one justified by the circumstances.

On one raft, a man with a broken back was still very much
alive, but there was no time to rig a special litter or strap him in
it. When told that hoisting him up by bowline might prove fatal,

[8] The first week of February was a black one. On the day that Group *Pfeil*
had made contact with SC-118, another U-boat 300 miles to the northwest had
torpedoed and sunk the troop transport DORCHESTER with a loss of 605 men.
The loss of two transports in one week cost nearly 1,000 lives.

he shouted back, "Go ahead, what have I got to lose?" The gamble paid off; he was hoisted on board, and survived.

As time passed, few people were found alive, and in the high seas, location of the scattered rafts proved difficult. More dead men than live ones were now on the rafts, and the dead were left as they were. Shortly before noon, one of BIBB's seamen slipped on the wet deck, and fell overboard. Before he could be recovered, the Asdic operator reported a contact and BIBB hurriedly got underway. After a fruitless 30-minute search with no further contact, the cutter returned and recovered the man, considerably the worse for his prolonged immersion.

After the delay caused by the Asdic search, BIBB worked hurriedly to locate any remaining survivors among the hundreds of dead. If her people needed further incentive, the thought of a U-boat coming up on the ship lying dead in the water provided more than enough, for as noon approached, BIBB was still working alone.

Meanwhile, five miles ahead of the convoy as an outrider on the starboard bow, INGHAM had had a relatively quiet night. Four times she had thrown out on sweeps as far as ten miles from the convoy, but there had been no firm contacts. The action was astern and on the port bow. She had been at general quarters several times, and throughout the night had seen the firing and pyrotechnics astern, but the burden had been carried by the rear guard. No one on INGHAM knew which or how many ships had been torpedoed. They were not alone. Neither did anyone else, including the escort commander. In combat, one tends to focus on the immediate pressing matter of staying alive, and getting the other man before he gets you. Everything else is secondary. A convoy battle, moreover, is spread out over a 15-mile patch of ocean, and events occurring in the far reaches, especially at night, may go entirely unnoticed. Each escort has its own piece of territory to protect, and it doesn't go running over to the next block unless it is told, or its neighbor obviously needs help.

Shortly after BIBB reported the sinking of MALLORY, ING-
HAM was ordered to sweep 50 miles astern of the convoy and
sink any derelicts found. Minutes later, speed was increased to 18
knots, and she pounded westward into the heavy 15-foot swells.
Two hours—and 35 miles later—she came on the first wreckage.
Lumber was stretched out for over a mile, while here and there
pieces of wreckage, an empty raft, or an overturned boat could
be seen. Of survivors there were no traces. Though it was not
known at the time, the wreckage was the remains of the Greek
ship KALLIOPI, sunk by Forstner 35 minutes after the
MALLORY.

Leaving the wreckage of KALLIOPI behind, INGHAM continued westward, zigzagging at high speed; 25 minutes later,
BIBB was sighted at a range of two miles. Two corvettes had also
arrived, and one was stopped while the other carried out an anti-
submarine patrol around the scene.

A call was made to BIBB on the TBS radio.

Whitehouse, this is Buffalo.[9] *Where are the survivors?*

Buffalo, this is Whitehouse. Everywhere. They are all around.

While BIBB was answering, the first man was sighted, a soldier
floating in a kapok lifejacket. At almost the same instant, the
starboard bridge lookout called out, "Two men about 50 yards
abeam!"

The captain ordered both engines backed full, and as the ship
trembled under the thrust of her backing turbines, binoculars
were trained on the men in the water. There was no need to stop
for them. Even at a distance of 50 yards, they were obviously
dead. One was staring at the ship with wide unseeing eyes, and
as he rocked slowly, his face dipped beneath the water, emerging
again slowly. Another, with a wool watch cap still on his head,
had his mouth wide open as though screaming. Their faces were
the color of white paper. With the ship stopped, other bodies
could be seen as they alternately rose on the top of the swells,

---

[9] In voice radio communications, vessels used code names in lieu of their
actual names to make identification by the enemy more difficult.

Commander Roy L. Raney, USCG. As commanding officer of the BIBB, he directed rescue of most of the survivors of the MALLORY, and on the night of February 8th, nearly caught U-402 on the surface. USCG/National Archives

INGHAM passes close under the quarter of BIBB during the fight around SC-118. The rugged long-range cutters of this class were the mainstay of the American escorts defending the merchant convoys during the winter crisis. USCG/National Archives

Survivors from a British merchant vessel await pickup by a Coast Guard cutter. Bringing the heavy crowded boat alongside in heavy seas was always a risky maneuver. USCG/National Archives

Sixteen survivors of the MALLORY wait on a merchant marine type raft for rescue by BIBB. This type raft provided far more protection than the Navy doughnut type. USCG

then disappeared in the troughs. A soldier floating dead in the water, so far removed from his element, is a hauntingly sad thing. For long moments there was silence, broken by the captain's voice.

"Let's get them on board."

The events of the next several hours are still engraved in the author's memory after the passage of many years:

> I was standing beside the Captain when he ordered rescue operations started.
> "Permission to take over the boat, sir?"
> "Granted."
> I started down the ladder, and the exec grabbed me by the arm. "Get away from the side as soon as possible; we're rolling pretty heavy. Ride out on the sea painter right from the start. When you are well out, then get out your oars."
> I nodded and scrambled down the ladder. I knew the drill well enough; the only trouble is that I had never done it in a heavy sea. In calm waters on a cadet cruise, yes. At the Academy, every morning before breakfast, there had been the long row across the Thames River. The last year there, I had put in many mornings as cox'n. But there is a world of difference between theory and practice, and between protected waters and mid-Atlantic, with 30 knots of wind and 15-foot swells.
> "Six volunteers!" I yelled to the men standing near the boats. Six quickly climbed into the boat, and the gripes were kicked free. I positioned the steering oar, then gave the signal to lower away.
> The seas had been steadily worsening during the day, and though the ship was now taking them on the port bow to give us a little protection, she was rolling badly. As the deck force began to lower away, we were first 30 feet above the swells, then as the ship rolled to starboard, received a good smack from one. The exec, Lieutenant Commander Jimmy Craik, was supervising the lowering from the aft end of the bridge, and he knew his business. He had to, for he needed to catch the right combination of roll and sea to let the boat drop. If he misjudged, and the seas dropped away too soon, or the ship rolled away at the wrong moment, the boat would be dropped too far. The result could be a broken boat, or a capsized one with the crew swimming. He held us for what seemed like an eternity at the

deck level, while the deck force tried to protect us with fenders as the ship rolled to port. Then as the ship reached her maximum roll to starboard, and a big swell rose, we were dropped, landing with a splash after a two-foot fall. Seconds later, the ship rolled away, and as we dropped into a trough, I glanced to the side and saw the red bottom paint of the ship's bilge, and the bilge keel above my head. As the boat rose again, I flipped down the quick release hook of the after fall block, and we were free aft. The boat dropped away again in the next trough, and the bilge keel flashed by inches away. If it ever came down and caught the gunnel of the boat, we would be flipped like a toy, and the crew would be spilled in between the boat and the ship; the next surge of the heavy boat could end it all. We rose again on a swell, and I yelled, "Let go forward!" With relief I saw the forward hook was free as we dropped again, and shoved the steering oar to bring the bow of the boat out and away from the ship. On the bridge, the exec was yelling through a megaphone for us to get clear of the ship. We were trying. Down we went again, and the boat crunched sickeningly against the ship. An eternity later, the bow came out, and the boat sprang clear of the ship, riding on the sea painter. As we moved out, I yelled, "Out oars!" and then, "Give way together!" The sea painter was cast off and we were living again. We headed away from the ship, the crew rowing with a strong steady stroke. I could feel an artery in my neck throbbing violently. It had been close. How would we get back aboard? Time enough to worry about that later. We had our hands full here right now.

I saw a body ahead and ordered, "Give way together!" As we neared the body, I swung the sweep oar to turn the boat and felt it hit something. Turning, I saw a sergeant bumping against my oar, his mouth open and his eyes staring. He bobbled stiffly. Rigor mortis had already set in. We were in the midst of perhaps a half-dozen bodies. Taking in our oars, we began dragging the people alongside. In a short time, the bodies began to interfere with the crew's rowing. Ahead, we saw more, but there was little room left in the boat.

"We have got to get rid of the dead men."

I looked carefully at each man's eyes. My hands were too frozen to feel for a pulse, so when their eyes and face looked dead, we tore off their ID tags and cast the bodies adrift. Soon there was room in the boat, and we resumed searching for survivors.

While this macabre task was going on, the pulling boat from a British corvette a half-mile away capsized as it was being lowered into the water. We were busy, however, and gave it little thought, knowing they were alongside a ship that could assist them.

One of the boat crew yelled and pointed to the ING-HAM about a mile off. At her truck was the boat recall flag, and she was sounding her whistle. Smoke belched from her stack as she moved ahead. The BIBB had sighted a periscope and all ships were getting underway. We began rowing rapidly toward her, not desiring to be left alone 500 miles south of Iceland on a mid-winter night. When it quickly became apparent that we were losing ground, we gave up and rowed more slowly to conserve our strength.

Continuing the search, we sighted a swamped boat with three men in it. Pulling alongside, we took aboard a private, a corporal, and a sergeant. The private was in surprisingly good shape. The sergeant was unable to speak and merely drooled and mumbled gibberish. Two men boated their oars and took the sergeant between them to keep him warm.

As we continued looking for more survivors, another boat was sighted. It was now getting dark, and the ocean was gray and lonely. We rowed toward the boat and, swinging alongside, found it was from the BIBB. The officer in charge was Lieutenant Bill Cass, the BIBB's navigator, and a football coach from Academy days. It was an awfully big ocean, our ships were nowhere in sight, and we had a load of dead and dying men. It was with considerable inner reluctance that I steered away in the gathering darkness. Unless INGHAM returned, we would not be much better off than survivors in other boats. It was a long row to Iceland.

But eventually INGHAM returned and took us aboard. As they hoisted us to the rail and took off the three survivors, Doctor Jim Smith was waiting with a glass tumbler and a bottle of rye for the boat crew. Climbing out of the boat, my hands were bloody and frozen into something resembling clubs from grasping the steering oar. The Doc extended a half glass of rye, and I managed to hold it between my hands and gulp it down. The fiery liquor burned down through my gut, but it felt good! Holding the glass back out, I said, "One more."

INGHAM's other boat had already returned. Two men picked up were already dead when they were hoisted aboard. One man was still alive, but thirty minutes of artificial resuscitation failed to revive him, and he died in the sick bay.

In the wardroom, the stewards mates peeled off my clothes. As they chaffed me with towels, my circulation began to return. After 20 minutes, the rubdown and the whiskey had taken effect and I was pretty well thawed out.

A pharmacist's mate hurried into the wardroom with his kit. Another group of survivors had been sighted on rafts. We were approaching to pick them up. I went topside in my long underwear, which, with the rye whiskey, was ample protection. A raft with five survivors was along the port side, and Ensign Jack Juraschek was in the water attempting to get a line on them. The ship rolled heavily to port, sucking Jack under the ship, and he emerged choking and yelling. Half drowned, he was hauled out. The survivors lay helpless in the raft. I told the bos'n mate to make up several lines and to tie a bowline on me. When the lines were ready, I took them and jumped into the water. Surprisingly, the shock wasn't too bad. I surfaced and climbed onto the raft.

The first survivor was a kid of about 18, with several days' growth of blonde beard. As I passed a line around him he said, "Please hurry, Mac." And I answered, "We've got coffee aboard." Not very inspirational; I should have mentioned the whiskey. The next man was more difficult, for my hands were refusing to function in the cold water, but soon he was in turn hauled up. The third man, a very fat, 300-pound merchant seaman, wore a rubber suit, but had cut the bottom half off due to its filling with water. I finally managed to get the line around him but couldn't tie a bowline, a knot I had tied hundreds of times. Between fatigue, cold, and the double whiskey, I was nearing the end of my usefulness. I compromised on a square knot, and they hauled the fat man away. After the fourth man was hauled up, my hands no longer worked.

Back in the wardroom, I changed into dry clothes, wrapped up in several blankets, and dropped off to sleep on the transom. Later, the messenger waked me to go on watch and mentioned that there were going to be burial services on the quarterdeck. After sandwiches and coffee, I went topside. The corpses were laid out on deck, sewed in canvas with a five-inch projectile lashed to each leg to take the bodies down. INGHAM plunged and rolled as she rushed ahead through the black night to catch up with the convoy. A body was placed on a plank by the rail held by four seamen, and covered with an American flag. The captain, reading from a prayer book lit by a small red flashlight, said a short prayer ending with the words, "Commit him to the deep." The plank was tilted, and an American soldier dropped into the sea, over 2,000 miles from home.

The rite was repeated and, as the last body splashed over in the darkness, life seemed very expendable. We silently dispersed. Some went down to the wardroom to help sort out personal effects taken from the bodies. Others went to grab a nap to prepare for what lay ahead. I headed for the bridge for the eight-to-midnight watch, exhausted physically, and drained emotionally. The war was getting very personal.

SC-118 was in darkness and seemingly undisturbed as ING-HAM approached. Earlier in the evening the Greek ADAMAS had been in column six when a submarine was sighted to starboard. ADAMAS turned away from the submarine into the path of the SS HUNTINGTON, and was rammed amidships, starting flooding in the engineroom and fireroom. The radio operator, thinking the ship had been torpedoed, sent a distress message. On receiving the signal, the convoy had made an emergency turn to port, and the escorts illuminated with starshells.[10] On ADAMAS, all hands fled the bridge and engine rooms, leaving the engines running. For 15 minutes, the ship ran uncontrolled across the rear of the convoy before the engines finally flooded and stopped. Though the ship was not taking water rapidly, some of the crew panicked. Three men were lost when a boat they were lowering capsized. Twelve more left the ship in rafts when the other boat

[10] The starshells were sighted by INGHAM while she was several miles astern of the convoy. At the same time, a radar target was picked up nearby which gave every indication of being a trailing U-boat. Swinging at a range of a half-mile to bring all guns to bear, the cutter challenged, and when no answer was received, a searchlight was thrown on the target. Then the captain shouted, "Fire!", which the gun boss promptly did. In the heavy seas, the salvo missed, and the target turned on all lights. It was a British corvette! The following conversation followed on the bridge:

"Mister, you were pretty quick on the trigger."

"But, sir, you said 'Fire'!"

"No, I didn't. I was talking to the searchlight. I said 'Higher'."

The gunnery officer involved has always been glad that his marksmanship that night was no better than his hearing.—J.M.W.

became fouled. Sixteen remained on board, where they were discovered by BABBITT, well astern of the convoy. After picking up the men from the rafts, BABBITT, very low on fuel, had to be relieved by the redoubtable little LOBELIA, which came limping up from astern, where she had spent an action-packed day.

After killing U-609 at 0505, LOBELIA had returned to the scene of HARMALA's sinking, which she had left hurriedly earlier on getting the submarine contact. Only scattered corpses were found. Among the many floating on the water were two dead seamen on a raft. They were from the JEREMIAH VAN RENSSE-LAER, which had been sunk the previous week in Convoy HX-224.[11] Finding no more survivors after a careful search, the corvette started back for the convoy. When still 60 miles astern, a tanker was sighted shortly after noon, lying dead in the water. As the corvette approached, a column of water rose beside the derelict tanker as a torpedo hit home. It was DAGHILD, still afloat 13 hours after being hit with three fish. LOBELIA steamed past and saw the crew nearby in boats.

"Which way did the U-boat go?" yelled the Frenchman.

The men pointed to a nearby squall, and LOBELIA headed toward it. The U-boat was sighted and LOBELIA opened fire, driving it down. When Asdic contact could not be made, the corvette returned and took aboard all 39 men of the tanker crew, and before leaving sank her with depth charges and gunfire. The job done, LOBELIA limped after the convoy at reduced speed, her machinery badly damaged by three days of shock and concus-

---

[11] The RENSSELAER was one more tragic example of premature abandonment. She was struck by three torpedoes in the early morning darkness of February 2nd. The ship was abandoned in disorderly fashion without orders. Two of the three lifeboats capsized while launching. Though the ship was not sinking rapidly, several men jumped into the icy seas. Fourteen hours later, a boarding party from one of the escorts came on board to examine the ship, and found one seaman who had elected to remain aboard. Of the other 69 men who abandoned ship, only 24 were found alive and brought to Scotland by the escorts. The boarding party reported that the vessel could have been saved and sailed into port except for the fact that the boiler fires had not been extinguished, causing the boilers to burn out.

sion from her own depth charges and gun fire. But there was no rest for the gallant little ship's crew and the 50 survivors aboard her. As she closed the convoy, the ADAMAS was sighted with BABBITT alongside, and when BABBITT requested relief, the corvette took over. After removing the survivors in a hazardous night rescue, LOBELIA was directed by the escort commander to sink ADAMAS. It was done with a depth charge placed close aboard, which proved to be the final straw. LOBELIA's engine stopped with a cracked thrust block. She was taken in tow by VIMY for the rest of the trip. In three days of continuous action, she had attacked seven U-boats, sunk one, seriously damaged another, and inflicted lesser damage on several others. Over 60 survivors had been picked up from three ships.[12]

INGHAM, after arriving back with the convoy near midnight, was moving toward her station when five rockets and a red flare were sighted ahead, and orders were received from VANESSA to rescue the survivors from the British NEWTON ASH, torpedoed in column five.

Ten minutes later, the crew was at battle stations with the ship zigzagging at 15 knots when a lookout sighted lights in the water ahead. Passing close aboard, they saw that it was a boat full of survivors. The captain swept the area for a mile around, echo-ranging for any sub which might be using the boat as bait, and at 0100, slowed and started an approach. Suddenly, there were two explosions, and heavy black smoke billowed up off the starboard bow where two torpedoes had "prematured." Speeding up, the cutter raced toward the scene, but found nothing and soon returned to the boat. Passing it, the men on the bridge yelled in unison, "Put out those lights!" One by one, they went out.

Captain A. M. Martinson, commanding INGHAM since January, was a veteran of over a year on the North Atlantic run as a

---

[12] Ironically, the first order of business after she reached port seems not to have been a hearty "well done" from the Admiralty but a Board of Investigation to determine why she had cracked her thrust block.

CO and escort commander. He had no illusions about the dangers involved when a man-of-war stopped to pick up survivors without a covering escort. Tonight there were none available to cover, and the area was hot. But he was a humane man and, with people in the water, was determined to get them. All on board knew that the U-boat was somewhere within a three-mile radius, and it had already proven that it had fangs. As INGHAM shuddered from her backing screws, there were a few shudders, also, among her crew.

In the darkness, a large white boat could be seen approaching through the heavy seas. Some of the cutter crew worked hurriedly, rigging the boarding nets while the gun crews closed up at general quarters. Martinson stopped upwind and drifted down slowly on the boat. The boarding nets and lines were thrown over. But the survivors got anxious and started rowing toward the rescue vessel. Just as they came alongside, a huge wave caught the boat and capsized it. Another wave followed almost immediately and smashed the boat against the ship, crushing a dozen men who were in the water between the two. Their screams could be heard all over the ship. The boat and people in the water began drifting aft, and men scrambled down the nets to grab them, only to have the sea snatch them away. The skipper ordered the searchlight on, and the big 24-inch light played on the water. In the light's beam, an arm was sticking out of the water with three gold stripes on the sleeve—probably the first mate or chief engineer. Then it sank slowly beneath the water. Of nearly two dozen men in the boat, only three were rescued. While the light was on the water, and swimmers were preparing to go over the side, the Asdic operator shouted, "Contact! Bearing zero two zero. Range one thousand eight hundred yards!"

"Both engines ahead flank!"

INGHAM began to shudder violently from the thrust of her engines, and for an eternity didn't move. Eighteen hundred yards off there was something beneath the water, and it required little imagination to guess what it was. At long last, someone turned off the searchlight. As the ship began to move ahead, the fire control phone talker kept repeating, "Oh Jesus, oh Jesus."

Soon she was up to 15 knots and all hands were beginning to breathe again. As the distance to the contact closed, it began to broaden and fade. Despite a half-hour of searching, the Asdic operator was unable to pick it up again.

Satisfied that the contact was non-sub, the captain returned to the area of the survivors, located another boat containing only one survivor, and backed down on it. Men on the stern threw a line and told the man in the boat to tie it around himself and jump in. He was hauled over the fantail soaking wet. As strong arms grabbed him, he piped up in a shrill Cockney voice, "Tyke it easy, mytes, tyke it easy!"

On deck, he broke down and started sobbing. Finally he straightened up, looked at the men gathered around him, and exclaimed, "Thanks Gawd we got a bloody Naivy!"

NEWTON ASH was Forstner's seventh victim in less than 24 hours. After sinking AFRIKA, MALLORY, and KALLIOPI shortly before dawn, and missing a shot at another ship due to a faulty torpedo, he had submerged to load his last torpedo. Surfacing soon afterwards, he set off after the convoy, but progress was slow due to numerous aircraft contacts and several close approaches by escorts. Seven times during the day he was forced to dive, but each time he surfaced and continued doggedly onward. Not only was his crew approaching a state of exhaustion, but air compressor and engine troubles had developed. In mid-afternoon, he received a radio message:

> *Forstner well done. Stay there and hold contact. All boats must arrive yet. The depth charges also give out. Stay tough. The convoy is frightfully important. Doenitz.*

The Admiral was right. Some of the escorts did not have enough depth charges for a full pattern, and others were approaching fuel exhaustion. Forstner drove on eastward and, shortly before midnight, saw the BABBITT stopped by the sinking ADAMAS. The sitting-duck destroyer was a tempting target, but only one torpedo was left, and the heavily laden merchantmen were up ahead. Just after midnight, Forstner was in position 1,500 yards on the starboard beam of NEWTON ASH and sent his last torpedo on the way.

Unable to make further attacks, Forstner took over the trailer's job and began transmitting continuous beacon signals. This tenacity nearly cost him his life, for BIBB, on the starboard flank, picked up the beacon signal on her radio direction finder and homed in. Her new SG radar made contact at 4,500 yards, and the cutter went to general quarters. At 1,700 yards, believing the U-boat to be in position for a shot at the convoy, Commander Raney of BIBB opened up with starshells. They lit off over the surprised U-boat, but the shock of the third salvo knocked out BIBB's radar, and her gunners were blinded by the gun flashes. Turning away, with the cutter only a half-mile off, U-402 escaped unseen on the surface. Had BIBB held her fire two minutes longer, it is likely that U-402 would have been caught on the surface and swift retribution exacted.[13]

Ireland-based Liberators and Sunderlands arrived at dawn, and at 1000, the last U-boat broke off the chase. Characteristically, it was U-402. She headed for the barn with one engine running on five cylinders, a hot thrust bearing, and both compressors leaking.

The battle of SC-118 against 21 U-boats had proven that a strong escort and sufficient air cover could, in most cases, protect a convoy against even massive wolf-pack attacks by average U-boat commanders. In five days, the escort—air and surface—had sunk three U-boats, heavily damaged four others, and allowed only three boats to penetrate the convoy screen to deliver torpedo hits. But one of these boats was U-402, and her superb commander had sent seven vessels to the bottom. A strong escort, aggressive tac-

[13] Forstner was indeed lucky. When BIBB opened fire, INGHAM was only two miles away, and in escaping, Forstner must have passed across her bow. But INGHAM's old SC-1 radar was not as efficient as BIBB's new SG, and the U-boat was not detected in the heavy sea.

Night illumination by a Coast Guard cutter on the North Atlantic. As a result of the illumination rounds, the gun crews were blinded by the flashes, and U-402 escaped. USCG/National Archives

In the wardroom of U-402, cruising at 100 feet, von Forstner celebrates with a cake the news of his award of the Knight's Cross, two days after breaking off from SC-118. The large cross around his neck was made by the crew while he slept. Frau Annamaria Rapp

U-402 enters La Pallice, France, following the attack on SC-118. Each of the small flags represents a ship sunk. Frau Annamaria Rapp

Baron von Forstner reviews an honor guard at La Pallice after receiving the Knight's Cross. Despite his experience, his days were numbered. Frau Annamaria Rapp

tics, and improved equipment could still not stop a determined professional of Forstner's caliber.

What was not realized at the time was that the battle had essentially been one between Forstner in U-402 and the 11 escorts of Group B2. With the torpedoing of the NEWTON ASH, his sinkings had passed the 100,000 ton mark, a fact that had escaped him, but not his crew, for that figure brought with it an almost certain award of the Knight's Cross, one of Germany's highest decorations. While Forstner slept an exhausted sleep after nearly 40 hours of continuous action, his first watch officer cautioned the radio operator to keep a sharp listening watch on the U-boat Command channel. During the night, the expected message arrived.

Forstner was awakened by the first watch officer, and asked to step into the control room. Somewhat puzzled, and still half asleep, he pushed aside the leather curtain of his tiny cabin, and stepped into the control room—to be greeted by his entire off-watch crew. On a red cloth cushion, the leading petty officer held an oversized version of the Knight's Cross, which the engineering force had just completed, while the radio operator held out the radio message from C-in-C, Navy, announcing the award. Behind them stood the cook with a newly baked cake. Rising to the import of the occasion, Forstner ordered that, after diving, a ration of eggnog with cognac be issued the crew. The celebration commenced as U-402 limped slowly toward La Pallice, unwilling to break radio silence before crossing the Bay of Biscay, where Allied aircraft patrolled continuously. When the battered U-boat finally sailed up the swept channel into her home port, a week overdue, a host of small flags flew from her periscope signifying her sinkings, while splashed across the port side of her conning tower in crude numerals was her total of shipping sunk—103,000 tons.

After Forstner had broken off, there were no further attacks. Group *Pfeil* drew off badly battered. Group B2 limped into port —spent and exhausted—with the LOBELIA, an awfully big little ship, on the end of a towline. Twelve merchantmen had been sent to the bottom. Neither side had "won."

Admiral Doenitz, gravely concerned at the punishment absorbed by his boats, said, *"It was perhaps the hardest convoy battle of the whole war."* [14]

The day after the pack broke off the attack, INGHAM, BIBB, and SCHENCK departed from Convoy SC-118 with seven merchant vessels for Iceland. After the battle, the next four days were, by comparison, uneventful, though the small convoy was battered by a full gale, which reached hurricane force on the 11th, and blew at over eighty knots for two days. The ships became badly scattered, and the weary escorts worked continually to keep them in some semblance of a formation.

On the first night of the hurricane, INGHAM barely escaped tragedy. One of the ready gun crews was huddled around No. 4 gun, hanging on as the ship rolled heavily in the mountainous seas. After dark, realizing that no U-boat could operate in such seas, the OOD ordered the gun crew to move away from the exposed gun, and seek shelter under the lee of the radio shack. A short time later, a huge sea broke amidships, and when the tons of water receded, the sponson around No. 4 gun, where the crew had been standing, was a mass of twisted metal. The wind-whipped, frozen men stared at the spot where they had been standing minutes before, and then at each other. When the relief gun crew took over and the weary men started below, the gun captain of the relief crew shouted after them, "You guys are sure lucky to be knocking off."

Boatswain Mate George Baker stopped on the ladder leading below, timing the seas before making a dash along the main deck for the safety of the nearby hatch.

"Yeah, we sure as hell are," he shouted back.

They dropped anchor in "Valley Forge" on the 15th of February. A gale was blowing, and was to continue for five days. No

[14] Karl Doenitz, *Memoirs of Ten Years and Twenty Days* (Bonn: Athenaum-Verlag Junkerund Dunnhaupt, 1958), p. 322. Italics author's.

boats could go ashore, and steam was kept at the throttle. During the first night, the anchor chain parted, and they were forced to hurriedly get underway, trailing a dense cloud of white smoke from a smoke tank accidentally ignited by the seas. But despite the atrocious weather, the time in port was welcomed, and the tired men tried to make up for weeks of interrupted sleep.

VII

FEBRUARY 16-28 / MORE ATTRITION

Five hundred miles to the south of Iceland, American Escort Group A3 was in rough straits and they were getting no rest. On the day after the Iceland section had broken off from SC-118, Group A3, which had enjoyed a few days' rest in Londonderry after the stormy eastward passage of HX-228 in January, picked up westbound convoy ON-166 off Ireland, and promptly plowed into a howling gale that lasted three days. But as quickly as the weather moderated enough to allow the convoy to close up, U-boats were detected by the HF/DF operators on cutters CAMP-BELL and SPENCER.[1] By February 21st, despite aggressive patrolling to keep them down, the convoy was surrounded by U-boats.

The escorts and long-range Liberators fought to keep them at bay. At 2014 that night, SPENCER, the escort flagship, commanded by Commander H. S. Berdine, USCG, and carrying the escort commander, Captain Paul Heineman, USN,[2] was in the van of the convoy when radar contact was made at a range of 8,600 yards. Increasing to full speed, SPENCER went to general quar-

[1] ON-166 had itself been located by Luftwaffe HF/DF stations, which had obtained bearings on the radio transmissions of the convoy's aerial escort. U-boats were vectored to the position, established contact, and began the pursuit which lasted for over a thousand miles.

[2] It would have been hard to find a better combination. Heineman, a hard and aggressive fighter, was probably the best escort commander the Americans produced. The flagship of Group A3, SPENCER, commanded by Berdine, participated in more engagements than any other American vessel during the winter of crisis, sinking two U-boats, and damaging several others.

ters and closed the contact. At 5,000 yards, the conning tower of a U-boat was sighted, and SPENCER opened fire. The U-boat dived and radar contact was lost at 1,800 yards. Less than a minute later, Asdic contact was made, and a nine-charge pattern dropped. Contact was not regained. The target, U-225, had been mortally wounded by the attack and went down with all hands.

So far, Group A3 had things well in hand. Though they had been able to function and work together as a team for some time, it was certainly one of the most "Allied" groups on the Atlantic. Besides the U. S. Coast Guard Cutters SPENCER and CAMP-BELL, it consisted of one British and four Canadian ships, and the Polish destroyer BURZA, and was commanded by an officer of a fifth service; the teamwork had been superb.

Heineman was a firm believer in the principle that aggressive action provides the best defense, and throughout the day had been casting out escorts to run down HF/DF bearings.[3] The tactic proved successful, and six U-boats were detected and driven off during the night. But the escort was not strong enough to stop them all. The seventh penetrated the screen and torpedoed the EMPIRE TRADER when only four escorts were left with the convoy, three others being away on offensive sweeps. Six hours later, the NIELSON ALONSO was torpedoed. The rescue vessel STOCKPORT went after one, and CAMPBELL was dispatched to help the other.

Arriving on the scene at 0405, the cutter picked up 50 men from four boats; three men had been killed in the engine room when the torpedo hit. After CAMPBELL started back to the convoy, the skipper of the torpedoed vessel came to the bridge and, under questioning, admitted that he had not destroyed the ship's confidential documents. CAMPBELL reversed course and started back to board the tanker, but just as the hulk was sighted, a column of water rose high in the air under her bridge. The U-boat

---

[3] Heineman was also a great believer in the value of HF/DF equipment on ships, and as a result of his efforts, the cutters CAMPBELL and SPENCER, which he rode as flagships, were the first two vessels in the U.S. Fleet to receive the gear.

had been hanging around to make sure of its kill. The cutter people had little time to worry about the derelict, however, for seconds later a torpedo exploded in their own wake. White smoke was sighted two miles off, and CAMPBELL gave chase. At 1,500 yards, it was determined to be coming from the Diesel exhaust of a U-boat, and the cutter barrelled in to ram. A searchlight was thrown on the diving U-boat, followed by a full depth-charge pattern.

The attack heavily damaged U-753, knocking out one engine and damaging the periscope and stern torpedo tube. The U-boat, which withdrew from the attack due to the damage, was the one that had fired a torpedo into the NIELSON ALONSO as CAMPBELL approached.

When contact was not regained, CAMPBELL abandoned the search and shelled the NIELSON ALONSO before hurrying off after the convoy. When last seen, the Norwegian was burning brightly in the night.

At 1107, while 50 miles astern of the convoy, an Asdic contact was made. As the range closed, and while turning hard right, a periscope was sighted close aboard to port. CAMPBELL let go with a full charge pattern which caught the U-boat in the left edge. The boil of water from its racing screws could be seen clearly between two depth-charge explosions. Asdic contact was regained and two more attacks made before contact was lost and the cutter took off again after the convoy, where Captain Heineman was calling urgently for all escorts to rejoin.

Less than two hours later, a U-boat was sighted on the surface, but dived before CAMPBELL could close, and the cutter continued toward the convoy. With the number of U-boats around, Commander James A. Hirshfield of CAMPBELL feared that if he went directly to the convoy, one might follow him and locate the merchantmen. He changed course to pass well off the port beam of the convoy, from where he would proceed to his assigned station. It was a smart move, for we now know that U-boats often trailed an escort, which would unknowingly lead them to contact with the merchant vessels.

CAMPBELL's radar was out of commission, but after dark on the 22nd, snowflakes and starshells were sighted just over the horizon. For the twelfth time in 48 hours, the weary crew went to General Quarters and the ship turned toward the convoy. The wolves were among the sheep, and the area between CAMPBELL and the convoy was alive with submarines. Several of the escorts had U-boats on the surface and the flashes of their guns and burning starshells could be clearly seen. In the magazines, far below decks, the ammunition handling crews could clearly feel the distant "crump" of depth charges. It was going to be another long night following on a lot of other sleeplessness. The previous night had been long enough.

U-606, which had started the ruckus, had been trailing the merchantmen all day, and shortly after dark, had closed the convoy and torpedoed three ships on the port side. CHILLIWACK picked up the U-boat as she turned away and delivered a depth-charge attack, then lost contact. The Polish destroyer BURZA, however, quickly regained Asdic contact and attacked. The U-606 went to 600 feet, at which extreme depth her damaged hull began to leak.

BURZA, coming in again like an avenging angel, plastered the U-boat with another pattern. One of the charges exploded just above the bridge of the U-boat, damaging the railing and conning-tower housing and bending the 20-millimeter anti-aircraft gun out of shape. Other charges shook the boat so badly that an oil line in the petty officers' quarters broke, spraying oil over the compartment. The boat was below test depth, and creaked and groaned in a terrifying fashion due to the water pressure. The engineering officer, accompanied by the warrant machinist, made a hurried inspection of the boat, and discovered the beginning of a crack in the hull, near the after diving tank. Becoming panicky, he rushed forward to tell the captain that the boat couldn't last.

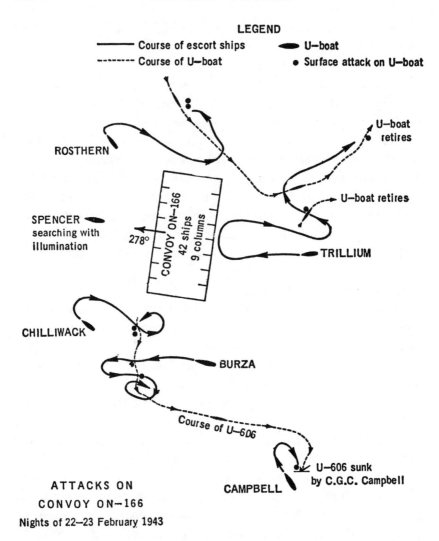

LEGEND

——— Course of escort ships   ◄■ U—boat

------- Course of U—boat   • Surface attack on U—boat

ROSTHERN

U—boat retires

SPENCER ◄■
searching with
illumination

U—boat retires

278°

CONVOY ON—166
42 ships
9 columns

TRILLIUM

CHILLIWACK

BURZA

Course of U—606

U—606 sunk
by C.G.C. Campbell

ATTACKS ON
CONVOY ON—166
Nights of 22–23 February 1943

CAMPBELL

Though the boat had been submerged less than an hour, the air was becoming bad, and there were reports of chlorine gas, caused by salt water reaching the batteries.

While the submariners were frantically trying to get matters under control, BURZA lost contact, and the depth-charging ceased. In similar circumstances, most U-boats would have crept silently away to fight another day. But U-606 was not like most boats. "Morale in this U-boat," reported the Allied Intelligence officers who interrogated her crew later, "was the worst we have encountered on any U-boat to date."

U-606 appears to have been an ill-founded boat from the beginning. On her first war patrol, she was barely out of sight of land before her captain was stricken with stomach trouble and forced to return to base. After a week in the hospital, during which time some of his officers consumed the captain's whiskey supply aboard ship, it became evident that he would be unable to continue in command. A substitute commander from another boat took her out to sea for the next patrol. Contact was made with an Arctic convoy, but no ships fell victim to the new boat. Instead, another boat, U-435, got into the convoy, sinking four merchant vessels and the destroyers HMS SOMALI and HMS LEADER. The other escorts struck back fiercely, but instead of hitting U-435, which had done the damage, caught and worked over the luckless U-606.

In October she sailed on her third war patrol under a new captain, Oberleutnant [4] Hans Dohler, a comparative youngster of 25 who had never served as a first watch officer, but had been upped from second watch officer on another boat to command of U-606 shortly before starting out on patrol.

He succeeded in sinking the big Norwegian whale factory ship KOSMOS II in Convoy HX-212.[5] The sinking less than two weeks after sailing with a new skipper should have pepped things up in the boat, but morale continued low. Shortly after sinking the KOSMOS II, U-606 had an easy shot at a freighter, but muffed it when the first watch officer gave the wrong bearing to the torpedo data-computer operator. Three torpedoes were fired and all missed. Another U-boat joined in the chase after the now fleeing freighter, and fired eight torpedoes. All eight missed! On arrival back in port, both U-boat commanders were to be given a severe dressing down for so ignominiously wasting so many torpedoes.

[4] Equivalent to senior lieutenant in USN.
[5] By strange coincidence, CAMPBELL was one of her escorts.

On U-606, there was much bickering between officers and men as to where the fault lay. Morale sank lower, and performance suffered even more. When the U-boat was surprised several days later by a destroyer, the watch officer sounded the alarm, but failed to give the order to flood the tanks and submerge. As the destroyer bore in, the U-boat continued on the surface, with the watch officer shouting, "Go deeper, go deeper!" Only the presence of mind of a machinist mate, who flooded the tanks on his own initiative, saved the U-boat.

After an in-port period in which the relations between the officers and men further deteriorated, U-606 sailed for her fourth war patrol. The crew was in a tense and hostile mood.

The first five weeks of the patrol passed uneventfully except for the horrible North Atlantic weather. On February 14, 1943, U-606 was met by a supply U-boat, and took aboard oil, bread, potatoes and other rations.[6] Doenitz was not calling a boat off patrol when she still had a full load of torpedoes remaining. On February 22nd, she at last sighted a convoy, ON-166, and that night closed in on the surface and torpedoed three ships. The attack was well executed, but her luck was fleeting, and now she was down deep, harassed by a determined and hard-hitting BURZA.

When the engineering officer burst into the control room, reporting the dire condition of the boat, Dohler did not hesitate. All tanks were blown, exhausting all the high-pressure air flasks in the process, and U-606 started up at a steep angle. On the way to the surface, one officer, according to some survivors, attempted to escape through the galley hatch, but was forcibly restrained by the skipper.

After reaching the surface, the Diesel engines were still functioning and interior lights were burning. Being now somewhat calmer, the engineering officer revised his estimate and decided

---

[6] During this period, two supply U-boats or "milchcows," U-460 and U-462, operating 500 miles north of the Azores, refueled and provisioned 27 U-boats, which as a result were able to stay at sea and attack Convoys ON-165, -166, and -167 on the North Atlantic routes.

Captain Paul Heineman, USN (left), the commander of Escort Group A3 (Heineman's Harriers) on the bridge of the CGC SPENCER with Commander Harold S. (Sloop) Berdine, USCG, the flagship's skipper. During the crisis of the Atlantic battle, no two American commanders saw more combat action. The flagship was in dozens of attacks and sank two U-boats during the winter. USCG/National Archives

CGC CAMPBELL after receiving the first HF/DF equipment provided an American escort. The antenna may be seen on the small mast near the stern. HF/DF was to prove a decisive factor in defeat of the U-boats. USCG

Commander James A. Hirshfield (left) on the bridge of CAMPBELL. USCG

A crewman from CAMPBELL goes over the side in the icy water to locate a hole beneath the water line. USCG/National Archives

that the boat could live for another two hours. His optimism was premature; it was soon discovered that the listening hydrophone was no longer working, and that the tremendous water pressure below 600 feet had caused the conning tower hatch to become jammed fast. U-606 was running on the surface both blind and deaf, with Allied warships all around!

The nearest was CGC CAMPBELL, only two miles away, and when U-606 broke surface, she promptly made radar contact. The manner in which she did was one more indication of the U-boat's continuing misfortune. CAMPBELL's radar had been out of commission for the entire day, and Chief Radarman Benjamin Stelmasczyk had been working feverishly to get it back in commission, for the ocean was "alive with U-boats." At 1955, he hopefully switched the set on, and minutes later picked up the convoy at a range of 13,000 yards. The chief continued his final adjustments on the set, and at 2010, only 15 minutes after the gear was turned on, picked up a small target at 4,600 yards.

"It is a small target. Looks like a sub," he reported to the bridge.

CAMPBELL heeled over under full rudder while the general alarm was sounding, and increased speed to 18 knots, homing on the target. It was her fifth attack of the day. The range closed rapidly, and radar contact was lost in the sea return at 800 yards. The racing cutter started a turn to starboard and at 400 yards Commander Hirshfield saw the U-boat broad on the bow and shouted across the bridge to the conning officer, Lieutenant Commander B. H. Brallier, to come right faster. No. 3 gun opened fire, and on the starboard wing, Chief Yeoman Pastrich opened up with a light 30-caliber machine gun that had been jury-mounted on the bridge wing combing. The submarine moved rapidly under the bow, and Hirshfield ordered two depth charges dropped from the stern racks. Before they could be rolled over, the U-boat hit the CAMPBELL a glancing blow under the bridge, then dragged along the side, its hydroplanes cutting a 15-foot gash in the cutter's engine room below the waterline. Then the two depth charges went off, lifting the U-boat about four feet.[7] CAMPBELL continued her right turn, the submarine slid off the quarter, and No. 5 three-inch gun pumped in two rounds before the pointer was blinded by the flashes.

U-606 was re-sighted at a range of 200 yards, and a 12″ signal light was thrown on her. At point-blank range, CAMPBELL cut loose with five-inch, three-inch, and 20-millimeter fire. Crewmen even grabbed Tommy guns and poured bullets into the U-boat. Twenty-millimeter tracers laced into the conning tower, blinking brightly as the explosive projectiles burst against the thin outer steel plate. Occasionally, the U-boat jumped as larger projectiles smashed home. Within minutes, 32 rounds of three-inch and ten magazines of 20-millimeter had been fired and some of the ready ammunition boxes were nearly empty. Then the searchlight went out as the electrical power failed.

The water had been rising steadily in the engine room after the collision and soon rose over the floor plates, stopping the turbines and shorting out the electrical supply generators. The engine room was abandoned, and below decks, emergency battle lanterns were switched on to enable magazine crews to pass up more ammunition, while on deck, the gun crews stood by their guns, searching the darkness.

During the time the cutter's full broadside was bursting on and around the U-boat, Oberleutnant Dohler had reached the bridge via the forward torpedo hatch, and with the assistance of those inside, succeeded in opening the conning tower hatch. As his men joined him on deck, he repeatedly exhorted them to remain calm. When CAMPBELL finally ceased fire, rafts were broken out, and the men looked around for their captain. He was nowhere to be seen. Men on the CAMPBELL had seen a three-inch projectile hit the conning tower just before cease fire, blowing a man overboard. It was undoubtedly Dohler. In spite of his

---

[7] The U-boat had been so badly beaten up by BURZA that some of the crew members did not recall being rammed, or the two depth charges exploding. They were only more jolts in a night full of them.

youth and inexperience as an administrator and commander, Hans Dohler in his last battle had sunk three ships, and in the final crisis, had died fighting.

Due to the list of the boat, the submariners were having a difficult time launching the rafts, and flashlights were broken out. CAMPBELL, fearing that the lights would attract another U-boat, ordered the lights extinguished or she would open fire again. The lights went out, except for a small one blinking SOS.

The other officers had remained below, and the warrant quartermaster found himself in charge of the men on deck. Fear seized him and he gave the order to abandon ship. Nearly a dozen men jumped overboard. CAMPBELL, with no power and disabled, drifted helplessly between the U-boat and the swimmers in the water, and attempted to throw lines to them. They were too far away, and disappeared into the night. One man called repeatedly, "Hey, boys," probably the only English he knew, but his voice soon faded in the night. None were ever seen again.

The officers and men who had remained below fared better. After some time had elapsed with no further gunfire, they decided it was safe to go on deck. One officer, feeling perhaps that discretion was the better part of valor, decided not to set the scuttling charges. He claimed to have opened the vents of the ballast tanks before joining the others on the bridge, leaving one rating below to open the main flood vent and to fetch the photographs of his girl friend from the officers' quarters.[8] The men on deck, having fortified themselves against the cold with sausages and bottles of rum and champagne, waited in relative comfort for their rescuers. There they were found by a boat from the CAMPBELL.

The cutter's regular boat crew was not available, for many of them were working in damage-control parties or standing watches on the guns as CAMPBELL lay helpless and vulnerable. A volunteer boat crew of officers and men was assembled under command of Lieutenant Arthur Pfeiffer, and included Lieutenant Alexan-

---

[8] The boat was still afloat several hours later.

der Stewart and Ensign Leroy Cheney. At 2130, the pulling boat was lowered, and rowed off into the night, steering upwind where the U-boat had last been seen. A half-hour later, a light gray conning tower was sighted, rolling slowly in the six-foot swells. The U-boat was well down by the stern, and by the long period of her roll, appeared to be well waterlogged. The Coast Guardsmen approached to within 100 feet of the U-boat and examined her with glasses. The anti-aircraft guns on the aft part of the conning tower could be clearly seen, but the U-boat men had no fight left in them. As the rolling of the U-boat made it impossible to go alongside, Art Pfeiffer shouted to them to jump in and swim to the boat. The men huddled on the conning tower pretended not to understand English, and repeatedly shouted back, "We do not understand; come nearer please." Finally two men swam out to the boat, and when they were pulled aboard, three more followed. Just before jumping over, one of the crewmen turned to an officer, and said, "I've waited a long time to do this!" With that, he punched him in the face and jumped over the side. When no more of the U-boat crew would leave the disabled craft, the boat headed back for the CAMPBELL. As they pulled away, the insignia on the side of the conning tower could be plainly seen. It was a map of England, with a hatchet stuck in the upper side. Below it were the words *Chop Chop.*

On the CAMPBELL, the damage-control parties had been working furiously under the supervision of Commander Ken Cowart, the engineering officer. Weight was jettisoned, and hundreds of gallons of fuel oil were pumped overboard to lighten ship and heel it over far enough to get at the hole in the hull. A party under Lt. (j.g.) Austin Wagner succeeded after great difficulty in getting a collision mat over the tear, but water continued to flood in faster than the pumps could handle it. Other parties cut away the 20-millimeter gun mounts, and magazine crews passed up ammunition to be thrown overboard. The plan was to lighten ship as much as possible, then build a cofferdam to keep out the water while the ship's welders put a patch over the hole.

Two hours after the collision, the BURZA arrived and commenced patrolling around the cutter. All hands breathed a little easier. Shortly afterwards, Lt. Pfeiffer and his boat arrived alongside with the five prisoners, who were taken aboard, given dry clothes, and locked up.

Now that the heat of battle had cooled, the CAMPBELL was still concerned about the Germans remaining on the slowly settling U-boat. Just after midnight, a running boat was lowered to go to their aid, but someone let the after fall go too soon, and the stern dropped into the sea. The boat was lost, but the crew was picked up by the other boat, which was still alongside. The BURZA later rescued seven of the eight men remaining on the U-boat. One drowned while attempting to swim to the destroyer.

In the early pre-dawn hours, some of CAMPBELL's crew were allowed to sleep for a couple of hours on deck, and a few of the more fatalistic officers went below to their staterooms.

Dawn brought a feeling of increased security, but it was short-lived. BURZA was near the limit of her fuel, and announced that she would have to break off that day. She proposed taking the CAMPBELL in tow for Newfoundland. Commander Hirshfield vetoed the idea; in his opinion, they would then be two sitting ducks rather than one. Through BURZA, he requested a tug and escort. CINCWA advised later in the morning that the tug could not arrive for three days, and suggested that after BURZA's departure, CAMPBELL remain alone until the arrival of the tug and escorts from St. John's. BURZA suggested that CAMPBELL abandon ship. Hirshfield countered with the suggestion that BURZA take fuel from CAMPBELL. This was rejected by the Polish skipper as impractical under the circumstance. They compromised by transferring 112 members of the CAMPBELL's crew, and the 50 survivors of the NEILSON ALONSO, whom the cutter had picked up earlier, by boat to the BURZA.

BURZA continued to stand by, and on the second morning, a newly arrived corvette took over the screening job after fueling from CAMPBELL, and the BURZA departed for Newfoundland. So short was her fuel that she was unable to divert even 20 miles enroute to St. John's, in order to pick up two boat-loads of survivors that had been sighted by aircraft. Over 400 people were on board, food was short, and the fresh water supply had been contaminated by salt water. But it could still be used for coffee, tea, and soup, and no one went thirsty. When the destroyer, which CAMPBELL's crew ever after maintained was "the fightenest ship we've ever seen," [9] finally arrived at St. John's, she had only seven tons of fuel left.

On the fourth day, CAMPBELL was taken in tow by the tug TENACITY, and under escort of two corvettes, headed for port. The following day, a submarine was sighted overhauling the crippled ship, and was driven down by one of the escorts. Nine days after her encounter with U-606, CAMPBELL was nudged into the dock for the beginning of emergency repairs which would enable her to be towed to a shipyard. She would live to fight again.

After Heineman broke off BURZA to screen CAMPBELL, ON-166 was left with only six escorts. Several attacks were repelled, but just before midnight of the 23rd, HMS DIANTHUS was forced to peel off due to lack of fuel. It was simply too rough to refuel at sea from the escort tanker. She left not a moment too soon. Two days later the fuel situation was so critical that her crew "emptied 120 gallons of Admiralty Compound into No. 6 tank, followed by gunnery oil, paint mixing oil, and two drums of special mineral oil." This additional half ton of inflammables enabled her to get in, and she coasted into wharf at St. John's with every tank bone dry.

With the escort reduced to five ships, the wolf pack got in and sank eight more ships. Some idea of the intensity of the

[9] The Poles were fierce fighters. After the rape of Poland, they had ample incentive. A story circulated among the escort forces about a Polish destroyer that picked up a number of survivors from a U-boat. When she arrived in port, none were on board. The author heard the tale from three different sources at the time. If there is any record to confirm the incident, it is well hidden.

Crew members of CAMPBELL prepare to lower a hastily constructed patch over a gaping hole below the waterline. USCG/National Archives

The Polish destroyer BURZA circles the disabled CAMPBELL screening her from attack. USCG

CGC CAMPBELL, disabled after ramming U-606, takes a tow line from HMCS DAUPHIN, but towing efforts were unsuccessful. Canadian Forces Photo

battle can be gained from the actions of the crew of the Norwegian tanker GLITTRE. She was hit by three torpedoes within an hour before the crew abandoned ship in two boats. Another tanker, the WINKLER, was hit at about the same time, and dropped aft, but her crew were men of stern stuff. When the U-boat surfaced, they opened fire, hit her conning tower, and attempted to ram, missing the diving boat by 25 yards. WINKLER then attempted to pick up the crew of the GLITTRE, but the survivors refused to come aboard, feeling that they were safer in the boats than on the WINKLER. They were right, for as WINKLER headed back for the convoy, she was hit by two more torpedoes and sank immediately. Only 19 of her crew managed to get a life raft that had been cut loose, to be picked up by the corvette DIANTHUS, which had also picked up the reluctant crew of the GLITTRE.

A particularly tragic loss was the little rescue vessel STOCKPORT, which had done such yeoman service three months before with Convoy SC-107. When the EMPIRE TRADER was hit and dropped astern during the first attack against ON-166, STOCKPORT had dropped astern to rescue her crew. The stricken freighter did not sink immediately, however, and under escort of the corvette DAUPHIN began limping toward the Irish coast. STOCKPORT headed back toward the convoy, and in the early morning darkness of February 23rd, ran onto U-604, which fired a four-torpedo spread at close range. Two hit, and STOCKPORT went down in three minutes with all her crew without getting out any distress call. They were gallant men, who had sailed often in dangerous waters, and their passing was not in vain. The epitaph of the little ship and her company would be engraved in the grateful memory of the hundreds of seamen she had saved.

In atrocious weather, and badly outnumbered, Group A3 had lost a total of fifteen of their flock, while sinking two U-boats and heavily damaging several others. Though the week-long battle had been a costly one, aggressive patrolling and prompt action when HF/DF bearings were obtained had prevented even heavier losses. As one result of the battle, prompt measures were taken to equip other American escorts with HF/DF. With the exception of radar, no other device proved more effective in the final defeat of the U-boats.

SPENCER had been just as busy as CAMPBELL. Nine depth-charge and gun attacks were made by her during the running battle, and on three occasions, she had narrowly avoided torpedoes. At 0652Z, February 23rd, SPENCER nearly got her second kill of the battle. Dropping on an Asdic contact, her depth charges caught U-454 and created havoc in the U-boat. The starboard quick dive tank was disabled and began leaking, water was flooding through the starboard shaft stuffing, and the attack periscope was disabled. The U-boat tried to surface at 0936, only to see SPENCER waiting. Finally, at 1100, his situation was so bad that he surfaced blindly. SPENCER, forced to hurry back to the thinly defended convoy, was just disappearing over the horizon.

SPENCER finally arrived at St. John's on the 27th of February. There was only time to replenish her fuel, ammunition, and depth charges before she stood out to sea four days later to take over the escort of Convoy SC-121. It was indicative of the state of the crisis that after three weeks of incessant battle, the tired escorts could be given no rest or maintenance.

Maintenance and repairs were also a problem for INGHAM. While ON-166 was fighting through, she lay in Hvalfjordur, buffeted by continual gales and waiting for an abatement to allow her to enter the floating dry dock to have the Asdic dome repaired. Nearly six weeks had elapsed, during which two convoys had been escorted, since the underwater detection gear had been rendered useless by the tear in the underwater dome. Though CTF 24 and CINCWA had been aware of the casualty, the escort situation was so tight that she could not be spared for repairs. Even a half-effective escort was better than none at all.

The weather finally moderated and she went into the British floating dry dock after defueling and off-loading ammunition. Once in, the crew discovered that there would be minimum heat and electricity, and no plumbing, for several days. The first two can be endured, but the last is well-nigh indispensable. The British had rigged up a nautical version of a three-holer, perched out over the edge of the dry dock, 80 feet above the water. Though protected topside from the winds by a canvas shelter, below the three holes the winter winds whistled by at 50 knots. It was no place to linger or read.

The second day in dry dock, repairs were rushed to completion, and tugs hustled over to move INGHAM out. After the tugs nosed her over to the destroyer tender VULCAN, the crew was told to expedite preparations for sea. They turned to loading ammunition and depth charges, and an oiler moved alongside and began pumping in fuel.

As the preparations were rushed, word was passed that the ship was sailing to recover survivors from a freighter that had been torpedoed while sailing alone 400 miles south of Iceland. By midnight, lines were cast off, and soon the ship was surging to the swells as she cleared the submarine nets and the harbor's protection.

During the morning watch, she passed the USS KEWAYDIN, an old Navy tug, courageously plowing south toward the sinking. As the tug was unarmed, and prime U-boat bait, INGHAM ordered her to return to Iceland. Only then did the tug skipper reveal that his chain locker was full of water, and he was having difficulty in the heavy seas. The cutter escorted her for a couple of hours until matters were under control, then reversed course and headed for the scene of the sinking.

By noon of the following day, INGHAM was in the area of the sinking and for two hours cruised through miles of debris. There were no people. At the far end of the debris, a large bulkhead and numerous rubber truck tires were sighted. Reversing course, she again searched through the wreckage without success. The evidence was mute but positive. One more ship and fifty more men.[10] In less than four weeks, 36 ships comprising over a quarter of a million tons of Allied shipping had been sent to the bottom on the North Atlantic. Somehow, the convoys were still going through, but the outlook was bleak. As March arrived, the crisis was imminent.

[10] So commonplace had sinkings become that the name of this unfortunate ship is not shown in INGHAM's log or war diary.

VIII

MARCH 1-19 / THE CRISIS

On March 3rd, only 4 days after arriving in St. John's from the grueling ordeal of Convoy ON-166, Heineman's "Harriers" sortied to take over Convoy SC-121 at WESTOMP for the eastward crossing. So critically short were escorts in the northern ocean that not even essential repairs had been made to many ships, nor any rest given the weary crews. Group A3 was a badly reduced shadow of the hard-bitten unit that had fought through ON-166. CAMPBELL was lying against a pier at St. John's, her engine room flooded, and her service with the Group ended. DAUPHIN was unable to sail and would have to catch up later. BURZA had been detached to another Group. The only replacement was the USS GREER, an old but experienced flush deck destroyer. HMS MANSFIELD was also assigned temporarily until DAUPHIN could join. In many of the ships, the radars and Asdics were either inoperative or working at reduced efficiency. The rust-streaked and battered ships had been driven too hard for too long, and by any normal criteria should not have been sailed. But the terrible winter and constant combat had taken its toll; dozens of escorts were damaged and laid up for repairs, and ships able to sail were sailed, even in a greatly reduced state of upkeep.

As soon as the ships of Group A3 cleared the headlands, they were met by heavy seas and gale winds, which, being from the west, did not slow them excessively at first. The following day, the gale worsened, and HMS WITHERINGTON, the escort commander of the western local escort which had been escorting SC-121, was sighted heaved to in the storm ten miles astern of the convoy. The British ship signaled only the bearing and distance of the convoy, and was not seen or heard from again by A3. When the mid-ocean escort reached the convoy, none of the western local escort were in sight. The convoy was completely unprotected and beginning to scatter in the gale. There being no one present to formally relieve, Captain Heineman assumed command of the convoy, and began to size up the situation. Fifty-six ships were counted in 14 columns. The new escort commander promptly requested the commodore to reduce the front to 11 columns, for with only six escorts, he felt unable to protect a convoy with a front of seven miles. Commodore H. C. Birnie, RNR, in the SS BONNEVILLE, was favorable to the idea, but felt that he would be unable to maneuver the heavily laden merchantmen until the weather moderated. During the few days remaining to him, the weather never moderated and the convoy remained in a widely extended formation. After his death, however, the vice-commodore took over and, with the weather no better than previously, promptly reduced the columns on request.

On March 5th, Group A3 was badly extended around the convoy; in the van, the flagship SPENCER was patrolling a sector seven miles wide. Her Asdic range in the towering seas was less than half a mile, and her radar range was also badly reduced by the sea conditions. As poor as the situation was, it quickly became worse when MANSFIELD developed boiler trouble late in the day, and had to return to Newfoundland.

As daylight broke on March 6th, the ocean was a raging wasteland of mountainous seas, with a heavy overcast, and snow blowing in a horizontal blizzard. Visibility was less than two miles, and the badly extended escorts could not even see each other in the storm, when, at noon, the HF/DF operators picked up loud radio signals from U-boats on the port beam and starboard quarter. In spite of the weather, the U-boats had established contact and early in the afternoon CINCWA warned that the shore HF/DF plot indicated they were gathering for an attack.

Aggressive Captain Heineman, without even enough escorts to adequately defend the convoy, refused to wait for the inevitable. Leaving the three slow corvettes with the threatened merchantmen, he sent SPENCER and GREER out on offensive sweeps to the starboard beam and port quarter, and after dark, swung the convoy 40 degrees to port to attempt to evade. It was indicative of the convoy's desperate plight that an escort commander would even attempt to turn the clumsy merchantmen in the stormy darkness, but the threatening situation demanded stern measures.

The course change was to no avail. At 0110, U-230 got into the convoy and slammed a torpedo into the freighter EGYPTIAN. No torpedo report was received, but two white rockets were reported by TRILLIUM, flashes of gunfire were seen within the convoy, and two reports of U-boats on the surface were received from merchant vessels, many of which turned on lights. Nearly an hour after the torpedo hit, the corvette ROSTHERN sighted lights three miles astern of the convoy, and soon reported that a merchant ship was picking up survivors. In the confusion of the stormy night, the escort commander was unaware that a ship had even been hit until advised by ROSTHERN, and the rescue vessel MELROSE ABBEY had not been alerted. The Good Samaritan was the British freighter EMPIRE IMPALA, whose decks were to prove only a temporary refuge for the survivors of the EGYPTIAN.

Dawn broke gray and overcast, with snow and hail being driven by heavy gale, but daylight brought no relief from the enemy. U-591 overhauled and hit a straggler, which was not identified, and after the explosion, gunfire again broke out astern of the convoy. SPENCER sighted a U-boat five miles ahead, and drove it down; an hour-long search of the area produced one

Asdic contact, on which a depth-charge pattern was dropped. Again in mid-morning, another U-boat was sighted by the cutter and depth-charged with inconclusive results.

During the rest of the day, and the following night, several attacks were made by U-boats, but in the heavy seas and blizzard, all the torpedoes missed. Reinforcements were also on the way. When CINCWA had received word of the torpedoing of the EGYPTIAN, he immediately requested that INGHAM and BIBB be sailed to beef up Group A3. BABBITT and MALLOW were relieved from other assignments, and also directed to join. Within hours, both cutters had cleared the headlands of ICELAND, the two destroyers had left their convoys, and all four vessels were plowing southward in heavy seas. BIBB's departure had been so hurried that 22 of her crewmen were left ashore.

A few hours after departure, the Asdic operator in INGHAM, echo ranging in the heavy seas, heard a sudden rise in the noise level. The temporary patch in the Asdic dome, installed only ten days before, had given way as the ship came down heavily in the seas, and the Asdic was once more useless at speeds over six knots. INGHAM would be of little help against submerged targets.

By an ironic twist, that was just what the escorts around SC-121 were faced with. At the beginning of March, increasingly concerned with the ability of the Allied escorts to locate surfaced U-boats by radar, Doenitz ordered his captains to adopt new tactics. As soon as they became aware of a radar transmission in their vicinity, they were to submerge for thirty minutes. It was an emergency measure, and was soon followed by a more drastic directive, ordering the U-boats to shadow the convoys at the maximum range at which the masts or smoke could be seen, from which position they were then to proceed around the convoy at maximum range of visibility to a position ahead, where they would dive and deliver a submerged attack. It was a radical change from the past two years of mass attacks on the surface, and SC-121 was one of the first convoys to encounter the new tactics. By a tragic coincidence, three of the escorts had inoperative Asdics and four had sick radars. Whether the U-boats came in submerged or surfaced, the crippled escorts were ill-equipped to deal with them. To make matters worse, some dozen ships had dropped behind in the wild weather. The merchant vessels were not the only stragglers, for the Canadian corvette TRILLIUM was also lost somewhere astern of the convoy.

The inevitable result of such large-scale straggling could not be long postponed, and the Yugoslav freighter VOJVODA PUTNIK, straggling somewhere astern of the convoy, fell victim to a U-boat. Later that Monday morning, the British GUIDO, which had surged out eight miles ahead of the convoy, was torpedoed in full view of SPENCER, cruising in the van position. SPENCER raced to the scene, made Asdic contact, and dropped two depth-charge patterns. When contact could not be regained, she stopped, and picked up 35 survivors. Ten others had died with the ship. While picking up survivors, a line was sucked into a condenser, crippling one of the cutter's engines, and an uneasy two hours passed before it was cleared.

By noon, only 33 ships and 2 escorts remained with the convoy. The rest were scattered over miles of ocean, and the storm showed no signs of abating. A straggler was hit during the afternoon, but BIBB, DAUPHIN, and INGHAM joined soon afterwards, boosting the escort strength considerably. The storm was also giving the U-boats trouble, and two attacks by them during the early evening failed due to the high seas. SPENCER chased down a surfaced U-boat and depth-charged it, and an hour later repeated the same kind of attack on another.

The U-boats couldn't get into the convoy, but astern, where they were roaming through the darkness, two stragglers were torpedoed, one of them for the second time. Shortly after 2100, a U-boat got into the convoy, and a merchant ship tried to ram it, missing by a matter of feet. The U-boat disappeared from sight under the bow, and the merchant seamen heard shouted commands in German as the U-boat skipper turned away at the last minute.

The escorts patrolled aggressively during the night. SPENCER, BIBB, and BABBITT made depth-charge attacks, and at midmorning Tuesday, ROSTHERN picked up a good contact on the starboard beam and delivered seven separate depth-charge attacks, a total of 44 charges being expended before the contact was lost. As a result, the only Allied casualty during the 24-hour period was a lookout on SPENCER, who suffered a broken leg as he was swept along the deck by a heavy sea.

The luck of the convoy continued through the afternoon of March 9th, when U-229 made a submerged attack, firing four torpedoes, all of which missed. BIBB and INGHAM were sent astern to sit on the U-boat.

But after dark, the bottom fell out. MALANTIC and ROSE-WOOD were torpedoed, and over half of the crew of the freighter were lost with the ship.[1] ROSEWOOD, the tanker on which the escorts were dependent for fuel, kept up with the convoy despite a yawning hole in her side. The U-boats were everywhere. BIBB sighted and chased down one astern, and DAUPHIN sighted another on the port quarter being fired at by a merchantman. ROSTHERN narrowly avoided a torpedo which she not only heard coming, but sighted visually as it sped by.

The escort commander gave the order *Zombie Crack!* and each escort swung out through a pre-planned search pattern. At the order to illuminate, all began pumping starshells into the night around the convoy, hoping to expose any surfaced U-boats. Nothing was seen and, in the heavy seas, it would have been a fluke had one of the low-lying U-boats been detected

---

[1] In the raging seas, the crew of MALANTIC behaved with great calmness and "executed orders splendidly" while abandoning ship. The second cook lost his life after holding his lifeboat to the rescue ship until all his shipmates in the boat were saved; then, too exhausted to climb the rescue net, he fell back into the sea and was lost.

visually. To make matters worse, in addition to the many inoperative radars and Asdics, two of the three HF/DF sets in the group were now out of commission. The debt incurred by months of running without time for maintenance was being called.

On INGHAM, off the convoy's port bow, there was little rest during the night. After returning from the late afternoon sweep astern, she had twice more been thrown out on sweeps ten miles ahead of the convoy, and had been at general quarters much of the evening, firing starshells on call. Just before midnight, the crew was secured from battle stations, and those going on the mid-watch had only time for a couple of cups of black scalding coffee (which had been allowed to boil all the time the crew was at battle stations) before going up to the bridge to relieve the watch. The thick black brew was guaranteed to keep anyone awake, but the first deep swallow caused a shiver down the spine, goose pimples on the skin, and an acid burning in the stomach.

A dull explosion came while the watch was being relieved, the bridge and Asdic hut crowded with oncoming and departing watchstanders. The oncoming OOD was still reading the captain's night orders, and coolly continued despite the obvious anxiety of the quartermaster, who was holding the red light, to dash out to the bridge wing and see what was happening.

"Don't get your bowels in an uproar," he said to the quartermaster. "We don't have the deck yet. Let that other crowd of heroes handle it."

But seconds later, he finished the orders, initialed them, and quickly stepped out to the bridge, just in time to be greeted with the loud clanging of the general alarm.

Breathlessly slipping on the headphones and steel helmet after reaching Fire Control, the gun boss received the orders, "Operation Raspberry. Bearings two-two-five to three-six-oh. Commerce firing when ready!"

Sixteen rounds of starshells were pumped out, and all around the convoy starshells from other escorts could be seen, their light mingling with the gunflashes. No U-boats were sighted, but in the convoy red lights had appeared, and word was received from Conn that two ships, the NAILSEA COURT and the BONNEVILLE, had been hit. The latter was the commodore's vessel.

Unfortunately, MELROSE ABBEY, the rescue vessel, was far astern picking up survivors of the MALANTIC, and was being covered by BIBB. DAUPHIN was therefore spelled off to pick up the latest survivors, and GREER was told to screen her. When GREER arrived in the area, lifeboats and rafts were sighted, and nearby was a sinking ship, her decks awash. Unable to locate the DAUPHIN, GREER asked permission to pick up survivors, but Heineman ordered her to locate DAUPHIN and carry out the original orders. Ten minutes after sighting the first survivors, GREER located another abandoned ship with boats and rafts alongside, but this one seemed to be in no danger of sinking. The crew, it appeared to GREER, had unnecessarily abandoned ship. (Later, they were to discover that it was the SS COUL-MORE, which had been torpedoed at the same time as the NAILSEA COURT and the BONNEVILLE.) Heineman, however, knew nothing of her being hit, and at this critical time, flagship SPENCER's radio gave up the ghost, isolating the escort commander from his other ships.

GREER finally located DAUPHIN, only to find that she had a broken steering gear and was unable to pick up survivors. Finally at 0300, two and a half hours after she had first sighted them, GREER came back to try to pick up the survivors of the NAILSEA COURT. A boat loaded with survivors came alongside, but the seas were rough, and the badly rolling destroyer was unable to maneuver to get the men aboard. Attempts to pick up men from the rafts were also futile. Two more hours passed before BIBB and MELROSE ABBEY, which were returning to the convoy after recovering 21 survivors from the MALAN-TIC, arrived on the scene and took over the rescue operations.

For several hours the two ships, aided by DAUPHIN, searched the howling night for survivors, but few were left. From NAIL-SEA COURT, only 3 of 48 were saved, and of BONNEVILLE's 43 men, a pitiful 7 were rescued. Among the dead were Commodore Birnie, and the master of the BONNEVILLE, both of whom had escaped from the sinking ship, and were last seen trying to reach a raft.

Shortly after dawn on Wednesday, March 10th, BIBB came upon the COULMORE, still floating high and safe, with a torpedo hole in her bow. The wound was not serious, and only her forepeak was flooded. Three survivors were rescued nearby, and they told a grim story. After being hit in the midnight attack, the crew had quickly abandoned ship. One boat had drifted away empty, while another capsized alongside with 14 men. Of a total of 43 men, only 7 who had managed to get aboard rafts were rescued. Many others had died during the night, while two miles away the ship they had left floated dry and safe.

Breaking off from the deserted derelict, BIBB raced westward, searching for the ROSEWOOD, which earlier in the day, unable to keep up with the convoy because of the torpedo hole in her hull, had dropped astern. For the rest of the day and night BIBB searched in an expanding pattern around the last reported position of the crippled tanker. Finally, at mid-morning on the 11th, the cutter sighted a ship on the horizon. It was the stern of the ROSEWOOD, with no sign of life, though a boat and a raft were still on board. Debris was scattered over the surrounding seas, and a swamped lifeboat rose silently on the swells. BIBB threw several salvos into the hulk, and left it sinking. Over 24 hours later, the cutter sighted the bow of the tanker, and finding no one aboard, sank it also.

Later in the afternoon, nearly three days after it had been torpedoed, the silently drifting COULMORE was once again sighted by BIBB and her position reported. The ill-fated COUL-MORE was later taken in tow by a tug, and arrived safely in port, a silent ghost ship without a crew.[2] Nearly 80 men had been lost by abandoning two ships which were in no immediate danger of sinking.

After the midnight attack, the strengthened escort and increasing air cover prevented any further loss within the convoy, and several attacks were made on U-boats attempting to approach.

When the convoy was turned over to the British local escort off Ireland, only 36 of the original 59 ships were present. Six had been torpedoed in convoy, and it was known that some of the stragglers had been hit. As the days passed, stragglers came into port, one by one. But many never arrived and were listed as "Missing, presumed lost." FORT LAMY, EMPIRE LAKE-LAND, LEADGATE, MILOS, VOJVODA PUTNIK, and EMPIRE IMPALA had fallen victim to the U-boats and storms while straggling. The loss of EMPIRE IMPALA, the brave ship that had rescued the survivors of the EGYPTIAN, was particularly tragic; when she went down, the crews of both ships were lost with her.

What made the loss of 13 fine ships even worse was the disturbing fact that, in contrast to Convoy SC-118, no retribution had been exacted from the attacking U-boats, despite every effort by the ships of an experienced ocean escort group. That this was due in large measure to the lack of maintenance and the resultant failures of radar, Asdic, and HF/DF equipment was obvious, but until the hard-pressed ships could be given more in-port time for upkeep, the situation was likely to recur. Loss of life in the stormy seas had been particularly heavy, and humanitarian considerations aside, we could afford the loss of trained personnel even less than we could the ships.

But in London, an event of potentially greater consequences had occurred on March 8th. A decoded Ultra signal contained the code word ordering all U-boats to change to a new code system using four Enigma machine rotors. Though the change was

---

[2] The COULMORE appears to be well-nigh indestructible. She was sold after the war to another company, and renamed the AVISFORD. In 1950, she became the Swedish STRIPPER. Later she was sold to a Panamanian company, under whose flag she sails today as the SS NAUTIC.

Convoy SC-121 battles an Atlantic storm. Badly scattered by the gales, the ships of the convoy were picked off by the trailing U-boats. In the heavy seas, few men were saved. USN/National Archives

The SS COULMORE, a ghost ship without a crew. USCG

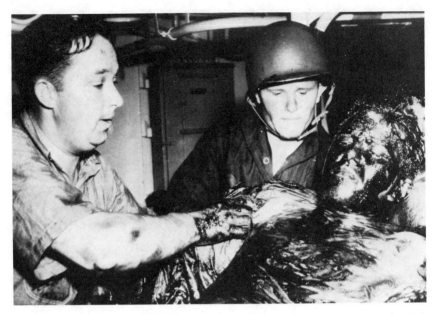

Hospital Corpsmen peel off the oil-soaked clothing of a survivor in the sick bay of an escort vessel. USCG/National Archives

Periscope view of an oncoming merchant vessel in perfect position for a bow shot. Until improved Allied radar and air cover made it too costly, most U-boat skippers preferred night surface attacks against escorted convoys, reserving submerged attacks for daylight encounters. USN/National Archives

not unexpected, all Ultra information on U-boats derived from the Triton code was immediately cut off, and crypto experts predicted that no further information would be forthcoming for months. Though this was to prove too pessimistic, the loss of the vital Ultra information at the height of the crucial battle was a heavy blow to the hard pressed Allied forces.

Arriving in the Fleet Anchorage, two days after leaving SC-121, INGHAM rapidly replenished her fuel, ammunition, and depth charges. The respite in the wind-swept fjord was to prove brief. The long expected all-out onslaught of the U-boats was upon us and the convoy routes from Newfoundland to Ireland had become one great battlefield, on which a bitter fight was raging with no quarters given by either the antagonists or the elements. The next fight, around HX-228, was typical of the merciless struggle.

While SC-121 had been heavily engaged, Convoy HX-228 was detected by a U-boat of Group *Neuland,* but in the heavy seas and storms, only a few U-boats were able to overhaul it. One of these was the highly successful Korvettenkapitän Trojer in U-221. In his War Diary, Trojer recorded:

March 10, 1943. In a snow squall came up at right angles to course of enemy, surfaced as soon as latter emerged from the snow squall. Reached an excellent position inside the convoy. Fired one torpedo which failed to detonate. A second, fired at a range of 3,100 yards, scored a hit.

2131. Fired two torpedoes at two large, overlapping merchant ships. First torpedo hit. Ship disintegrated completely in flames and a vast cloud of smoke. Hundreds of steel plates flew through the air like sheets of paper. A great deal of ammunition exploded.

Shortly afterwards scored another hit on a freighter, which also exploded. From bow to bridge the ship was under water. Heavy debris crashed against my periscope, which now became difficult to turn. The whole boat reechoed with bangs and crashes. In disengaging, went deep, but came back to periscope depth in time to see torpedo hit.

My target for No. 3 tube, a modern five-thousand-tonner with several twin masts, went full astern in order to avoid running into the exploding ship. The shot was too chancy. My periscope went completely black. I could hardly see a thing, while all the time heavy fragments of debris continued to shower down upon us. The noise inside the boat was terrific. It felt as though we were being hit by a stream of shells. Heard clearly the noise of a sinking ship, and then all was quiet. Tried to lower my periscope in order to clean the lens. It came down about five feet and then stuck. It was obviously bent. At that minute the listening-room reported the sounds of propellers, which could be heard where I stood in the conning tower, and at once gave the order: "Dive! full ahead both!" Depth charges, two patterns of four, were already falling, and pretty close to us. The conning tower hatch started to leak, and a mass of water came down into the boat. The boat plunged and jumped, but she gained depth steadily.

Locked in a death struggle, the few U-boats that had made contact and the escort, composed of British, Polish, and Free French vessels under Commander A. A. Tait, Royal Navy, in HMS HARVESTER, stood and slugged it out in the stormy seas.

Running down a radar contact the following morning, HARVESTER sighted U-444 on the surface and rammed, driving up and over her. The submarine became wedged in the destroyer's propellers, and the two vessels lay locked together. When she finally broke clear in the heavy seas, HARVESTER's propellers and shafts had suffered so much damage that she was barely able to limp along on one engine at slow speed. The Free French Corvette ACONIT arrived to find U-444 still miraculously afloat, and finished it off by ramming.

Tait, in the meanwhile, despite his badly damaged ship, had rescued 50 survivors from a merchant ship, and was crawling along on one engine, vulnerable and without protection. The ACONIT had been ordered by Tait to rejoin the convoy, which he felt was in greater danger than his own ship. HARVESTER's good shaft cracked soon after daylight, however, leaving her lying helpless. ACONIT was ordered back to assist, but while still several miles away, the Frenchmen saw a column of smoke on the horizon, and intercepted HARVESTER's last radio signal, reporting that she had been torpedoed. Racing toward the scene, ACONIT made Asdic contact, and commenced dropping depth charges. U-432 broke surface, and Lieutenant Levasseur of

ACONIT for the second time that day drove his crumpled bow into a U-boat. But the trade of U-432 for HARVESTER was not an equal one, for the loss of life among the destroyer crew and the many merchant survivors on board was heavy, and included the gallant Tait.[3] In the short and violent action around Convoy HX-228, four merchantmen and a destroyer had been sunk, while the wolf pack had lost two boats with a third heavily damaged.

Doenitz pulled out the U-boats from the fight, and on March 14th, deployed them along a patrol line south of Iceland, with orders to sweep westward. He was not working in the blind, for B-Service had intercepted a message reporting Convoy HX-229 southeast of Cape Race steering a course of 067 degrees. The following day, another deciphered Allied signal revealed to the Germans the detailed instructions to another convoy, SC-122. All available U-boats were ordered to the attack. Groups *Stürmer* (18 U-boats) and *Dranger* (11 U-boats), augmented by a number of new U-boats which had sailed from French and German bases, hurried westward to intercept the convoys while they were in the air gap. *Dranger* was to operate against HX-229, and a third group, *Raubgraf*, was to hit SC-122.

But in the stormy weather, the U-boats had to reduce speed, and the leading convoy, SC-122, passed the intended patrol line before the U-boats could get on station. HX-229, behind the slow SC convoy and somewhat to the south, also slipped by the patrol line during the night of March 15th without being sighted. It is likely that both convoys would have gone through undetected had not U-653, on its way home to France after a long patrol, accidentally fallen in with HX-229.

Doenitz promptly acted on the sighting report, sending 21

---

[3] Many brave men died when the HARVESTER went down, and none stood higher than Captain J. C. Ellis, the master of the WILLIAM C. GORGAS. When his ship was torpedoed, he stayed at the searchlight until all hands had abandoned ship, then went into the water. He was picked up by the HARVESTER, and after she was hit, was again in the icy water clinging to a life ring. When a seaman asked him to take his place on a life raft, he replied, "No, son, keep your place." Shortly afterwards, Ellis slipped from the life ring and was lost.

boats of *Raubgraf* and *Stürmer* Groups homing in on U-653, which had taken up a trailing position astern of the target. Seventeen other boats were ordered to form a patrol line ahead of the convoy.

By nightfall on the 16th, eight boats had made contact with the HX convoy. The battle began in a howling gale, which had scattered the convoy widely, and the U-boats rampaged among the many stragglers. The weak escort, consisting of a variety of ships scraped together to make up the ad hoc group, was unable to protect the merchantmen scattered over such a large area, and during the night, the U-boats reported scoring 18 hits, sinking 6 ships, and damaging 4 others. On the following day, U-91, acting as cleanup man, sank all the damaged vessels by submerged attacks. No rescue ship had been assigned to the convoy, and the escorts were faced with the bitter choice between leaving the crippled ships to their fate, or helping them and thereby further weakening the already inadequate screen around the besieged convoy. In the first two days, 13 ships went to the bottom, and in the cold stormy seas, without adequate rescue vessels, the loss of life was heavy. The same day, some 150 miles ahead of HX-229, contact was made by several U-boats with Convoy SC-122. For the first time, U-boat Command realized that their boats were now in contact with two convoys.

The escort of Convoy SC-122 was a stronger one than that of HX-229, and the attackers were at first beaten off. Early on the morning of the 17th, however, contact was re-established, and four ships were torpedoed in the SC convoy. At the time of the attack, only six of the eight escorts were present. One of the escorts, CAMPOBELLO, had developed a bad leak and sank on the 16th. Another escort, GODETIA, had taken aboard the survivors and had not yet rejoined. During the daylight hours of March 17th, numerous aggressive daylight attacks were carried out by submerged U-boats, and several ships from both convoys were sunk.

The faster HX-229 had continued overhauling SC-122, and

during the night of March 18th-19th, had come up with the slow convoy so that the two made up a very large mass of ships in a small area of the ocean. In this 50-mile stretch, some 80 merchantmen, 18 escorts, and 38 submarines were cruising, while overhead Liberators, Fortresses, and Sunderlands from Iceland and Ireland searched for the hard-to-see submarines among the thousands of whitecaps and huge swells.

The escort of British, Canadian, and U. S. destroyers, British frigates and sloops, British and Canadian corvettes, and U. S. Coast Guard cutters had been beefed up on the 18th by support forces rushed at full speed from Iceland, and they arrived at the height of the crisis.

INGHAM was one of the new arrivals. After reaching Iceland following the battle around SC-121, divers had been sent down to check the still ailing Asdic head. They reported it damaged and inoperative, and plans were made to enter the dry dock and, after two frustrating months, at long last have it repaired. Once more, however, the crying demand for escorts took precedence, and on March 15th, with the Asdic still inoperative, she moved into Reykjavik Roads. On the following afternoon, when the U-boats made firm contact, she was ordered to sail with BABBITT to augment the escort of SC-122.

Clearing Skagi Point, and turning south, they worked up to speed in the heavy seas. BIBB, which had arrived only the day before after several action-packed days cleaning up behind SC-121, was in Hvalfjordur, and would follow as quickly as she could be refueled, repaired, and provisioned. By dark, the winds were gusting to 70 knots, and BABBITT, pounding badly, requested that speed be reduced. The larger INGHAM, which was also taking a beating, immediately complied. The following morning, a whole gale was blowing, and in the towering seas, speed had to be further reduced. Messages describing the attacks on the two convoys flowed into the Code Room, and CINCWA urged that the join-up be expedited. Early in the afternoon, the gale moderated a little, and speed was increased first to 13, then to 15 knots. Through the night, the two escorts drove on, suffering considerable damage to their lifelines, boats, and topside gear as the seas broke over the decks.

On Thursday morning, the wind had dropped to a relatively mild 20 knots, and the opportunity was taken to test-fire the guns and conduct drills. A large empty raft was sighted close aboard, but there was no time to investigate; too much debris was adrift on the North Atlantic to become excited by one more raft. During the morning, BABBITT broke off on a slightly diverging course, her orders changed, to join HX-229. INGHAM continued toward SC-122.

With the improving weather, the two sorely tried convoys began receiving air cover, and some escorts from other convoys not under attack had joined. Thirty-two U-boats were still in contact, but only nine managed to get within sight of the merchantmen during the day. Trojer, in U-221, still at sea despite his near fatal encounter a week earlier with ACONIT, was the only one able to score, getting two ships from HX-229 during the day with a submerged attack.[4]

As INGHAM closed the convoy, HMS HAVELOCK, the escort commander of SC-122, ordered her to a position 40 miles from the convoy to create a diversion after dark by firing starshells and pyrotechnics, and dropping depth charges, hoping to decoy away some of the shadowing U-boats. The tactic had been used before during the winter, with what success no one could say, but some U-boats may have been led astray. To make the ruse more effective, orders were issued to the convoy and screening vessels that no starshells or snowflakes would be fired during the night except to directly illuminate a target.

At 0550, the SS CARRAS was torpedoed. Starshell spreads were fired by the escorts, and the rescue vessel ZAMALEK, screened by the corvette BUTTERCUP, went to her aid. On

---

[4] Trojer was a fine U-boat commander, and his brush with ACONIT was not his only close shave. In December, his boat had been in a night collision with U-254, and the latter had gone down with most of her crew.

arrival, the rescue vessel reported that the CARRAS was still afloat and salvageable, but that the master and crew had taken to the boats. They had also neglected to destroy the confidential books and papers. The rescue ship rejoined, while the disgusted corvette returned to the ship and put people aboard to destroy the code books and papers.

The rest of the night passed quietly and Friday morning dawned bright and clear. Even the wind and seas had subsided, and the temperature of 53 degrees was just nippy enough to make the coffee taste better. As though the day wasn't reward enough, a Liberator could be seen far out on the horizon. With the excellent visibility, moderating seas, and covering aircraft, there seemed little chance that a U-boat would be bold or brash enough to make a pass at the convoy in broad daylight. The convoy was now only 450 miles from the Irish coast, and past experience had indicated that Doenitz usually ordered the wolf pack to break off when the convoys came under coverage of land-based aircraft. After three black days, things were looking up.

INGHAM took advantage of the fine weather to hold gun drill at 0900, and at 0925 stood down between the columns of the convoy to take up station astern. Ten minutes later she swung smartly and reduced speed to 12 knots, commencing a patrol of the stern sector. After the continually terrible weather of the past four months, this day made sea-going a pleasure, and in the bright sunlight, some of the bridge gang had removed their jackets and rolled up the sleeves of their dungaree shirts.

At 1054, the OOD gave an order to the helmsman for a routine change of course, and stepped to the port wing of the bridge to take a look around the horizon, which was clear. Out of nowhere, a column of white water rose from beyond the horizon. Binoculars were trained on the bearing, but nothing else could be seen. It seemed likely that an aircraft had dropped a bomb, but there was not a dot in the sky. Seconds later, a white rocket rose in the air, making it obvious that something was out there on the surface. Turning quickly and increasing to

18 knots, INGHAM stood toward the scene after reporting the sighting to the escort commander. Thin smoke could soon be seen on the bearing, and shortly afterwards, two masts, making it seem likely that a ship had been torpedoed. The ready-gun and depth-charge crews were closed up for action. By 1130, the torpedoed ship was close enough to be identified as the American freighter MATHEW LUCKENBACH. Three boats and two rafts of survivors were sighted, and one man was swimming, with none of the boats making any move to pick him up.

The submarine was close by, and INGHAM slowed in order to better utilize her sick Asdic, and circled the wreckage while awaiting the arrival of the destroyer UPSHUR, which would screen her while she rescued survivors. The American destroyer was four miles away, and coming fast with a bone in her teeth.

The MATHEW LUCKENBACH was a "romper" from Convoy HX-229, and all things considered, her crew was extremely lucky. She had been in convoy when the attacks of March 16th had occurred. After five ships had been torpedoed, the officers and men of the American freighter, dismayed that no evasive course change had been ordered by the escort commander, and dissatisfied with the way things were going, held a meeting and decided to leave the convoy and proceed independently. For two days and nights, they had been running alone through the heaviest U-boat concentration yet seen on any ocean, and despite the odds against them, had almost made it.

But the odds and U-527 caught up with them. The U-boat had surfaced at dawn, and was promptly driven down by an approaching Liberator. Seventeen minutes after diving, four aerial bombs were heard to explode at a great distance, and the U-boat eased up to periscope depth for a looksee, continuing its search submerged. Later in the morning, the masts of the MATHEW LUCKENBACH were sighted through the periscope, and an approach was started. The freighter was running on a straight course at its full speed of ten knots, and the submerged U-boat had to push to get into firing position. Twenty minutes after the first sighting, the submarine, which had dropped ten degrees aft of the freighter's beam, was losing the race and the angle aft of the beam was increasing. As the angle increased further, the range would begin to open, and the freighter would present an increasingly difficult target from astern. It was then or never. Kapitänleutnant Uhlig, peering through his attack periscope, snapped out the firing data.

"Range one thousand, eight hundred yards, angle starboard one-oh-oh, speed ten. Bearing, mark! Three-fan spread. Tubes one, two, and four."

When the torpedo officer reported the data cranked into the firing computer, Uhlig took one last bearing.

"Shoot!"

At three-second intervals, the three torpedoes shot from their tubes, and the attack team looked at their watches and waited. Two hundred and thirty-four seconds after firing, one torpedo hit in the vicinity of the forward mast, raising a column of water several hundred feet in the air, and a second hit amidships, wrecking the bridge.

"Got him!" said Uhlig, stepping back from the periscope to let his first watch officer have a look.

"Captain from Hydrophone. Screw noises have ceased."

"She's stopping and letting off steam," reported the first watch officer, stepping back from the periscope to let the captain have another look.

In his hurry to get off the spread, Uhlig had badly underestimated the range. The actual distance had been 4,000 yards He decided to close for a finishing shot.

"Steer three-two-two. Slow ahead together."

The U-boat crept toward the stricken ship.

"Captain from Hydrophone. Noise bearing one-four-five. High-speed screws."

"Let's have a look."

Uhlig pressed his face against the eyepiece and followed the periscope up.

"That's good. Oh, oh, here is a destroyer coming, but a good ways off yet."

He swung the periscope around the rest of the horizon, then stopped it on an easterly bearing.

"Aircraft coming in also. Down periscope. Take her down to 150 feet. Port fifteen. Half ahead both."

Turning to the first watch officer and the quartermaster, who was busy entering the data in the log, he said, "We will retreat to the horizon to survey the situation. When things quiet down, we'll make another approach under water and finish her off."

The "destroyer" he had heard and seen was INGHAM, and by the time she arrived at the scene, the U-boat was three miles away and opening. After UPSHUR had arrived and began screening, the cutter stopped and commenced taking aboard survivors. The merchant seamen were not too helpful, and made no attempt to row toward the rescue vessel, forcing her to maneuver alongside each boat and raft to take them on board. Not knowing where the U-boat might be, the cutter men worked quickly, and 30 minutes later had everyone aboard, including the man in the water, who had been left on the freighter when she was hurriedly abandoned, and had been forced to leap into the water and swim for the boats. One of the merchant ship's survivors had taken a bottle into the boat with him, and while awaiting rescue, had consumed a sizeable portion of it. He was helped on board well stoned.

The merchant captain and several survivors were brought to the bridge. They confirmed that there had been no damage to the engine or boiler rooms. The freighter was sitting on an even keel, with smoke rising from her funnel. The only visible damage was to the starboard wing of the bridge, which was in considerable disarray. The ship was heavily loaded, and her decks were jammed with Army trucks and other valuable cargo.

A suggestion that the merchant crew might wish to go back aboard and get underway to join the convoy met with little response. They had had enough. Their chance sighting by an escort from another passing convoy when no one else even knew they had been hit had been stretching their luck too far.

Lieutenant Al Martin turned to Captain Martinson, "Captain, if you will give me two officers and twenty men, I'll take that ship into Iceland. The weather is good, and I think we can make it OK."

"Well," said the Captain, "you know we won't be able to give you an escort. There aren't any lifeboats left aboard either."

"Yes, sir. Perhaps we can put a couple of life rafts aboard."

Two junior officers, whom Martin had indicated when he specified the composition of the salvage crew, were in a hasty huddle in a far corner of the bridge.

"Big deal!" whispered one. "A freighter with two holes the size of a barn door in her, the ocean lousy with Krauts, and this weather sure as hell won't hold. What in the hell's wrong with him?"

"I'm with you, buddy. If the merchant crew won't go back, why stick our necks out on a hairy one like this. If anything happens we won't last two hours on those rafts."

Al continued expounding his plan, while the captain listened. One of the J.O.s worked around behind the captain's back where he could catch Al's eyes, and began vigorously shaking his head and giving him a thumbs down. The captain suddenly turned, and saw him as he froze in the middle of his negative signaling. If the captain had been seriously considering the idea, the J.O.'s obvious reluctance may have had a dampening effect. Turning back to Al, he said, "No. It's too much of a chance. We'll ask for a tug to come out. She looks like she'll float indefinitely."

As the INGHAM got underway and worked up to speed returning to the convoy, the two J.O.s huddled around the bridge wing compass repeater.

"That was," said one, "the closest shave of the winter."

"Yeah. Old Al must be hungry for a hero medal."

"Or prize money."

"What the hell you mean, prize money. You don't get prize money unless it's an enemy ship, and the cheap bastards have even knocked that off now. The only way you'll get any money is to be in the merchant service and salvage another guy's ship. In this outfit, you get two hundred bucks a month and glory. And I don't want any of that posthumous glory."

A tug was sent out to tow in the MATHEW LUCKENBACH, but was unable to locate her. After the war, we learned why. U-527 had lurked nearby all day, and began closing the scene of the torpedoing after dark. Two hours after sunset, she surfaced and saw the freighter six miles away, where it had been driven by the winds. Uhlig was a conservative man, and dived in order to make a submerged attack on the derelict. He was taking no chances on a trap.

Another skipper, Pietzsch in U-523, had sighted the masts of the freighter at 1625, and had promptly retreated. Diving soon afterward, he commenced a cautious approach and, determining the ship was a derelict, by 2000 had worked within 1,500 yards. At 2008, he sent one torpedo crashing into the hulk, to the great surprise of the people in U-527, who were themselves preparing to deliver the *coup de grâce!* Eleven minutes after being hit, the freighter rolled over and sank. There had, as things turned out, never been a chance to bring her in, and but for the Old Man's conservative judgment, two dozen of his crew would have bought the farm.

The MATHEW LUCKENBACH was the last ship sunk from the two convoys. The following morning, Doenitz called off the wolves due to the increasing pressure of covering aircraft and the augmented surface escort. One U-boat had been sunk by a Liberator during the day, and several had been heavily damaged by escort attacks. But the German Commander in Chief was highly pleased.

"It was," said Doenitz, "the greatest success that we had so far scored against a convoy." [5]

What was particularly gratifying to Doenitz was the fact that it had been possible to bring three-quarters of the total of 44 U-boats into contact with the convoys despite bad weather and poor attack conditions, and a surprising number of boats had been able to get in daylight submerged attacks in the face of an increasingly strong surface and air escort.

While U-boat Command was happily totaling up the sinking reports, the Allies surveyed the situation with gloom. In the last ten days of February, 21 ships of 183,650 tons had been lost; in the first ten days of March, 41 ships of 229,949 tons; and in the second ten days of March, 44 more ships of 282,000 tons. What was even more alarming was that of the 85 ships sunk so far in March, 67 had been lost in protected convoys, and only four U-boats had been sunk around the four heavily hit ones. The convoy system was nearing the breaking point.

Captain Roskill, the British Navy historian, says, "One cannot look back upon that month without feeling something approaching horror over the losses we suffered."

Reviewing the battles, some of the Naval staff concluded that, "It appeared possible that we should not be able to continue convoys as an effective measure of defence."

"It [the convoy system] had," continued Roskill, "during three and a half years of war, slowly become the lynch pin of our maritime strategy. Where would the Admiralty turn if the convoy system had lost its effectiveness? They did not know; but they must have felt, though no one admitted it, that defeat then stared them in the face." [6]

Winston Churchill, not one to rattle easily, messaged President Roosevelt, "Our escorts are everywhere too thin, and the

---

[5] Karl Doenitz, *Memoirs of Ten Years and Twenty Days* (Bonn: Athenaum-Verlag Junkerund Dunnhaupt, 1958), p. 329.

[6] S. W. Roskill, *The War at Sea*, Vol. II (London: H. M. Stationery Office, 1954-61), pp. 368-9.

strain upon the British Navy is becoming intolerable." The
Prime Minister declared that until the balance had been restored
in the Atlantic, no more convoys could be sent to Russia, and
neither Stalin nor Roosevelt could make him alter the decision.

But at this black moment, when the Admiralty believed the
U-boats were ". . . very near to disrupting communications
between the New World and the Old," the pendulum began
to swing. Though no one realized it at the time, the U-boat
offensive had hit its apogee at 1042, March 19, 1943, when the
torpedoes slammed into MATHEW LUCKENBACH, the 21st
and last ship to be hit in the battle around SC-122 and HX-229.

After that bright March morning, the fortunes of the U-boats
started down, and within the amazingly short space of ten weeks,
the Battle of the Atlantic was to end in victory for the Allies.
Speaking of the battles of March, Admiral Doenitz says, "The
success achieved in this month was destined to be the last decisive
victory won by the Germans in the battle of the convoys." [7]

But those few of us who saw that column of water rise high
in the sky on the northwest horizon could little know at the
time that it was the high-water mark of the German U-boat
offensive, just as surely as the fight in a grove of trees on a ridge
at Gettysburg 80 years before had constituted the furthest advance of the Confederacy.

---

[7] Doenitz, *op. cit.*, p. 330.

IX

MARCH 20-MAY 22/TURN OF THE TIDE

After the morning of March 19th, the escorts around SC-122 and HX-229 gained a clear upper hand. At 2248 on the evening of the 19th, an HF/DF fix showed a U-boat to be 20 miles from the convoy. INGHAM threw out on the bearing, and less than an hour later obtained radar contact. As she approached, the target faded out, and when no Asdic contact was made, a depth-charge pattern was dropped on a time-distance estimate with no apparent results. Later, the Liberator which was providing night coverage was sent out to the same area, and jumped the U-boat nine miles from the convoy. Once more, on the following night, the night patrol aircraft was vectored out an HF/DF bearing on the starboard beam and attacked and drove down a surfaced U-boat.

After that the convoy was not further molested. With the 42 merchant seamen, and 25 naval personnel of the armed guard from MATHEW LUCKENBACH aboard, INGHAM was so crowded that she was ordered to Londonderry to discharge the survivors. The "hot bunk" system was implemented, allowing survivors to use the bunks of crew members when the latter were on watch. The chief mate of the sunken freighter, Willy Heyme, had proved to be an interesting shipmate during the few days he was on board. An officer in the Imperial German Navy during World War I, he had first served on destroyers, participating in the Battle of Jutland in 1916. When the High Seas Fleet became virtually immobilized after that battle, he had volunteered for U-boat duty and had fought the rest of the war as a U-boat officer. After World War I, he had migrated to the States, becoming a naturalized citizen, and a Merchant Marine officer. His stories of life in U-boats drew an attentive audience. Commenting on his recent experience at the hand of his former countrymen, Willy wryly concluded that they were "a very efficient crowd."

The first three weeks in March had left no doubts on that score. Every eastbound convoy had been intercepted, and a heavy toll extracted. With so many U-boats at sea, it no longer appeared possible to avoid them by evasive routing. Convoys turning away from one concentration merely ran into another.

The last week of March, INGHAM arrived in Liverpool and went into dry dock to have the Asdic dome repaired at long last. During eight long frustrating weeks of constant action, she had been like a fighter with one hand tied. Her North Atlantic days, however, were numbered. Upon leaving Liverpool, she was to report to Task Force 63, engaged in escorting convoys from the States to the Mediterranean. The American surface escort groups were to be withdrawn from the North Atlantic, which would henceforth be wholly a British and Canadian responsibility, aided by American Hunter-Killer Groups built around escort carriers. As INGHAM eased into the Herculaneum Dock at Liverpool, the first of the American escort carriers was already moving into action.

From intercepted radio intelligence, Doenitz knew that the next two eastbound convoys, SC-123 and HX-230, would be entering the air gap about March 25th, and Group *Seeteufel* was deployed to wait for them. The SC convoy sailed into the waiting U-boat line on the evening of March 26th, and two U-boats sent out contact signals, one reporting a carrier of the ILLUSTRIOUS class with the convoy. Actually, it was the escort carrier USS BOGUE.[1] In addition to the new escort carrier, SC-123 also had Captain J. W. McCoy's newly formed 3rd Support Group of five Home Fleet destroyers beefing up the regular escort. Using HF/DF, the destroyers of the British support group ran down the bearings, forced the U-boats to dive, and sat on them. So promptly had the destroyers acted that the contact U-boats were unable to even transmit the course and speed of the convoy, and for the first time in a month, an eastbound convoy slipped through without being attacked or identified. When the convoy was well clear of the U-boat patrol line, the support group hustled back at high speed and joined up with HX-230 to see it through the danger area. This convoy was sighted by the northernmost boat of the patrol line, and Group *Seewolf* of 28 boats was ordered to hit it. But again the destroyers of the support group located the signaling U-boats by HF/DF and forced three of them to dive during the night.

On the morning of the 28th, the month of March, contrary to tradition, "went out like a lion," with a full hurricane enveloping the convoy. The U-boats were unable to operate in the seas, but Doenitz refused to call off the battle, believing that the hurricane would scatter the convoy so badly that the trailing U-boats could reap a heavy crop of stragglers.

The War Diary of U-260 (Korvettenkapitän Purkhold) describes the first night of the hurricane as follows:

> March 28, 1943. Wind Force 11. Sea force 9, SW hurricane. 2030 Sighted steamship estimated 8,000 tons running before the storm. Range 4,000 yards. Remained to starboard of her and decided to attack on the surface before darkness fell. With the very heavy sea running there is very little likelihood of her sighting me. Spray has reduced visibility to something between one and two miles. At 2105 delivered my attack obliquely into the weather. Attack failed as I had underestimated target's speed and range. Did not realize

[1] This was not Bogue's first convoy. She had been with HX-228 two weeks before when HMS HARVESTER was lost, but the heavy weather prevented her launching aircraft during the battle.

that the opportunity was as good as gone, since the heavy seas sweeping over me had prevented me for a long time from seeing the ship. I set off in pursuit intending, if possible, to attack before dark, because in a heavy sea and with poor visibility the danger of losing her altogether in the darkness of the night was too great. 2200 Pursuit broken off. While trying to run before the storm at full speed, the boat dived twice. By blowing tanks, putting my helm hard over and reducing speed I managed to hold her reasonably on the surface. To remain on the bridge was impossible. Within half an hour the captain and the watch were half drowned. Five tons of water poured into the boat in no time through the conning tower hatch, the voice pipe and the Diesel ventilating shaft. The ship was running directly before the storm. I myself had to turn away, and with a heavy heart I abandoned the chase.

The severity of the storm was such that Convoy HX-230 was badly scattered and the ship carrying the convoy commodore capsized in the raging seas, carrying down all hands. But only one U-boat managed to torpedo a straggler. One of the reasons was the splendid work of the Iceland-based RAF Liberators, which provided cover throughout the storm and prevented the trailing U-boats from keeping up with the convoy.[2] When the storm abated, they were too far astern to catch up. The contrast of the last 10 days of March with the previous 30 days was obvious, but the implications were not yet clear. Two convoys had passed through the battle area with the loss of only one ship to U-boats. That this was partially due to the weather was clearly recognizable, just as the terrible storms of January had given a few weeks' respite. But the appearance of the support groups, the first escort carriers, and long-range air cover in the air gap had all had an immediate effect that was as yet not realized.

The establishment of support groups had long been planned by CINCWA, but the ships simply were not available. Finally, in March, as more ships came from the repair and building yards,

---

[2] They were from No. 120 Squadron, Royal Air Force, probably the best ASW squadron of the war.

withdrawals were made from the hard-pressed escort groups to provide part of the resources, and after Churchill's decision to cease Russian convoys, additional destroyers were loaned to the Western Approaches Command from the Home Fleet. The United States Navy contributed the escort carrier BOGUE and five attendant destroyers. Six support groups were formed, and thrown into the battle.

Aside from the advantages inherent in each group being able to train and work together as a team, fully familiar with each group commander's doctrine and plan of action, each support group was a mobile striking force, which could be dispatched where it was most needed. Once in the vicinity of a threatened convoy, it could roam at will among the shadowing U-boats, raising havoc with their attempts to concentrate and deliver a coordinated attack. Equally important, not being tied down to the close defense of the convoy as was the escort group, the ships of a support group could sit on top of a contact until the U-boat was destroyed or forced to surface due to exhaustion of its batteries and air supply.

A second factor in reversing the tide of battle was the arrival of the escort carriers, which were able to operate in the vicinity of a threatened convoy and provide air coverage throughout the passage. With their arrival, the air gap ceased to exist, and the U-boats were no longer able to operate on the surface without a constant fear of attack from the air.

In very heavy weather, however, the relatively small escort carriers were lively ships, and in the stormy northern ocean often could not operate aircraft. To afford air cover at such times, very long-range Liberators were required, and during the winter crisis, only the few aircraft of Coastal Command's No. 120 Squadron in Iceland were available. In the spring of 1943, as a result of very strong British representations, a drastic reallocation of Liberators for anti-submarine warfare was made by the United States, and by summer, their weight was being felt. The allocation of very long-range bombers to the anti-submarine

program was highly controversial, and the failure to provide
even the bare minimum requirements of these aircraft was, in
the opinion of many naval officers and historians, one of the
primary reasons the Allies were in the critical position they occupied in March, 1943.[3]

As April arrived, despite the past ten days' respite, no one on
the Allied naval staffs dared hope that it had been other than
a brief interlude. But the first ten days of April also passed without serious attacks. We now know that after the bitter battles
of March, most of the U-boats were withdrawn from the North
Atlantic for rest and repairs, creating a temporary U-boat vacuum
on the northern convoy routes. Ashore, the cryptoanalysts at
Bletchley Park, working in an information blackout since the
German code change of March 8th, miraculously broke back into
the German Triton code at the end of the month. The breakthrough, which has never been publicly explained, once more
provided the Submarine Tracking Room with an accurate picture
of U-boat dispositions and allowed them to divert many of the
convoys around the more dangerous U-boat concentrations. Even
as mid-April approached and fresh U-boats again were deployed
in strength, the convoys were pushing through with only light
losses, thanks to strengthened escorts, augmented by the presence
of support groups, and increasing air coverage. As the favorable
situation extended into the third week, the Allied outlook, which
had been one of extreme pessimism in mid-March, brightened
considerably. Confidence had so improved that a decision was
made to send a heavily protected convoy through a U-boat concentration, and have it out on the spot. It would be both cold-
blooded and incorrect to describe Convoy HX-233 as a decoy,
but it would draw the U-boats, and when they came in, the Allied
command felt certain the strong escort could deal the U-boats a
heavy body blow. HX-233 was to prove the most significant eastbound convoy of the month.

The mid-ocean escort was Captain Paul Heineman's experienced A3 Group, with a number of new faces, including the

[3] See Appendix III, "The Long-Range Aircraft Controversy," p. 257.

Canadian destroyer SKEENA and the Coast Guard cutter
DUANE, which had replaced the crippled CAMPBELL. A3 was
still a badly overworked group, and on April 11th, with only
three days' rest in St. John's after a westward crossing, they
stood out past the breakwater enroute to a rendezvous with
HX-233. The next day, they took over the convoy from the local
escorts off the Newfoundland banks, and headed eastward. The
routing was to take them far south of their accustomed beat, and
into calmer and warmer waters. On the second day, ARVIDA and
DIANTHUS, which had been delayed in sailing from St. John's,
joined up, raising the escort's strength to eight ships. Unlike the
previous month with SC-121, the escorts' radars and Asdics were
now up to snuff and operating. Advantage was taken of the good
weather to refuel several escorts from the accompanying tanker.

Heineman's ships were engaged in their usual aggressive patrolling around the convoy when at 0240 on the 16th, SPENCER
made radar contact and took off after a target. The U-boat dived
at 3,200 yards, and Commander Sloop Berdine took in SPEN-
CER, delivering an 11-charge attack. Regaining contact a short
time later, he fired a hedgehog pattern without results. Contact
was again lost. Throughout the night, the veteran ship continued
the search, and at 0416, made Asdic contact, and delivered
another attack. At dawn, she was joined by a Canadian frigate.
The escort groups were at long last reaching a strength that
would permit detachment of vessels to stick with the contact,
and not until mid-morning did the two ships give up the search
and head back to the convoy. The U-boat had been unable to
get out a sighting report, and the merchantmen remained
unmolested during the night.

As 0312 the following morning, another radar target was
detected and SPENCER raced out to intercept. The U-boat
dived, and SPENCER and DIANTHUS set up a search pattern
to hold it down. The hunt had continued for over two hours
when, at 0539, ARVIDA reported the FORT RAMPART torpedoed. SPENCER closed the scene to screen ARVIDA while
she recovered survivors, and almost immediately picked up an
Asdic contact. A hedgehog attack was unsuccessful, contact was

lost, and the two escorts began a box search. With dawn came the welcome news that Captain McCoy's crack 3rd Support Group of Home Fleet destroyers had arrived, and were already after another U-boat 14 miles away. With evidence of more U-boats around the convoy, and with a support group to follow up and work over any contacts, Heineman ordered the flagship to return to the convoy.

SPENCER had just arrived back on station when, at 1050, she made Asdic contact 5,000 yards ahead of the convoy. Turning hard left after the U-boat, which was trying to escape toward the convoy, she dropped an 11-charge pattern, opened out, quickly regained contact, and dropped another full pattern. Badly shaken by the one-two punch, the U-boat dived under the convoy, and Spencer, smelling a kill, went in after it, dodging in and out among the merchant vessels while her Asdic operator tried to regain contact.

When contact was made again between columns six and seven, a hedgehog pattern was fired, and at 1138, the U-boat broke surface 2,500 yards away. The cutter's ready guns opened fire, and her crew raced to battle stations to man the other guns. The U-boat gunners scrambled topside as she surfaced, and began spraying the cutter with 20-millimeter fire. SPENCER replied with all guns, DUANE rushed in firing broadsides, and several merchantmen at the rear of the convoy opened fire at the U-boat. SPENCER was between the merchantmen and the U-boat, and the accuracy of the Armed Guard crews of the merchantmen left much to be desired; their shells were falling over and around SPENCER, and one five-inch projectile hit SPENCER on the starboard side, spraying shrapnel and splinters around the deck. Shot at from both sides by friends and enemy, SPENCER kept blasting away, and three minutes later, the accurate fire of the two cutters had left the conning tower of the U-boat a smoking wreck. The submariners leaped into the water, leaving the U-boat running in a wide circle.

Berdine bore down on the U-boat intending to ram, but as they closed, and it became apparent that no one remained aboard

A depth charge dropped from the stern racks explodes as SPENCER attacks
U-175. USCG/National Archives

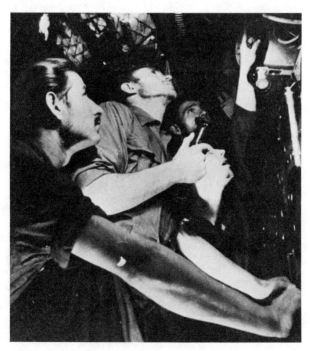

As depth charges explode around them, members of a U-boat crew attempt to
locate and repair a leak. Imperial War Museum

Following U-175 through the convoy, SPENCER (foreground) and DUANE set up a search pattern astern. USCG/National Archives

U-175, surfacing, is taken under fire by SPENCER and DUANE. USCG/National Archives

SPENCER bearing in to ram the U-boat. At this point, seeing the Germans abandoning ship (several may be seen one ship-length aft in the wake), Commander Berdine swung hard left, exclaiming, "I don't have to ram that damn thing." USCG/National Archives

Smashed by shellfire, U-175 moves ahead slowly. A crewman can be seen at the base of the conning tower. USCG/National Archives

Away the boarding party! A boat from SPENCER casts off to try and salvage the U-boat. In the stern is LCdr. Oren, while in the bow with rolled up sleeves and a sack of grenades is Lt. Bullard. USCG/National Archives

The boat stands by while Bullard climbs into the conning tower. USCG/National Archives

the boat, he ordered left full rudder, saying to the officer of the deck, "I don't have to ram that damn thing!"

Eight of SPENCER's crew had been wounded, one fatally, but she paralleled the U-boat and the loudspeaker call, reminiscent of the days of sail, rang throughout the ship, "Away the boarding party!"

This party had been specially trained for some months by Lieutenant Commander John B. Oren, the cutter's executive officer, to board and if possible capture intact any U-boat that might be blown to the surface. The training had included sessions in a mockup of a U-boat at Londonderry, Ireland, and each man had his duties clearly in mind. As the boat containing the boarding party came alongside the U-boat, which was still moving slowly ahead, Lieutenant Ross Bullard jumped onto the conning tower, a .45 automatic tied to his wrist by a lanyard, and a sack of hand grenades over his shoulder. His first job was to lob a grenade down the hatch to take care of any U-boat men who had any fight left. Looking down the hatch, he saw three dead men inside, and the interior of the conning tower a mess of blood and wreckage. No grenade was necessary. Water began to lap into the conning tower as the U-boat slipped lower in the water, and Bullard was forced to give up his attempt to get into the control room. It was too late to save the U-boat, but the Coast Guard lieutenant became the first American in over a century to board an enemy man-of-war underway at sea. He removed the clip of cartridges from his pistol, fired the round that was already in the chamber, threw the pistol across the water to the boat, and jumped into the water as the U-boat slid under. Being the ship's gunnery officer, and thus responsible for all firearms, he was taking no chance on losing the pistol.

The two cutters began picking up the German survivors from the water. Nineteen were rescued by SPENCER and 22 by DUANE. All were badly shaken, some were wounded, and many were in a state of shock. One extremely nervous officer began talking freely and rather fluently in English. Even after being assured that all survivors would be picked up if possible, he voiced his fears that the cutter would not stop in spite of his crew's shouting and arm waving.

"It is not easy down there," he repeated several times. "The bombs were bad. Inside it was all bad. Everything shaking, things fall down, it smelled and hurt the eyes."

Describing the U-boat's approach, he said, "We came up and saw you in the periscope, but you saw us and we knew it was all over. Our chance to get you was gone. We don't like the bombs. It is hard when they shake the boat. We went down and the bombs started going off—things stopped and would not work—a lot of things broke."

Control had been lost, the hull was leaking, and one shaft was fractured. With full-up planes, the U-boat had blown all tanks to surface. When the unequal gun fight started on the surface, he had jumped into the water.

As he drank coffee and thawed out, he told how much they had wanted to get a shot at a large escort vessel like the SPENCER.

"If you had not seen us so quick," he said, "maybe you would not be the lucky one."

Another survivor was greatly agitated, accusing the cutters of machine gunning the survivors and leaving them in the water. In fact, the cutter had ceased firing at the U-boat when it became apparent that the crew was abandoning ship, and at the first opportunity began picking up survivors. Of such mistaken impressions are "atrocity" stories born. That the survivors would be well treated was taken for granted by another of the U-boat's officers, who said he expected that "any honorable soldier would treat a weaponless enemy soldier decently."

Most of the crew were well indoctrinated and not as talkative, the officers even refusing to give their rank and serial number as required by the Geneva Convention. However, when one of the cutter's crewmen forcibly took a ring from a German sailor, and when this was reported and the ring located and returned, the grateful German volunteered the information as to which survivors were officers. The senior surviving officer, Lieutenant zur See Peter Paul Moeller, said little, apparently unable to understand English, or his captors' attempts at German. However, when the prisoners were put ashore in Ireland, he came up to Commander Berdine, and in a flawless British accent, thanked him for the treatment given the U-boat crew. Another officer was nearly as closemouthed; when he was hauled onto the deck of SPENCER, he looked up at the radar antenna revolving on the mast, and pointed at it, exclaimed, "Goddamn radar!" After that, he too clammed up.

One of the officers was critical of his captain for attempting a submerged attack in daylight and calm weather. In actual fact, U-175 was tricked into the approach by an odd situation. When the U-boat first sighted the convoy, SPENCER was coming up between the columns from her night's work astern, and no escort was ahead. The U-boat started its approach through what appeared to be a wide hole in the screen. At that moment, SPENCER emerged from between the columns and moved out ahead into the gap, where contact was made on the surprised U-boat. The cutter had arrived back on station in the nick of time.

Following the sinking of U-175, only one other U-boat contact was made near the convoy. Shortly after midnight on the 18th, a patrolling aircraft reported a U-boat diving 7,000 yards ahead of the convoy. SPENCER investigated, following the contact into the convoy in the darkness, and dropping harassing depth charges. No ships were torpedoed.

Commenting on the SPENCER's actions, Rear Admiral Samuel Eliot Morison, the United States Navy historian says, "It was significant of the training and discipline of these [HAMILTON] class cutters. A year earlier, no escort commander would have dared dash up and down convoy columns at night for fear of collision." [4]

The same could not be said of all the merchant vessels. Two American freighters, attempting to avoid a torpedo, collided in broad daylight, and the crew of one promptly abandoned ship,

[4] Samuel E. Morison, *The Battle of the Atantic, Vol. 1* (Boston: Little, Brown and Company, 1947), p. 346.

leaving her to be towed in by a disgusted British tugboat crew. But lest the landsman draw a hasty and unfavorable comparison of the merchant seamen versus naval crews, it should be realized that the merchant fleet was expanding at such a rate that a master often had to make do with whatever crew could be assembled. Many of them were green, and their training was hurried. While ships were sometimes prematurely abandoned, it was not always without reason. The merchant seamen were often sitting on top of highly explosive cargoes of munitions or aviation gasoline, and after a torpedo hit or collision, the ship could explode at any moment. In their slow and vulnerable vessels, they cruised month after month as prime targets, while the men-of-war, with their high speed and maneuverability, were seldom hit. Though the merchant seamen were paid higher wages than the escort sailors, few of the latter would have traded places with them. By any measurement, they were brave men, and engaged in a perilous trade.

On April 20th, the convoy was turned over to the British local escort off Ireland, minus only one U-boat victim. The contrast with March, when only 36 of an original convoy of 59 ships had been delivered by the same escort group, was one more indication of the changing situation.

As Group A3 stood toward Loch Foyle and Londonderry for a well-earned breather, they had every reason to feel satisfied. The one merchantman which had been lost to U-boat attack had been rapidly avenged, and U-boat Command could ill afford an even tradeoff. Even more important, however, had been the thorough manner in which the escorts, surface and air, had quickly jumped every U-boat which attempted to penetrate the screen, and had not only driven them off, but sat on them until the convoy was well clear. Of eight U-boats directed onto the convoy, only one had been able to launch an attack.

Doenitz believed that the weather was to some extent responsible for the failure of the U-boats to get inside the screen, and when the next convoy, following the same route as HX-233, was

A German crewman yells for help alongside SPENCER. USCG/National Archives

A boat from the Group flagship maneuvers alongside a Canadian corvette loaded with merchant ship survivors. USCG/National Archives

An injured U-boat officer being assisted by crew members of SPENCER.
USCG/National Archives

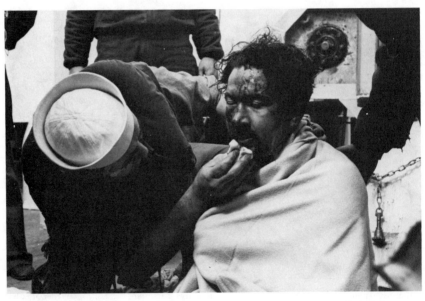

A U-boat petty officer being assisted by a sailor. USCG/National Archives

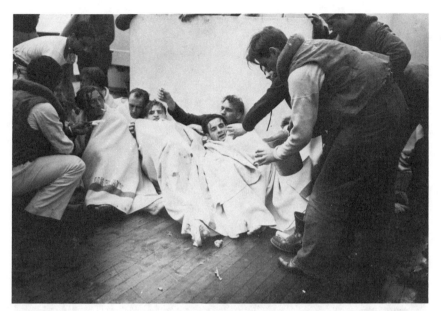

The battle over, U-boat crewmen are given coffee and cigarettes. USCG/
National Archives

SPENCER crew member killed in the battle is buried at sea as Commander
Berdine reads the service. Facing him is the Group Commander, Captain Paul
Heineman, USN. USCG/National Archives

Captured German prisoners are offloaded from SPENCER and DUANE into custody of British military police. USCG/National Archives

Even after the Battle of the Atlantic had been decided, the U-boats were a menace. A tanker in a heavily escorted convoy burns, while in the foreground a destroyer escort carries out a sweep, attempting to locate the submerged U-boat. USCG/National Archives

sighted on April 18th, he refused to allow an attack because "the dead calm sea and the complete absence of wind would have been too great a handicap.[5]

The U-boat Command Diary for that day commented that "Meager success, achieved generally at the cost of heavy losses, renders operations in these areas inadvisable."

As April neared its close, Allied losses for the month had dropped to less than half that of the previous month, while U-boat losses, 15 in all theaters, remained the same as March. The battle was far from won, but the pendulum was once more near dead center.

The beginning of May found the U-boats' strength on the North Atlantic at the highest point of the entire war. Sixty boats in four great patrol lines lay to the southwest of Iceland, off Newfoundland, and in the Bay of Biscay and Gibraltar approaches. But the Allied HF/DF net was able to locate the deployed U-boat groups with unusual accuracy, and three convoys for which they were waiting were safely guided around them by radical course diversions.[6]

But with so many U-boats at sea, there was little hope that the convoys could continue to escape detection, and on May 4th, a fourth convoy, ONS-5, steamed into the middle of a patrol

[5] Karl Doenitz, *Memoirs of Ten Years and Twenty Days* (Bonn: Athenaum-Verlag Junkerund Dunnhaupt, 1958), p. 336. The combination of calm seas and the new American SG radar was indeed a formidable handicap. Several months later, while escorting a Mediterranean-bound convoy, our new SG radar picked up a momentary contact 11,000 yards astern, but nothing could be seen visually. The information was passed to the escort carrier BOGUE, which was with the convoy. Refusing to believe the contact was legitimate, BOGUE did not launch a torpedo bomber, but sent instead a more handy fighter, which had no depth bombs. A short time later, the fighter excitedly reported a U-boat cruising at periscope depth. In the calm seas, our SG radar had picked up the U-boat periscope at a range of more than five miles. Though certainly an exceptional range, it was indicative of the difficuties experienced by the U-boats in absolutely flat seas.—J.M.W.

[6] During May, the Allies finally changed their radio codes for the first time in over a year, and B-Service was unable to break the new ones. Doenitz was thus deprived of one of his most valuable sources of intelligence on Allied movements, and the result was evidenced by a rapid drop in contacts made with Allied convoys.

line and was sighted. The tactical situation was highly favorable to the Germans, for 30 boats were within close range of either side of the convoy, and 11 more boats of another group were just ahead of it. If Doenitz had been concerned with the calm seas in the month of April, he had no such worry now. The convoy had been harassed by U-boats as well as badly delayed and scattered by a gale, and only with great difficulty had Escort Group B7, under Commander Peter Gretton [7] in HMS DUNCAN, been able to round up 30 of them into some semblance of a convoy. A dozen stragglers had been formed into two groups, which were well astern of the convoy, each protected by only one escort. To add to their woes, the terrible weather had made refueling of the escorts from the convoy tanker impossible. On the very day that the main U-boat pack made contact, Gretton was forced to break off in his own ship, DUNCAN, and head for Newfoundland to refuel, and he was followed shortly after by three of the destroyers of the 3rd Support Group, which had just arrived to reinforce the escort, but were low on fuel. CINCWA immediately ordered the 1st Support Group out from St. John's, but they would not arrive before the attack began. U-boat Command looked forward with high confidence as the night of May 4th approached and the storm abated.

Eleven boats fell onto the convoy during the night and sank five ships. The next day found the convoy badly scattered and four more ships were sunk in daylight attacks. As night approached on May 5th, only seven escorts remained with the scattered convoy, and they were worn out after days of action and severe weather. All were short of fuel and some had only a few depth charges remaining. The convoy was out of range of land-based air cover, and the 1st Support Group would not arrive until the following day. With 30 U-boats gathered for the

---

[7] Gretton, now Vice-Admiral Sir Peter Gretton, K.C.B., D.S.O., O.B.E., D.S.C., RN (Ret.), was one of the outstanding escort commanders of the war. "Peter could," says a fellow officer, "smell a U-boat 40 miles away and go straight to it."

attack, one of the destroyer commanders felt that, "The convoy seemed doomed to certain annihilation."

But as night fell, fog set in, and the escorts with their radars had an advantage denied the U-boats. As the U-boats groped through the thick fog and darkness, unable to see anything, the escorts picked them up on the radar screens and attacked fiercely. In a wild all-night action, 24 attacks were attempted by U-boats, and all were driven off. Four U-boats were caught by the escorts and sunk, two by ramming and two by depth-charge attacks, and three others were heavily damaged. By 0400, the U-boats had completely lost contact with the convoy.

After daylight, the 1st Support Group got within range, surprised several shadowing U-boats, and sent one to the bottom. A Canso flying boat of the RCAF also got in its lick, sinking another near the convoy. The little corvette PINK, escorting four stragglers by herself, was not to be outdone, and not only got all her flock in safely, but sank U-192 when it tried to interfere. To make the German disaster complete, U-439 and U-659 had collided with each other on May 3rd while closing the convoy, and both went down.

As more reports of what had occurred were received by U-boat Command, Doenitz broke off the engagement. Twelve convoy vessels had been sunk, but seven U-boats had been destroyed, and two others lost while trying to close.

Disappointed though he was by the crushing defeat in the fight around ONS-5, Doenitz re-formed the survivors of the three Groups, of which only 18 boats were in condition for battle, and directed them against eastbound convoys HX-237 and SC-129.

Three ships were sunk in HX-237, but the escort, beefed up by the 5th Support Group, the escort carrier HMS BITER, and long-range aircraft, sank one U-boat.

The SC convoy was protected by veteran Escort Group B2, once again under Commander Donald MacIntyre in HMS HESPERUS. MacIntyre was second only to the famous Captain "Johnny" Walker as a killer of U-boats, and his victims had included Otto Kretschmer's U-99 and Joachim Schepke's U-100, the two top-scoring U-boats of the war. In the face of this aggressive escort, only our old Nemesis from SC-107 and SC-118, Siegfried von Forstner, in U-402, was able to penetrate the screen and sink two ships in a daylight submerged attack. But he was later depth-charged and heavily damaged, and the surface and air escort sank two other U-boats.

Another U-boat was almost destroyed, and her escape is one of the real sagas of World War II. Caught on the surface by HESPERUS, U-223 was chased down and plastered with depth charges, and when her situation became desperate, her skipper, Oberleutnant Gerlach, elected to surface and fight it out. MacIntyre took HESPERUS in with all guns blazing and dropped a pattern of depth charges alongside the U-boat, which was wallowing helplessly on the surface. Despite the punishment he was absorbing, Gerlach got his engines started and as HESPERUS came in again to drop another pattern of charges, the U-boat fired torpedoes at the destroyer. When they missed, Gerlach steered straight at the destroyer, which was blazing away with all guns, and attempted to ram it. Finally the U-boat was brought to a standstill, unable to maneuver or fire torpedoes. HESPERUS was running low on depth charges, and her gunfire seemed to be having little effect on the U-boat. Having just come out of three months' repairs as a result of ramming U-357 in December, and not wishing to again cripple his ship, MacIntyre was not eager to ram the U-boat. Instead, he decided to try to roll it over by gently ramming it and then applying ahead power. The U-boat rolled on its beam end, but then the destroyer's bow slid along the hull, and the U-boat righted itself. Gerlach gave the order for his crew to muster on deck, believing the boat was doomed. A wounded man fell overboard, and a second man, misunderstanding the order, jumped overboard. HESPERUS, seeing the Germans apparently abandoning ship, concluded that the U-boat was sinking, and departed to return to the threatened convoy.

Almost miraculously saved by the destroyer's departure, the Germans turned to with a will, and by the next afternoon, had effected emergency repairs and got underway for St. Nazaire, which they reached safely 12 days later. Just as strange was the fate of the crewman who had jumped overboard, and vanished in the night. He had floated for several hours in his lifejacket when, to his amazement, another U-boat surfaced 50 yards away, picked him up, and eventually brought him back safely to port.

The final one-two blow to the U-boats came when Gretton's B7 Group, flushed with success after Convoy ONS-5, took Convoy SC-130 eastward through the wolf packs and sank three U-boats without the loss of a single ship. Following close behind, Convoy HX-239, protected by a strong escort, as well as the 4th Support Group and an escort carrier, went through without loss, and two more U-boats paid the price.

The U-boat offensive collapsed. When the two convoys reached England, the submarine tracking room reported that wireless transmissions by U-boats on the North Atlantic had ceased.

On May 22nd Doenitz, faced with the loss of 31 boats in the first three weeks of May, recalled all U-boats from the North Atlantic. The combination of improved radar, HF/DF, strong escort and support groups, and the increasing number of aircraft around the convoys had made it impossible for the U-boats to continue to stay on the surface, and with the loss of surface mobility, the deadly wolf packs could no longer form in overpowering numbers.

"We had," says Doenitz, "lost the Battle of the Atlantic." [8]

Only eight weeks and three days after the U-boat offensive reached its high noon, it had been shattered, and so quickly did the tide change that many weeks were to elapse before the full extent of the Allied victory was realized. But as the summer passed, and the convoys went through virtually unmolested, the effects of the triumph of the escorts were increasingly felt from the deserts of Africa to the far-off atolls of the Pacific, and the

[8] Doenitz, *op. cit.*, p. 341.

way was clear for the massive build-up of men and matériel for the great land offensives that brought final victory.

The absence of the U-boats from the Atlantic shipping lanes after May continued until late autumn, during which time they were fitted with increased anti-aircraft armament and radar detection devices. Late in the year, they returned to renew the fight, but in the face of overpowering Allied strength, the wolf-pack tactics were, with few exceptions, a thing of the past.

The Battle of the Atlantic as a decisive influence on the outcome of the war ended in May, 1943, but the U-boats fought a holding operation until the bitter end, and paid a horrible price. In all, 785 were lost, and of 39,000 U-boat men who sailed on war patrols, 32,000 failed to return. Allied ships and aircraft, growing increasingly stronger, roamed the oceans, striking the U-boats wherever they showed themselves. Yet, the U-boat men continued to sail in the face of the forbidding odds, and their morale remained for the most part unimpaired. In the annals of war, few finer examples of sustained courage or of higher *élan* are to be found. How was the U-boat fleet held together while suffering losses that by any normal standards should have caused disintegration? Faced with an increasingly hopeless situation, why was the fight continued?

The principal reason for continuation of the battle was the huge Allied forces tied down by a relatively small U-boat fleet. Though they seldom managed after May, 1943, to inflict any significant damage on Allied convoys, their mere presence at sea forced the Allies to provide strong escorts, and the men, aircraft, and ships thus committed were not available for the coming invasion of Europe.

The men of the U-boat Command were certainly aware of the losses being sustained within their flotillas, and the seriousness of their situation was apparent to the veterans who returned from the combat areas. But in most cases, before the high morale and discipline in a boat began to crack, the boat met its end. The replacements boats were usually skippered by younger officers in their first command, and with the optimism and resilience of

A U-boat goes down after an attack by an American destroyer escort. USCG/
National Archives

In a desperate bid to counter the increasing Allied airpower, the U-boats were
recalled and equipped with powerful anti-aircraft armament, and instructed
to fight back at the aircraft on the surface. These tactics proved a costly
failure. This U-boat, her superstructure bristling with flak guns, and her
conning tower riddled by gunfire from a surface escort, settles slowly while
her crew prepares to abandon ship. USCG/National Archives

An aircraft bomb hits beside a U-boat before exploding. Pursued by increasing numbers of long range aircraft and by escort carrier groups, often guided by Ultra information, after May, 1943, the U-boats could find little sanctuary. USN/National Archives

youth, they were more concerned with hitting the enemy than about being killed themselves, the latter contingency being one that the normal person seldom admits in any event. Predictably, many of the new skippers died on their first patrol, before they had developed the necessary experience and caution to survive, and after two or three patrols, all were living on borrowed time.

Perhaps the main thing that sustained them through their months of trial were the promises of their leaders that their desperate situation was only a temporary one, and that new weapons would be introduced which would once again swing the tide of battle. Chief among these were the new high-speed U-boats, the "Snorkel" [9] breathing device that allowed the U-boats to cruise for days without surfacing, and the acoustic homing torpedo. Research on means of nullifying the effect of Allied radar was also being conducted.

New tactics were introduced, the most significant being the equipping of the boats with heavy anti-aircraft machine gun armament to enable them to stay on the surface and fight it out with the aircraft rather than dive. A few early successes were obtained, but the aircraft quickly changed their tactics and in the ensuing months turned the air-surface battles into a slaughter before the Germans abandoned the attempts to fight it out on top.[10] The new high-speed U-boats finally reached the operating areas in 1945, and achieved some success. That they were a dangerous new weapon is undeniable, but they came too late and in too small quantities to effect an outcome that had long since been decided.

In retrospect, the immensity of the Battle of the Atlantic dwarfed all other sea battles of history, and its pivotal effect in many respects exceeded Waterloo, Trafalgar, Gettysburg, or the Marne.

Roskill, commenting on the battles of May, says, ". . . because

[9] Snorkel—English adaptation of the German *Schnorchel,* nose or snort.

[10] The decision to fight back at the aircraft on the surface was one of Doenitz's greatest tactical errors. During the 94 days that the order was in force, 57 aircraft were shot down by U-boats, but 28 submarines went down and 22 others were damaged by aircraft attacks.

convoy battles are marked only by latitude and longitude, and
have no names that ring in the memory like Matapan, the victory of May, 1943, is scarcely remembered. Yet it was in its own
way as decisive as the Battle of Britain in 1940; for never again
was the German Navy able seriously to threaten our lifeline—
let alone come within a measurable distance of severing it." [11]

Not only in its broad strategic implications, but in the very
number of merchant ships involved, it was of gigantic proportions. A total of 85,775 ships in 2,889 escorted merchant convoys ran to and from the United Kingdom across the trans-ocean
routes. Of these, 654 ships were lost from the convoys, and 1,578
others while sailing independently, a total of 11,899,732 tons
of shipping on the North Atlantic alone. Over half of these
were British, and 30,248 men of the British Merchant Navy gave
their lives that the Islands might continue to fight.

In this struggle, whose losses were borne in large part by the
British merchant sailor, the credit for the victory must be largely
given to the two Royal Navies, which for most of the 45 months
before the spring of 1943 fought alone, with help from the
Americans coming only in the last third of the crisis. A few hundred warships and aircraft and less than 50,000 men of the Allied
escort forces were the fulcrum on which the Free World's cause
was so precariously balanced.[12] Few of their countrymen then
knew and even less now remember the desperate fight waged by
them on the cold and cruel northern seas. But had they failed,
the results would have been catastrophic, and total defeat must
surely have followed. The clear measure of the devotion and
courage of the men in those "storm-tossed and far-distant ships"
shall always be that, in that dark and bloody winter of crisis, they
did not fail.

[11] S. W. Roskill, *The Navy at War* (London: William Collins Sons & Co., Ltd.,
1960), p. 277.
[12] When victory came in May, 1943, in addition to 12 ocean escort groups,
there were only 6 support groups, 2 or 3 escort carriers, and about 40 long-
range Liberators.

APPENDIX I / THE WEAPONS

ASDIC

Asdic, developed through the work of the Allied Submarine Detection Investigation Committee, from which it derived its name, was the primary underwater detection device used by Allied escort vessels throughout the war. The first crude models were turned out at the end of World War I, and perfected in the years following by the Royal Navy. The equipment was basically a transmitter-receiver sending out a highly directional sound wave through the water. If the sound wave struck a submerged object, it was reflected back and picked up by the receiver. The length of time from transmission until the echo was received was utilized to measure the range, which was shown as a flickering light on the range scale. By mounting the transmitter head so that it could be directed like a searchlight, the bearing of the target could be read from a compass receiver.

The transmitter (sound) head extended below the ship, and was encased in a large metal dome to minimize the noise of water rushing past when the ship was underway. This dome was filled with water, through which the sound traveled, but the water inside the dome was stationary, and thus the noise level remained relatively low at moderate speeds. Above 18 knots, however, noise became so high that good results were not obtained, nor were they favorable in very rough weather when the ship was rolling, pitching, and heaving.

During escort and screening operations, the Asdic operator searched through an arc of about 45 degrees each side of the base course. But unlike a searchlight, the Asdic had to be stopped on each bearing long enough for the relatively slow sound waves to go out and the echo return should there be a target. The usual practice was to train to a bearing and transmit a sound impulse, which could be heard as a distinct noise or "ping." If no echo was received after several seconds, the sound head was trained five degrees more, and another "ping" sent out. This was repeated throughout the watch, searching in five-degree steps through the arc to be guarded.

If the outgoing impulse struck a submerged target, the echo would be received as a distinct "beep." When this occurred, the Asdic operator would give the alarm, and feed ranges and bearings to the conning officer. By training right and left until no echo was received, right and left "cuts" were determined, fixing the width of the target, and more quickly determining if it were moving to one side or the other. A change in the pitch of the returning signal from that of the outgoing one gave the skilled operator an indication of whether the target was closing or opening out. This change in tone, known as "doppler effect," can be observed on a train whistle as it approaches and then passes. If the target is approaching, the tone is higher; going away, it is lower.

Echoes could bounce back from many things other than U-boats, and whales, schools of fish, rocks, vertical currents, and ships' wakes caused many false alarms, especially with green operators. The old timers, however, were adept at classifying a target as "sub" or "non-sub," and the conning officers quickly learned who the reliable operators were. But even the best were sometimes fooled, and occasionally a whale fled the area, well shaken up by a depth-charge pattern. An even more serious problem than non-sub contacts were the frequent times when a U-boat could not be detected due to water conditions. Asdic was not very effective in rough water, or when water layers of different temperature deflected the sound waves. A U-boat could often dive below such a layer, and be immune from detection.

Asdic could be utilized for listening as well as "pinging." The propeller noises of a U-boat running submerged at high speeds could sometimes be heard, as could the operation of its machinery, diving planes, and ballast tanks. But contact by listening was unusual, for U-boats when confronted by an escort would usually go deep, rig for silent running, and creep along at a speed low enough to prevent cavitation of their propellers.

When Asdic contact was made on a U-boat, the attacking vessel steered straight at the target, usually at a speed of 15 knots. As the target moved left or right, the escort's heading was altered to keep it dead ahead, and bearings and ranges were plotted to determine the course and speed of the U-boat. At about 500 yards, the conning officer hoped to have a good mental picture of what the U-boat was doing, and if it was moving left or right, he would alter course and take a lead, much as a hunter leads a flying bird. The lead had to be sufficient to allow for the movement of the sub after contact was lost and while the depth charges were sinking to exploding depth. As the escort came close, the U-boat would pass beneath the beam of the Asdic, and contact would be lost. The deeper the U-boat, the further out would be the range at which contact was lost. On an average, a firm contact was lost at about 300 yards.

The time to begin firing depth charges was determined by a unique "black box" called the chemical recorder, in which the returning echoes inscribed marks on a moving special chemically-treated paper. By aligning a special arm parallel to these marks, the rate of closure and hence firing time was determined. When the marks came under the scribed mark on the arm, the officer operating the recorder began firing depth charges.

Even if an attack was delivered with the correct lead angle and firing time, there was no assurance of damage, for the U-boat was often at a different depth from that at which the charges were set to explode. The depth of the U-boat could only be guessed, or roughly estimated, from the range at which contact was lost.

The U-boats became adept at evasive measures, and the best time to evade was after the escort had taken its lead angle and lost Asdic contact close in. A widely used German tactic was to run straight away from the escort, forcing it into a stern chase. The escort was forced to ping through the disturbing water of the U-boat's wake, often producing multiple echoes When the escort was very close, the U-boat would turn hard left or right, and more often than not would escape the lethal area of the depth-charge pattern. Another tactic was to turn hard with a great deal of power so as to create a disturbing knuckle of water, which would reflect echoes, and sometimes lead the attacker astray. The Germans also released chemical pellets, which would produce clouds of bubbles to reflect the sound waves and decoy the escort away from the U-boat. Still another highly effective tactic was to dive very deep, hiding beneath a thermal inversion, or beneath the settings at which depth charges were usually set. At great depths, the escort lost contact sooner beneath the Asdic beam, and the time in which the U-boat could take evasive action was greater. As the war progressed, the newer U-boats were able to routinely dive as deep as 600 feet.

The battle of wits between the escorts and U-boats was a constant one, with the advantage shifting back and forth as new tactics and weapons were developed.

RADAR

Though the basic principles of radar—the reflection of radio waves from a solid surface back to the sending set—had been known since 1922, it was not practically applied for over 17 years, when shore-based radars were installed and played an important role in saving Britain during the great air battles of 1940. The first primitive shipboard search sets were installed in American and British ships in 1941. They were crude, unwieldy contraptions with huge antennas, of little use in detecting a small target such as a U-boat, but of great help in maintaining station on a convoy. By 1942, the British began installing a short wavelength radar capable of detecting surfaced U-boats at several miles, and the greatly improved American SG radar was being readied for issue to the fleet.

In the earlier radars, the antenna was rotated until a pip showed on a grassy green line on an oscilloscope, indicating a target. The bearing could be read from the antenna position compass, and the range measured by the distance of the pip along the base line. The information was then relayed to the conning officer to plot or work out in his head. Only one target at a time could be reported.

With the new SG radar came the PPI (plan position indicator), on which the radar information was displayed, with a dot at the center representing one's own ship. Other targets were represented by small white dots, which reappeared each revolution of the radar antenna. The observer, looking into the PPI scope, had roughly the same view that an aviator high over the convoy would have enjoyed. On the darkest night, the conning officer had only to look into the scope to quickly see the situation of all surface targets simultaneously.

Of all the weapons developed during the Battle of the Atlantic, none was as effective in defeating the wolf packs as the microwave radar. After the newer sets were installed during 1943, a U-boat could rarely run in on the convoy surfaced without being detected and attacked. With their surface mobility restricted, concentrated pack attacks on the surface at night were no longer feasible, and the boats again had to resort to the less-effective submerged attacks.

RADAR COUNTERMEASURES

Surprisingly enough, though the Germans early in the war had excellent fire-control radar on their large combatant vessels, they never installed radar on U-boats until the very end of the war. By that time, U-boats were seldom able to operate on the surface in the face of overwhelming Allied air strength, and radar proved of little use in submerged operations. American submarines, on the other hand, received the equipment at an early date and employed it to good advantage against the Japanese. Part of the reason for German failure to develop U-boat radars earlier, when it may have been a most useful device, may have been their emphasis on radar countermeasures. Being acutely aware of the ultimate effect of Allied radar on the ability of the U-boats to operate, the Germans worked desperately for an answer. By October, 1942, they had developed the first radar warning device, called METOX. This radio receiver, with its antenna set up on the conning tower after surfacing,[1] picked up the radio signals transmitted by Allied radars, much as a common radio receiver will pick up a signal when turned to the frequency of a commercial broadcasting transmitter. By manually rotating the antenna, the rough bearing from which the radar signal was coming could be determined. The device did not provide a range, but by noting if the bearing remained steady and listening for an increase in the strength of the signal, the U-boat was often able to determine if a radar-equipped escort was approaching in time to take evasive action. The METOX gear, however, received only the long wave length band used by the early Allied radars. When, in May, 1943, the Allies came out with the new short wave length radar, the METOX was unable to detect it. U-boats cruising on the surface, with no signals or warnings coming from their METOX receivers, were caught flat-footed by aircraft with the new radar, and U-boat losses from night air attacks rose steeply.

---

[1] METOX was a very cumbersome portable device, with cable leading down through the conning tower hatch. When the boat dived, the antenna and cable had to be first taken below before the hatch could be closed. A German friend tells of nearly drowning when, after ordering a crash dive, he became entangled with the METOX antenna and cable when halfway through the hatch. As the boat went down, the water began pouring over him and into the hatch. Only then did the control-room watch tumble to what was happening and hurriedly stop the dive.

The Germans, being unaware that a new radar, not detectable by METOX, was being used by the Allies, were greatly puzzled, and their confusion was supposedly compounded by one of the interesting hoaxes of the war.

A captured Allied pilot under interrogation, according to the story, volunteered the information that Allied aircraft were no longer using radar to locate the U-boats. Instead, he said, they had found that METOX was giving off a telltale radio signal on which the aircraft could home. The Germans immediately issued warning about the emissions from METOX, and many U-boat skippers quit using it for fear of being detected. In actual fact, the captured pilot's story was an ingenious prevarication. The METOX, being a receiver and not a transmitter, did not give off detectable radiation. But the hoax helped dissuade the Germans from using a device that was still effective against some radars, and may have postponed their solution of the short wave radar dilemma. Even today, many former U-boat men will swear that our planes were homing on their METOX gear.

By the year's end, however, German scientists had partially solved the problem, helped greatly by the opportunity to analyze the new radar equipment from an Allied bomber shot down near Rotterdam. The answer was a new receiver called NAXOS, capable of detecting Allied radars on a wide band of frequencies. After its installation, U-boat losses from night air attacks dropped to a more acceptable level.

In addition to the radar detectors, much work was done, unsuccessfully, to insulate U-boats by providing coatings of special paint or non-reflecting material that would make the boat more difficult to detect by radar. The most successful countermeasure to radar, however, was the introduction in 1944 of the snorkel. Essentially an air tube sticking above the water while the U-boat cruised at periscope depth, the snorkel enabled air to be taken into the boat to run the Diesel engines, while exhausting the Diesel discharge. As the batteries could be recharged by the Diesels, using the snorkel for a few hours daily, the U-boat was never required to surface at sea. After the daily battery charge, the U-boat could dive deep on its electric motors. Allied radars were able to detect the snorkel only under exceptionally favorable conditions. Fortunately, the snorkel came into use too late to seriously affect the Atlantic battle, but it gave the U-boats considerable immunity from air attacks while traveling to and from station.

HF/DF

Next to radar, no single device played a greater part in defeating the U-boat than the high-frequency direction-finder (HF/DF), called "Huff-Duff" by escort sailors. Radio direction finders were not new, and had been used for years to obtain radio bearings on low and medium frequencies for navigation purposes. The Royal Navy, however, was the first to develop equipment to take bearings on the high frequency radio transmissions used by U-boats. Numerous shore HF/DF stations were located on both sides of the Atlantic as well as in Greenland, Iceland, and Bermuda. The U-boats at sea communicated frequently and at great length with U-boat Command, especially after contact was made with a convoy. If bearings were taken by a number of widely separated HF/DF stations on a U-boat's radio signal, the bearings could be plotted and the approximate position determined. What the U-boat was saying in code was immaterial; the mere fact that it was transmitting gave away its position. Special plotting teams analyzed and plotted these positions, and a daily secret bulletin was sent out to the escort groups giving estimated positions and direction of advance of U-boats at sea. While the positions were accurate only within 50-100 miles, the information allowed the convoys to take evasive courses away from heavy U-boat concentrations and often avoid them.

In 1942, HF/DF equipment was installed aboard ships, and with these the escorts were able to take bearings on radio signals close aboard, and with much more accuracy than possible from shore stations hundreds of miles away. If two or more ships in the escort had HF/DF, cross bearings could be plotted, and a very accurate fix obtained. An escort would then be sent out to chase down and attack the U-boat. It proved highly effective against a U-boat making contact with the convoy and sending radio signals for other U-boats to home in.

Surprisingly, the Germans throughout the war made only token attempts to minimize their radio transmissions. The reasons for this were twofold. They believed that fixes by shore HF/DF stations were not accurate enough to obtain usable fixes, and they were unaware that we were using the more accurate close-range shipboard HF/DF. But wishful thinking was also involved. U-boat Command itself constantly called for reports of U-boat positions, which were essential for the exercise of centralized control, on which the wolf pack system depended. The imposition of radio silence would have crippled this system, yet in retrospect, the failure to do so was one of the German Navy's more serious tactical mistakes. After 1943, Allied air power rendered the wolf-pack system ineffective in any event, and the continued use of radio at sea caused the loss of dozens of U-boats.

DEPTH CHARGES

The oldest of anti-submarine weapons is the depth charge, a barrel-like casing containing high explosives, and detonated by a "pistol" actuated by water pressure at a selected depth. The first 300-pound depth charges were developed during World War I, and could be set to explode as deep as 300 feet. At the very end of that conflict, larger ones of 600 pounds were produced. The first means of delivery was by simply rolling them over the stern from special racks. Later, depth-charge projectors, or "K-guns," were developed which, by means of an explosive propellant charge, hurled the depth charges out to the side of the ship approximately 50 yards. These side-thrown charges, together with those dropped over the stern, enabled the escort to lay nine- or ten-charge patterns covering a wide area, to compensate for the submarine's maneuvering.

Despite the terrific explosive power of the charges, the U-boat's pressure hull was so strong that a depth charge had to explode within 10 to 20 feet of it to inflict lethal damage. To put a depth charge this close to a submerged U-boat was extremely difficult, and most boats were sunk only as a result of accumulated damage from many charges. By 1943, Torpex, half again more powerful than TNT, was introduced as the explosive filler in streamlined depth charges which sank faster and thereby reduced the dead time. But despite its impressive appearance, and unnerving effect on U-boat crews, the depth charge was not the answer to the submarine. In 1942, the "Hedgehog" was developed to overcome some of the obvious inadequacies of the depth charge.

HEDGEHOG

The hedgehog is a projector-type weapon which throws 24 small projectiles several hundred feet ahead of the attacking escort. After entering the water, the 32-pound projectiles arm, and explode on contact with the submarine or the bottom. The hedgehog can be trained to the bearing of the U-boat, and Asdic contact can often be maintained until the time of firing. Not only did this weapon eliminate the long loss of contact before firing, and the vexing problem of guessing depth, but as the charges did not explode in case of a miss, the escort had a much better chance of regaining Asdic contact than with the water churned up and disturbed by depth-charge explosions. The hedgehog proved to be a deadly weapon, but it was neither as thrilling nor as impressive as dashing in with depth charges exploding. So effective have ahead-thrown weapons and homing torpedoes proven that depth charges are no longer used by modern anti-submarine vessels.

Though never a decisive weapon, the acoustic homing torpedo was a constant threat to attacking escorts. The Coast Guard manned USS MENGES under tow, after she was hit by an acoustic torpedo. USCG/National Archives

TORPEDOES

Surprisingly enough, the Germans started World War II with a torpedo that was less reliable than those used in the Kaiser's War. Not only did they experience trouble with the depth-keeping mechanism, but the magnetically actuated firing pistols in the warheads proved ineffective. This type pistol was intended to explode beneath the ship as the torpedo passed through its magnetic field, breaking the ship's back and causing far more damage than a hit against the side. Under actual combat conditions, there were many failures, especially during the Norwegian Campaign. Ship after ship escaped due to faulty torpedoes, while the U-boat skippers ground their teeth in frustration. To make matters worse, the air-propelled torpedoes left a clear trail of bubbles, and the escorts would come barreling down the torpedo wake with blood in their eyes to work over the attacking U-boat. As a result of prompt and severe action by U-boat Command and the technical people, fixes were made. The Germans soon came out with an electric torpedo which left no telltale wake, and it proved to be a highly reliable and effective weapon. In early 1943, they introduced the new FAT torpedo, which could be set to zigzag or circle after running a set distance, and promised to create havoc in the convoys. Late in the year, the acoustic torpedo came into use. Designated primarily for use against escorts, it homed on the noise of the surface vessel's propellers. In its first use against Convoy ON-202, several escorts were sunk; but within a matter of weeks, the Allies had come up with a countermeasure in the "Foxer" gear, a noisemaker streamed astern of the escort to divert the homing torpedo. Though it was to prove a dangerous nuisance, the acoustic homing torpedo was never a decisive weapon.

The Allies came out with their own acoustic homing torpedo in 1943. Dropped by aircraft, it homed on the noise of the U-boat's propellers, and proved to be a deadly weapon. Over 20 years later, the improved acoustic torpedo is still a primary anti-submarine weapon.

APPENDIX II | ULTRA—RIDDLE
WITHIN AN ENIGMA

No secret of World War II has been more closely guarded than the Allies' penetration of the Axis radio codes and much of the information is still classified 40 years after the events. The conflict involved, for the first time, common use of radio at all levels of command, and this allowed interception by the other side and perhaps decoding. Though less secure than telephone lines, both sides were forced by geographic necessity to use radio with the attending risks. Strangely enough, the experts on both sides, while themselves successfully penetrating enemy codes, discounted the possibility that their own codes were also being broken. This strange complaisance and blindness to the other's cryptoanalytic ability brought tragic consequences.

The German B-Service's penetration of the British fleet codes and the British and Allied Merchant Ship (BAMS) code was not a surprising accomplishment. Given the relative simplicity of these manual codes and the large volume of British traffic, the success of the German cryptoanalysts was predictable. In 1940, however, the British converted to an electro-mechanical encoded fleet system, which was not again compromised for any significant period.

But the BAMS code, used in a less secure environment subject to compromise, was retained for nearly four years. German traffic decoded by the British provided strong evidence that the Germans had broken BAMS and were reading the convoy routing traffic. But no action was taken to change the code until June 1943, and thousands of Allied seamen and hundreds of fine vessels paid for the delay with their lives.

Unlike the British, the Germans began to war with a highly sophisticated code system using the Enigma machine, an electro-mechanical coding device highly resistant to penetration. The principal of the machine had been known since 1919, was used by several countries, and in fact some models were commercially available. In 1928, the U.S. Army Signal Corps purchased one for only $144 from the German manufacturer. Unfortunately, the following year the army decoding team was broken up by Secretary of State Henry Stimson because, "Gentlemen do not read other gentlemen's mail."

The Poles were not as naive or idealistic. After discovering that the Germans were using machine produced cipher, a team of brilliant scholars was recruited from the University of Poznan, and began working on the German codes in 1928. A covert examination of an Enigma machine being shipped from Berlin to the Warsaw embassy was made over a weekend by removing it from the Polish customs house, and rewrapping it for delivery on Monday. Additional machines were covertly acquired and by 1934 the Polish code team had penetrated the German procedures. During the "Night of the Long Knives," leading to the murder of Nazi Brownshirt leader Ernst Röhm, Polish Intelligence operators were fully informed through their decrypts. By 1938, over 75% of intercepted German traffic was being decoded.

This was an astonishing achievement, for it involved not just the physical possession of the Enigma machines, which was only a start, but the solution of the German operating procedures, construction of their rotors, and determination of the daily rotor settings. Using a three rotor Enigma, the number of possible code permutations was 3×10^{18}, and the incorporation of a fourth wheel raised this to 4×10^{20}.

On September 15, 1938 the Germans added two rotors to

Enigma, and for the first time in five years the Poles were unable to read the German traffic. The Poles were confident that given time they could also break into the new code, but time was running out. With war looming, the Poles on August 16, 1939 turned over to the British and French two Enigma machines together with documentation on their years of work. When Poland was overrun in September, the Polish code experts made their way to France via Roumania, and were soon back in operation under French command. Their work on the Enigma system was probably Poland's greatest contribution to final victory.

At the outbreak of war, the British Government Code and Cipher School (GCCS) moved from London to its wartime station at Bletchley Park, north of London, and from there was directed the massive attack on the Axis ciphers. The operation, which became known as Ultra, was to have a profound effect on the outcome of the war. By April 1940, the brilliant team of professional intelligence operators, academics, and world-class chess experts had broken into the first Luftwaffe ciphers, and by the time of the German blitzkrieg into France, was regularly feeding vital intelligence to the Army and RAF.

Unfortunately, no real inroads had been made into the German Navy ciphers. In early 1941, the Royal Navy made a determined effort to capture enemy vessels at sea in order to seize their Enigma machines and codes. Three trawlers were seized with documents, but all had jettisoned their machines.

The big break came on May 8, 1941 when HMS BULLDOG attacked U-110 and forced it to the surface. The Germans set explosive scuttling charges before abandoning ship, but failed to jettison their Enigma machine and code books. The detonators failed to explode, and the British boarded the drifting submarine, seizing the entire code setup including the Enigma machine and the daily settings through the end of June! The U-boat sank while in tow, and the Germans were never the wiser.

Within days after receiving the material, Bletchley Park was fully into the German Navy Hydra Code, and continued to read it throughout the war. The results were nearly instantaneous. By June 23, tipped off by Ultra, British warships had sunk six tankers and three supply ships used to supply German raiders. Though the coming months would see the British privy to much of the German secret maritime radio traffic, no amount of intelligence could make up for the critical shortage of warships and aircraft required to adequately act on the information. Losses at sea continued high.

On February 1, 1942, the Atlantic U-boats were detached from Hydra and put on a new cipher, Triton, which linked them directly to U-boat command. For the next ten months this code change produced a nearly total stoppage of direct Ultra information on U-boats, though from other sources using Hydra, HF/DF bearings, sighting reports, and deductions, the Admiralty's Submarine Tracking Room was able to make many accurate estimates. But this was second best, and by November 1942, shipping losses had climbed to 730,000 tons monthly.

After months of arduous effort, Bletchley made its first break into the Triton cipher in December, and within weeks the Admiralty was receiving a steady flow of decrypts.

With the Germans reading BAMS, and the British the Triton, Hydra, and other German codes, both navies were leaking badly, and suspicions on both sides should have been aroused. The broken German messages contained detailed information on British convoy routings and the makeup of cargoes; the BAMS traffic broken by the Germans included the daily British estimates of U-boat positions and they were exceedingly accurate. A German staff report at the time stated, "The decoded signal from the British Admiralty on probable positions of German U-boats is completely true and can only have been gained by reported sightings and radio reports. *An insight into our own cipher does not come into consideration.*" Repeated German investigations into their code security reached the same conclusion.

They simply could not believe that the complex Enigma system, with its tight security and frequent changes of settings and ciphers, could be broken for any length of time.

The British were just as complacent, but with far less justification, for BAMS was a much simpler code, and in the hands of the merchant service was more subject to error and compromise.[1] After the penetration of Triton, it became more evident to the British that something was amiss; the broken German signals made it clear that B-Service was routinely reading BAMS. But long months were to pass before it was finally and mercifully changed.

As the Bloody Winter of 1942–43 approached, however, each side was "reading the other's mail." At the height of the battle, an event anticipated by Bletchley occurred—the Germans changed to a new form of Enigma using a four rotor system. On March 8, 1943, an Ultra decrypt revealed the code word ordering the change, and Ultra information on U-boats rapidly dried up. No worse time could have been chosen, for the battle had now reached its ultimate fury. But during the next three weeks a miracle occurred and Bletchley made its way back into the new cipher; by April, real time decrypts were back on line. The previous major code shift had required ten months to master. How this miracle occurred has never been revealed.

Following the victory of the escorts in May 1943, Ultra fed a steady stream of intelligence to the Allied forces, which now had enough ships and aircraft to promptly act on the information. Their routing, positions, and operations now laid open to the Allied code breakers, the U-boats could find no rest or safety. Pursued by forewarned ships and aircraft with advanced detection and ASW gear, the U-boats suffered terrifying loses without inflicting significant damage in return. Hunter/Killer groups

---

[1] On a number of occasions, merchant vessels were hurriedly abandoned after being hit and code documents were not destroyed. Escorts had to be dispatched to sink the still floating vessels, or place boarding parties aboard to insure destruction of the documents. On at least one occasion, the crew of a sinking warship failed to account for destruction of the code wheels of its decoding machine.

built around escort carriers roamed the ocean, directed to the U-boats by Ultra, and were able to stay with their prey until destruction.[2] The German heavy units were also betrayed by Ultra, and by 1944 disappeared from the high seas.

In the secret battle of the codes, a major factor in the war's outcome, both sides displayed a remarkable genius in breaking the other's ciphers. The reluctance of the experts to admit the vulnerability of their own ciphers and take timely corrective action is still an unexplained tragedy.

[2] To avoid compromise of Ultra, the Allies had to avoid too overt a reaction to vital Ultra intelligence. When the positions of several refueling submarines were revealed by Ultra, a decision was made to kill them in sequence over a period of time rather than at one stroke, which might have alerted the Germans that something was seriously amiss.

APPENDIX III / THE
LONG-RANGE
AIRCRAFT CONTROVERSY

During the winter crisis, perhaps no mistake of the Allies was so glaring as the failure to provide enough VLR (very-long-range) four-engine aircraft for aerial escort of convoys in the mid-ocean areas. Long before America came into the war, the problem of allocation of aircraft resources had arisen in Britain. RAF Coastal Command, charged with conduct of maritime air reconnaissance and convoy air escort, was at the bottom of the totem pole when four-engine aircraft were handed out, and Bomber Command stubbornly refused to turn over enough additional long-range aircraft for convoy escort. The Royal Navy, having no land-based aircraft of its own, was forced to rely on Coastal Command for all air cover except that provided by its carriers, and they were dissatisfied not only with the quantity of long-range aircraft assigned by the RAF, but with the quality of the services provided. The RAF and Navy finally compromised by setting up joint command centers, in which the Navy had the final say on maritime operational matters. But the RAF still retained control over allocation of personnel and aircraft.

At Casablanca in January, 1943, the Allied leaders agreed that since no lasting objectives could be obtained until the U-boats were defeated, the war against them would henceforth have first call on Allied resources. Surprisingly, the decision did not result in the diversion of long-range aircraft from the continental bombing offensive to escort convoys, where the stark lessons of combat had conclusively shown that merchantmen were rarely lost when covered by both sea and air escorts. Instead, between January and May, 1943, in an effort to cripple the U-boat offensive, Allied bombers dumped 19,000 tons of bombs on German U-boat bases and building yards *and not one single U-boat was destroyed.*[1]

It was not a failure chargeable solely to Bomber Command. For over two years, the Admiralty and Coastal Command had pressed for the bombing of the U-boat bases on the French Biscay coast, and a considerable portion of Bomber Command's effort had been devoted to this mission. It soon became apparent, however, that high-altitude bombing had little effect against the strongly constructed concrete U-boat shelters, and that any worthwhile results could only be obtained by razing the adjacent towns and dockyards, a measure that would result in heavy casualties among the French civilian population. Not until January, 1943, did the British Government, faced with a rapidly worsening situation on the convoy lanes, give Bomber Command a green light. After several weeks, the lack of results was evident to Bomber Command, but the raids were ordered continued by the Air Staff until mid-April, and the American Eighth Air Force did not ease up until midsummer. During the long and costly operation, not one submarine shelter in any Biscay port was penetrated by a bomb, nor were the U-boat crews, sheltered safely in the countryside, seriously inconvenienced. Attacks were also aimed at the building yards in Germany with little effect, and not until April, 1944, was the first U-boat destroyed in a builder's yard.

In retrospect, the concentration on continental bombing at the expense of convoy protection probably cost the lives of thousands

---

[1] Two hundred and sixty-two Allied aircraft were lost in these strikes. At that time, in addition to the 18 very-long-range Liberators, the Allies had only 312 long-range aircraft of all types for Atlantic convoy protection. How much effect the 262 aircraft squandered to no purpose might have had if assigned to convoy escort can be imagined when we consider that, with the hours made available by that number of aircraft, and U-boat sightings by aircraft escorting convoys occurring an average of once every 29 flying hours, over 700 U-boat sightings would have been theoretically possible.

of seamen and hundreds of fine ships. During the height of the
winter crisis, with the Allies facing defeat on the North Atlantic,
there was exactly one squadron of very-long-range Liberators
based on Iceland to cover the entire mid-Atlantic air gap.

But if we are inclined to point an accusing finger at Allied and
RAF mission priorities, we should first look to our own house,
where inter-service jealousies and self-seeking were rife. By a
long-standing post-World War I agreement, the Army had been
given control over most land-based aviation, and the Navy operated all seaplanes, an arrangement more appropriate in 1922 than
in 1942. Finally, with shipping being slaughtered along the American East Coast, the Army, which had started out waging a semi-
independent anti-submarine war, agreed to placing its land-based
ASW aircraft under Navy operational control. But the change
gave the Navy little voice concerning the quality of pilots and
crews, and Navy airmen loudly contended that the Army pilots
were poorly trained in maritime warfare and tactics. Admiral
King, a man who seldom minced words, said in a letter to General "Hap" Arnold of the Army Air Force:

"I am told that your experienced personnel is now diluted to
such an extent that air crews of Army planes cooperating with
the Navy are not doing the work which you would expect of
them. Compare this situation with our proposal that an appropriate number of our patrol-plane squadrons be equipped with land
planes which will enable them to perform their common task
with greater effectiveness in the cause which we have in common."

Though his implied great superiority of Navy crews over their
Army contemporaries is at least open to debate, that the Army
Air Force was at that time zealously working for independent
service status to the detriment of effective cooperation is certain.

"I . . . am interested to note that you look to what Senator
Wadsworth said in 1920 to support your views," King wrote
Arnold. "All of us—no matter what uniform we wear—must go
to work to win the war. I stand on the grounds that whenever the

use of land planes will enable naval air units more effectively to perform their tasks, they should have land planes." [2]

Arnold was adamant in his refusal to meet the Navy's request for Liberators, and countered with a proposal to set up an Air Force maritime organization similar to RAF's Coastal Command, to which King replied:

"I note that you propose the establishment of a Coastal Command, which is surprising to me in the light of the common knowledge as to what the experience of the British Navy has been in its association with the RAF for the past twenty-five years and, particularly, during the past three years." [3]

The organization question was only a part of the breach that separated the Army Air Force and the Navy. The Army did not relish what they considered the drudgery of routine convoy escort, and wished instead to establish "killer" groups to go after any submarine sighted, believing such tactics to be a greater deterrent to the U-boats than close escort of convoys.

In March, 1943, the Army staff issued a report, prepared by a prominent American physicist employed by them, which aimed to "win for Army aircraft the autonomy and full naval cooperation needed for a prosecution of offensive operations." [4] The report maintained that convoying was at best a most inefficient procedure, and that aircraft could be used more effectively by carrying the attack to the enemy wherever he might be found.

This, of course, was in direct disagreement with the views of the U. S. Navy and the British Admiralty, who insisted that around the convoys was where the U-boats would be found, and not in a wild goose chase over the wide expanses of ocean. That

---

[2] Ernest J. King and Walter Muir, *Fleet Admiral King* (New York: W. W. Norton & Company, Inc., 1952), pp. 454, 455.

[3] *Ibid.*, p. 454. King was expressing the same opinion of Coastal Command held by many officers of the Royal Navy at that time. Prior to the assumption of operational control of Coastal Command by the Navy, its record in ASW and maritime reconnaissance left a great deal to be desired.

[4] Henry Stimson and McGeorge Bundy, *On Active Service in Peace and War*, Vol. II (New York: Harper & Brothers, 1948), p. 512.

the Navy men were right was later conclusively proven by a British analysis of aircraft effectiveness around convoys as contrasted with the "offensive" operations over vast expanse of empty ocean.[5] Aircraft operating in close escort of convoys made a U-boat sighting on the average of once every 29 flying hours. Those engaged in "offensive" sweeps not connected with convoys made a U-boat sighting only once every 164 hours of flying; and after the Germans began using the METOX radar receivers, only *once every 312 flying hours!*

In this bickering and disagreement, the underlying issue was one of power. The Navy feared that should the Army Air Force attain its goal as an independent service, operating "everything that flies," the Navy would lose its air arm and with it the war at sea. If Admiral Doenitz was aware of the schism, he must have viewed it with mixed feelings of glee and at least professional sympathy. The separate Luftwaffe and the lack of naval air reconnaissance was, according to him, the principal reason for Germany's defeat at sea.

In the British case, Coastal Command was not a Navy organization, but one over which the Admiralty usually had the last word, and the British with their genius for compromise were able in the end to attain excellent Air Force-Navy cooperation.

The Army-Navy issue came to a head in May, 1943, when Admiral King asked General Arnold to send to Newfoundland a group of bombers in order to strengthen the air coverage of the North Atlantic convoys. Arnold did so, but ordered the squadron commander to engage in only "offensive" operations and forbade him to cover convoys. A showdown conference was called, as a result of which the Army declared they wanted out of the ASW picture. The Navy quickly accepted, agreeing to give the Army a number of Navy Liberators from future production schedules in return for the ASW-equipped Liberators then being flown by the

---

[5] Neither the first nor the last time that the professional combat men were proven right, and the whiz kids wrong.

Army. Both parties got what they wanted, and the Navy, for the first time, took complete control of American ASW air efforts.

The Navy, however, did not come out of the fight with clean hands. While hard-working Coastal Command No. 120 Squadron was attempting with its paltry dozen Liberators to stem the on-slaught of the U-boats in the mid-Atlantic air gap, the U. S. Navy had 112 of the big aircraft, 70 of which were operating from the West Coast of the United States and the Pacific Islands, often on reconnaissance missions and in rear areas of little combat activity. Only when British pressure increased, and the President himself inquired into the uses to which U. S. Navy Liberators were being put, did Admiral King agree to release more to the Atlantic. Bombers were commandeered from the Army Air Force, Navy, and RAF Bomber Command and thrown into the Atlantic battle.

The results were immediate. The number of VLR aircraft available in the North Atlantic rose from 18 in February to 70 during May, and U-boat Command in its War Diary of May 6th ruefully noted that the Allies were able to supply convoy air cov-erage nearly continually for the entire Atlantic crossing. Con-stantly threatened from the air, the U-boats could find little rest or respite, and their areas of sanctuary shrank rapidly.

But all jurisdictional problems were not yet resolved. Admiral King, a fiercely loyal Navy man who saw many problems in hues of Navy blue and gold, did not improve his popularity with the British when he refused to authorize British operational control of U. S. Navy anti-submarine aircraft based in Morocco, a British area of strategic responsibility. His stand was quite different from that which he had taken with the U. S. Army Air Force only months before, when he had insisted that Army aircraft be under Navy operational control for efficient mission coordination. The Moroccan matter was unresolved throughout the war, and U. S. Navy and RAF Coastal Command aircraft operated in the same area without centralized direction and with considerable duplica-tion of effort.

The crisis had been too grim and the possible consequences too great to deal in service parochialism, and though honest professional differences of opinion were the basic underlying causes of the controversy, some of the in-fighting reflected to no great credit on the participants.

Summarizing the results of the VLR aircraft shortage, Roskill says, "For what it is worth, this writer's view is that in the early spring of 1943 we had a very narrow escape from defeat in the Atlantic; and that, had we suffered such a defeat, history would have judged that the main cause had been the lack of two more squadrons of very-long-range aircraft for convoy escort duties." [6]

[6] S. W. Roskill, *The War at Sea*, Vol. II (London: H. M. Stationery Office, 1954-61), p. 371.

APPENDIX IV / RETRIBUTION

The following U-boats have been mentioned in the discussion of the actions around the convoys during the winter crisis. The aggressive U-boat commanders were in the minority, but they did most of the damage. They went often in harm's way, and few survived. For most, death followed quickly after their successes, and six months was to be their average life expectancy after the actions. Of the 59 U-boats in this narrative, 52 perished at sea.

U-boat	Commander	Date Sunk	Sunk By	Where
U-520	Schwartzkopf	10-3-42	RCAF Sqdn 10	N.A. (North Atlantic)
U-658	Senkel	10-30-42	RCAF Sqdn 145	N.A.
U-132	Vogelsang	11-3-42	Explosion	N.A.
U-626	Bade	12-17-42	USCGC INGHAM	N.A.
U-187	Munnich	2-4-43	HMS VIMY and BEVERLY	N.A.
U-609	Rudloff	2-7-43	FFS LOBELIA	N.A.
U-442	Hesse	2-12-43	RAF Sqdn 48	Off Portugal
U-225	Leimkuhler	2-21-43	USCGC SPENCER	N.A.
U-606	Dohler	2-22-43	USCGC CAMPBELL and ORP BURZA	N.A.
U-522	Schneider	2-23-43	HMS TOTLANE	N.A.
U-432	Eckhardt	3-11-43	FFS ACONIT	N.A.
U-444	Langfeld	3-11-43	HMS HARVESTER and FFS ACONIT	N.A.
U-384	v. Rosenburg-Gruszcynski	3-19-43	RAF Sqdn 120	Off Iceland

U-boat	Commander	Date Sunk	Sunk By	Where
U-632	Karpf	4-6-43	RAF Sqdn 86	Off Iceland
U-175	Bruns	4-17-43	USCG SPENCER	N.A.
U-192	Happe	5-5-43	HMS PINK	N.A.
U-438	Heinsohn	5-6-43	HMS PELICAN	N.A.
U-465	Wolf	5-7-43	RAAF Sqdn 10	Off Cape Ortegal
U-89	Lohmann	5-12-43	HMS BITER's Sqdn 811 HMS BROADWAY and LAGAN	N.A.
U-456	Teichert	5-13-43	HMS LAGEN HMS DRUMHELLER RAF Sqdn 423	N.A.
U-266	v. Jessen	5-14-43	RAF Sqdn 86	N.A.
U-753	v. Mannstein	5-15-43	Unknown	SW of Iceland
U-381	v. Puckler	5-19-43	HMS DUNCAN and SNOWFLAKE	N.A. N.A.
U-521	Bargsten	6-2-43	PC-565	Off Virginia coast
U-435	Strexlow	7-9-43	RAF Sqdn 179	W of Figueria
U-409	Massman	7-12-43	HMS INCONSTANT	N of Algiers
U-527	Uhlig	7-23-43	USS BOGUE's Sqdn VC-9	S of Azores
U-614	Sträter	7-29-43	RAF Sqdn 172	Off Cape Finisterre
U-591	Zeismer	7-30-43	USN Sqdn VB-127	Off Pernambuco
U-462	Vowe	7-30-43	RAF Sqdn 502	N.A.
U-454	Hackländer	8-1-43	RAAF Sqdn 10	N of Cape Finisterre
U-604	Höltring	8-11-43	Scuttled after attack by VB-129, VB-107, and USS MOFFETT	E of Pernambuco
U-84	Uphoff	8-24-43	USS CORE's Sqdn VC-13	Off Azores
U-523	Pietzsch	8-25-43	HMS WANDERER and WALLFLOWER	SW of Iceland
U-338	Kinzel	9-20-43	RAF Sqdn 120	W of Vigo
U-229	Schetelig	9-22-43	HMS KEPPEL	N.A.
U-221	Trojer	9-27-43	RAF Sqdn 58	SW of Iceland
U-460	Schnorr	10-4-43	USS CARD's Sqdn VC-9	N of Azores

U-boat	Commander	Date Sunk	Sunk By	Where
U-643	Speidel	10-8-43	RAF Sqdn 86 and 120	N.A.
U-402	v. Forstner	10-13-43	USS CARD's Sqdn VC-9	N of Azores
U-631	Krüger	10-17-43	HMS SUNFLOWER	S of Greenland
U-600	Zurmuhlen	11-25-43	HMS BAZLEY and BLACKWOOD	N of Azores
U-377	Kluth	1-?-44	Unknown	N.A.
U-305	Bahr	1-17-44	HMS WANDERER and GLENARM	SW of Ireland
U-91	Hungerhausen	2-25-44	HMS AFFLECK, GORE, and GOULD	N.A.
U-603	Bertelsmann	3-1-44	USS BRONSTEIN	N.A.
U-653	Kandler	3-15-44	HMS VINDEX's A/C, STARLING and WILD GOOSE	N.A.
U-223	Gerlach	3-30-44	HMS LAFOREY, TUMULT, HAMBLEDON, and BLENCATHRA	Mediterranean
U-68	Lauzemis	4-10-44	USS GUADAL-CANAL's Sqdn VC-58	Off Azores
U-441	Hartmann	6-18-44	Polish Sqdn 304	NE of Ushant
U-413	Sachse	8-20-44	HMS WENSLEY-DALE, FORESTER, and VIDETTE	S of England
U-230	Eberbach	8-21-44	Scuttled in Toulon during invasion.	
U-262	Laudahn	Captured in French port following invasion, 1945		
U-260	Becker	3-12-45	Mine	SW of Kinsale
U-298	Gehrken	Surrendered Bergen, May, 1945		
U-758	Feind	Surrendered Kiel, May, 1945		
U-267	Knieper	Scuttled Flensburg, May, 1945		
U-704	Nolte	Scuttled Vegesack, May, 1945		
U-530	Wehrmuth	Surrendered in Argentina, July, 1945		

APPENDIX V / PROFILE

OF AN ACE

In the arena of combat, be it the life-and-death struggle of war, or the less final competition of athletics, a few individuals rise clearly above their contemporaries, exhibiting a special and often indefinable gift of body, nerve, mind, and desire that permits them to repeatedly achieve goals that are denied to ordinary men. A few perform with such apparent ease as to seem born to success. Others reach stardom only by dogged determination and rigorous training, spurred on by driving desire. Almost certainly, the great ones must start with some inherited talent, but the degree will probably always be open to question, for the parents from whom the child inherits his traits are also the ones to establish the environment in which he grows to manhood, and the relative effects of the two can never be clearly separated.

With Korvettenkapitän Siegfried Freiherr von Forstner, the question was merely academic, for he was born and raised to one tradition—a military career and service to the Fatherland.

The son of a regular army general—a World War I regimental commander and winner of the Pour le mérite with cluster—the young von Forstner was the fourth generation of an aristocratic Prussian family to enter the military. His grandfather and great-grandfather before him had also been army officers, and an uncle had commanded U-1 and U-28 in World War I, a conflict that took the life of another uncle in the Imperial Navy. When the time came to enter officer training, Siegfried and the next younger son, Wolfgang-Friedrich, entered the Navy, while the two youngest brothers entered the Army.[1]

Graduating from the German Naval School in 1933, service on the pocket battleship ADMIRAL SCHEER and specialized gunnery training followed for Siegfried, then three years on the cruiser NURNBERG as ordnance officer. On the outbreak of war, seeing that action was more likely to be had in U-boats than in a light cruiser, he applied for U-boat school. When the NURNBERG was laid up for repairs in December, 1939, after being torpedoed by the British submarine SALMON, he was ordered to U-boat training, reporting to the U-boat school in March, just weeks before the Norwegian campaign began, in which the entire German Fleet was to be involved. The climax of any naval officer's career, and the entire reason for his professional existence, is combat at sea, and Forstner read the reports of the Norwegian action with growing impatience and frustration. When the Battle of France followed and ended with the quick French capitulation, the opportunity for him to see combat action appeared to be fading. But Operation Sea Lion, the planned German invasion of Britain, was cancelled in the autumn, and the brunt of the war against England fell increasingly on the U-boats. In September, von Forstner, then a Kapitänleutnant, graduated from U-boat school, and was promptly sent into the thick of things—as a student commander under Korvettenkapitän Otto Kretschmer in U-99. Kretschmer, a Naval School classmate, who had entered U-boats shortly after the arm was re-established in 1935, was at the time the German Navy's top-scoring ace, followed closely by Joachim Schepke in U-100, and Günther Prien, whose U-47 had sunk the battleship ROYAL OAK at Scapa Flow.

Because of his seniority, Forstner was slated to receive command of a new boat without first serving time as a watch officer, and in order to obtain the minimum of combat experience needed, was assigned to Kretschmer as a student and extra num-

---

[1] Of the four, only Wolfgang-Friedrich, captured when his U-472 was sunk in 1944, survived the war.

ber. The cruise was a short one, but he had the opportunity of seeing a U-boat handled by an expert during several actual attacks.

Returning in the late fall, Forstner was given command of a small training U-boat for five months until his new command, U-402, was ready for acceptance in Danzig. He had been detached from U-99 none too soon, for shortly afterwards, she was sunk, and Kretschmer was taken prisoner.

After accepting the new U-402, the summer was spent in shakedown training, and she sailed on her first patrol in October, 1941, an uneventful ice reconnaissance cruise. The second war patrol, off the Azores, produced only one sinking—the LLONGIBBY CASTLE. The third cruise was also quiet until the last day on station, and Forstner fumed inwardly, his sense of frustration being summed up in a letter to his wife, Annamaria:

"This is a war, not a holiday trip. Yet here we sit in an endless expanse of blue water under a smiling sun—no enemy, no nothing—and others have to do all the fighting. It is simply disgusting!"

Impatient though he was, the several quiet patrols gave Forstner, still a relative novice in U-boats, a chance to learn and train his crew. Throughout the war, the highest casualty rate was among boats on their first patrol. If they could survive the first couple of cruises, they learned enough to look after themselves. More than most, Forstner needed the time to acquire the experience that his daring nature would later demand. One of his former watch officers recalls the Forstner of those days:

"Baron von Forstner became a U-boat commander without ever serving as a watch officer, and because of this, his successes at first were not great. His lack of experience he made up for with *Draufgangertum*.[2] He easily disregarded the necessary caution."

But the label of incautiousness was not an apt one for Siegfried von Forstner. Intelligent risk-taking has little in common with

---

[2] Translated roughly as *aggressiveness*, or as we old China hands would say, *Gung Ho*—J.M.W.

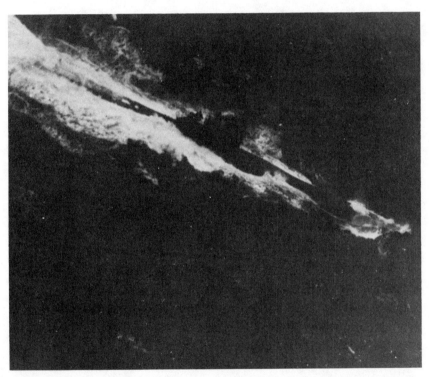

U-402, surprised on the surface by a TBF from the USS CARD, clears the bridge before starting its last dive. Twenty-five seconds after diving it was hit by a homing torpedo dropped by a carrier aircraft, and went down with all hands. USN/National Archives

bravado and foolhardiness, or with impulse and dumb luck. It is based on fact and preparation, and guided by reason, though these do not diminish the courage required to take the risks.

"The most salient characteristic of the ace," said a leading American psychologist, "was his risk-taking ability. Throughout his life he had kept testing the limits of his abilities."

Combat experience repeatedly proved that such men were not only highly resistant to accidents, but suffered fewer combat casualties for the results obtained than those who tried to play it safe.

The sinking of the USS CYTHERA (PY 26), which occurred on his last day on station, was a good example. U-boat commanders generally avoided attacking armed escort vessels, for if they missed such an elusive and hard-to-hit target, they could find themselves the prey instead of the hunter, with a long series of depth-charge attacks by an aroused warship a distinct possibility.

But on May 2, 1942, on his third war patrol, and with nothing to show for the long weeks of waiting, Forstner was ready to tackle anything to get a kill. At 0425, in the pre-dawn darkness 100 miles east of Cape Fear, North Carolina, the bridge watch of U-402 sighted a warship at four miles, zigzagging at 14 knots on a southerly course. Remaining on the surface, Forstner moved out ahead of her, plotting her course and speed. Two hours later he was in good position ahead and dived to begin a submerged attack. At first, he was unable to see anything through his attack periscope, but at 0641, he had the target in sight at 1,900 yards with a perfect beam shot setup. Three torpedoes sped on the way, and two of them hit the unfortunate vessel midships. Her depth charges, set for 150 feet, exploded as the stern went under, and less than a minute later, her bow also sank beneath the waves.

Forstner surfaced and stood in toward the site of the sinking, now marked with a spreading oil slick. Only two survivors were found, clinging to a raft, and both were rescued. The vessel had been a large yacht, which several months before had been taken over by the Navy and converted into an escort vessel. It was the 250-foot, 850-ton CYTHERA, enroute from Norfolk to Pearl

Harbor via the Panama Canal, and all but 2 of her 71 officers and men went down with the ship. The survivors were a pharmacist mate and a seaman, and the former had seen more than his share of trouble, having been a member of the crew of the OKLA-HOMA when it was sunk at Pearl Harbor only five months before.

Writing to his wife, Forstner said, "We should really have kept them locked up and all that, but a U-boat is not spacious as you know and they were nice chaps and friendly—they joined us in our meals, and we brought them home in our own way, and nobody the worse for it. At our arrival, they were met by an escort and taken away in the usual manner thought fit for prisoners of war, much to the consternation of my crew, whom they had invited to come and see them back home in the States after the war."

On the next patrol, Forstner was heavily depth-charged off Cape Hatteras, and limped back to La Pallice, considerably the worse for wear.

After the depth-charging, he wrote, "You know, it is far easier to limp back successful, though somewhat the worse for wear, than to return to port safe and sound after a completely uneventful war patrol—and yet under such adverse conditions, maintain discipline, or rather establish it [as the inexperienced young commander you are] in a crew still waiting to be welded together by action and built up to a high level of morale."

Four quiet patrols to learn the ropes, with two kills and a depth-charging to season them, had made the crew of U-402 as ready as they would be without the tempering of really heavy fighting, which could only be gained around the protected convoys. Thus, when Forstner fell in with Convoy SC-107 on his next patrol in November, the first large group of targets he had encountered, he drove in hard, venturing where few U-boat commanders would go, and reaped a heavy kill as a result of his reckless daring and tenacity. On the next patrol in February, faced with an exceptionally strong escort around Convoy SC-118, the now completely confident Forstner put on one of the great U-boat performances of the war, sinking seven ships, and pulling out only after his last torpedo was expended.

After the battle, von Forstner limped home to a hero's welcome, receiving the Knight's Cross on the day of his arrival. In the afterglow of his latest victory, he became even more reticent than usual about his successes, but when the performance of his crew was mentioned, he warmed to the subject, especially the performance of his warrant machinist, Fischer, who had worked around the clock, fitting in by hand a new port thrust bearing, which had enabled them to continue and make contact with the convoy. Pressed as to what role he had played, an acquaintance recalls that he replied with a smile, "As a matter of fact, I slept most of the patrol. You see, I have to—well—sort of sleep in advance, because once things start happening, there won't be any sleep for me until it is over."

But the willingness to give to his crew a major share of the credit did not prevent him from being a stern disciplinarian [3] and one intolerant of carelessness, for already the menacing shape of things to come was becoming clear to the combat skippers. Many of the new draft coming aboard were full of the "superman" concept implanted by the Hitler Youth, much to the exasperation of the captain, who felt that they were all "too willing to assume authority without the accompanying sense of responsibility and self-control." [4] Particularly frustrating to him was the necessity to continually correct some of the new men.

"At their age and in their position," he said, "whenever I had given cause for admonishment, you bet I took good care it wouldn't happen a second time!"

---

[3] A former subordinate recalls him as ". . . an extremely correct officer, and very Prussian through and through."

[4] As the war progressed, many of the new men coming into U-boats were hard-shell Nazis. This was in contrast with the older Navy men, who had been commissioned before Hitler came to power, and were as a group aloof from the Nazi ideology, though they served its leaders. At the time, the Germans had a saying that the Wehrmacht consisted of the Prussian Army, the Imperial Navy, and the National Socialist Luftwaffe.

Recovering his sense of humor, he added, "This complaining about the shortcomings of the junior officers without doing anything about it is a silly business. If indeed, we have reason to believe that they fail to come up to requirements in some respects, we, their seniors, are the ones to tell them—in as tactful and as comradely a manner as possible. If we shirk this trouble, the fault is ours as well as theirs."

So during the two months availability in La Pallice, von Forstner worked on the new men, molding them in as part of his experienced crew, knowing full well that one weak link in a submarine crew could mean death for them all. That he had succeeding in developing a high sense of *esprit de corps* in his crew by the constant training and the victories at sea was evidenced by the pride they showed in their captain and boat. Ashore in La Pallice, the crew boasted to the French girls, and the substance was promptly reported by the French underground to the Allies. An American intelligence report of mid-summer, 1943, contains the information that the crew of U-402 all wore distinctive red pom-poms on their hats, which were made by the Baroness Annamaria von Forstner, whom Forstner had married in Hamburg in December, 1940, while waiting to take over command of U-402.

U-402 sailed for her seventh war patrol in April, and early in May fell in with Convoy SC-129, escorted by none other than Group B2, their old enemy of February, now under command of Commander Donald Macintyre, next to Walker, the most successful of the U-boat killers. Of all the U-boats that made contact with the convoy, only U-402 managed to get to the merchantmen, sinking two. But the escort struck back savagely, and U-402 was given a severe pasting with depth charges, and was badly damaged. Out of control, the boat sank far below her test depth, and when it seemed that the groaning, creaking hull must collapse from the terrific water pressure, finally checked her dive and leveled off. As the depth-charging continued, and the end seemed near, Forstner called most of his crew into the control room, and led them in prayer. The escorts finally lost contact, and U-402 crept away and made her way back to La Pallice.

From another crew member, Forstner's wife learned of the boat's narrow escape, and of the gathering in the control room. To her anxious inquiries, he replied, "You see, whatever happens, we are not forsaken out there, though it may seem so one day."

As a result of the damage, U-402 was forced to spend over three months in the repair yard, and Forstner arrived in Hamburg for what was to be his last leave. The strain of nearly three years of combat action was showing, and his increasing disillusionment with the Nazi propaganda handouts came to a head when he was called in for a briefing. He came home in a sullen and depressed mood, and exploded:

"This is really the limit! We are called to a briefing to be told that we should hate and despise the enemy, otherwise we cannot do our duty. My sense of responsibility needs no bolstering by such sentiment. The mere suggestion is an outrage. Why should I hate the enemy? They are standing by their country as I am by mine. Despise them? What for? None of us out there in his right senses would dream of underestimating what we are up against—indeed, if we did, it might well prove our undoing. What is more, how very stupid it would be—belittling the enemy means but detracting from one's own achievement, if you have been lucky enough to get the better of him."

Toward the end of his leave, the heavy British air raids on Hamburg began and all the homes in the vicinity went up in flames except for the small one in which the von Forstners had their flat, and a neighboring twin. Forstner and his wife, Annamaria, sat on the roof during the raid attempting to put out the fires started by the incendiary bombs. Two bombs were extinguished, and in the interval between, they talked.

"This is beastly," said Forstner, looking at the burning city. "Out there is bad enough, but if someone starts attacking me, at least I can fight back with all that I am worth, and you bet I do!

But here you can only sit tight and hope for the best—a sitting duck to shoot at . . . and to think, that whatever we do out there, we cannot prevent this!"

As the leave drew to a close, Forstner was increasingly preoccupied with the fate that he realized was probably inevitable. Under the Allied onslaught the list of U-boats "overdue and presumed lost" grew daily, and the crews were leaving their valuables ashore and making out their last wills and testaments before departing, but still they sailed. He was also becoming more and more concerned with the course his country was taking, but like most professional officers, could not bring himself to speak out in the area of politics, though increasingly he noticed and disliked the things he saw while he was home.

On one of the last nights of leave, he talked about the possibility of the enemy getting him. "Whenever I realize," he said, "that I have lost the game and have absolutely no chance left, you may rest assured that I won't do anything foolish—and I shall try to save my men and myself. The war will be over for us, and there will be more than enough for us to do after the war is ended. However, should it happen that the boat is sunk, and we are trapped, do not torment yourself with visions of slow suffocation. I have sufficient means for the entire crew to prevent this. But that is a last resource, as you know me well enough to be certain that I shall not make use of it unless I must."

U-402 sailed for her eighth and last patrol in September, and joined Group *Leuthen* attacking Convoy ON-202 in the North Atlantic, using the new acoustic homing torpedoes for the first time. Six merchantmen and three escorts were sunk with heavy loss of life, but three U-boats were sunk by the escorts. During the battle, a Liberator attacked and badly damaged U-377 twelve miles astern of the convoy, and would have probably finished it had not Forstner closed in and thrown up a heavy barrage of flak to drive the aircraft off. The successful anti-aircraft defense may well have influenced his subsequent thinking.

On the morning of October 13th, Forstner, who had then been at sea for over five weeks, was on the surface several hundred miles north of the Azores racing southward for a rendezvous with a "milch cow" to replenish his nearly empty tanks. By an interesting coincidence, ahead of him lay a westbound GUS convoy, escorted by Task Force 63, with Captain Roy L. Raney, USCG, as task force commander in CGC BIBB, and which included CGC INGHAM, the two ships Forstner had narrowly evaded on the night of February 8th. The escort carrier, USS CARD, was screening far to the north of the convoy. Just after noon, a TBF from the carrier, piloted by Lieutenant Commander Howard M. Avery, USN, the squadron commander of CARD's VC-9, sighted the U-boat 25 miles south of the carrier and dived in to attack with guns blazing. When the U-boat failed to dive, Avery, who had a homing torpedo, but no bombs, circled a mile astern to avoid the German fire, and called for help.[5] Another TBF, piloted by Ensign B. C. Sheela, arrived and attacked, catching U-402 by surprise, but missed by 200 yards with a depth bomb. Forstner saw his chance and pulled the plug. As the rusty conning tower sank beneath the sea, Avery banked steeply and raced in, dropping a new type Mk. 24 homing torpedo 100 feet beyond the swirl where U-402 had disappeared. The torpedo homed on the propeller noise of the speeding U-boat, and 25 seconds later went off with a violent detonation. Minutes later, only a spreading oil slick and two cylindrical metal objects marked the grave of U-402 and her captain and crew.

In the aftermath of war, the men of the U-boat arm were painted as the blackest of villains, guilty of the wanton killing of thousands of defenseless merchant seamen. Undeniably, they, like our own submariners, inflicted great destruction and much human misery, but that death from a torpedo is more grievous or stealthy than a bomb dropped from the sky at night is no more support-

---

[5] The Mk. 24 homing torpedo was ineffective against a surfaced U-boat.

able than the contention that a convoy of armed merchantmen screened by warships is a defenseless target. The contrast between the submariners' notoriety, and the almost chivalrous reputation of some of the lone German surface raiders can be largely attributed to the fact that the latter usually sank a victim only after giving warning, and picked up the survivors afterwards.

By the physical and tactical limitations of their boats, submariners were prevented from doing this, and from this circumstance were born accusations of deliberate cruelty and callousness. Yet we in the escort forces, under less handicaps, sometimes did not pick up even our own survivors, and more than one escort commander was dressed down for rescuing survivors to the detriment of his tactical objective.[6]

Long after the passions of battle have cooled, the bravery, the fighting spirit, and the dedication of the men who fought in the U-boats of the Kriegsmarine compel the respect of other fighting men. That they served a government bent on an evil design was their misfortune and later shame, but like us, most of them fought for their country and their people, professionals carrying out their duties with little knowledge and even less control over the political direction of the war. Regretfully, we did not meet under other circumstances, but those of us who once fought

---

[6] Repeatedly, combat commanders on both sides placed the destruction of the enemy above the rescue of survivors. One of the most famous examples was the sinking of the British transport LACONIA in August, 1942. After surfacing, Hartenstein, the commander of U-156, found that she had been carrying 1,800 Italian prisoners of war, as well as 971 Allied crewmen and passengers, including 80 women and children proceeding on leave. He began rescue operations and broadcast the location of the sinking to the British, promising not to molest any ship that would assist in the rescue. U-boat Command ordered other boats to help, and asked the French to send aid. While the U-boats were surfaced, their decks crowded with survivors, and displaying large Red Cross flags, an American Liberator arrived, circled for nearly an hour, then attacked, dropping bombs among the hundreds of survivors. Although damaged, the U-boats continued the rescue work, and hundreds of survivors were saved and turned over to French warships. As a result of the attack, Doenitz issued orders that no rescue operations would be undertaken in the future. This order was the basis for one of the charges against him at the Nürnberg trials. On this particular charge, he was found not guilty.

against them, while despising all that the Nazi political regime stood for, would be the first to agree with their former Commander in Chief when he said of the German combat sailor, "Let no man denigrate the fighting men of this last war. To do so is to besmirch the honour of those who gave their lives in the execution of their duty." [7]

---

[7] Karl Doenitz, *Memoirs of Ten Years and Twenty Days* (Bonn: Athenaum-Verlag Junkerund Dunnhaupt, 1958), p. 478.

BIBLIOGRAPHY

Chalmers, W., *Max Horton and the Western Approaches*. London, Hodder and Stoughton Ltd., 1958.

Churchill, W., *The Second World War*. Boston, Houghton Mifflin Company, 1950.

Doenitz, K., *Memoirs of Ten Years and Twenty Days*. Bonn, Athenaum-Verlag Junkerund Dunnhaupt, 1958.

Easton, A., *50° North*. London, Eyre and Spottiswoode (Publishers) Ltd., 1963.

Frank, W., *The Sea Wolves*. New York, Holt, Rinehart, & Winston, Inc., 1954.

Gretton, P., *Convoy Escort Commander*. London, Cassell & Co. Ltd., 1964.

Jacobsen, H., and Rohwer, J., eds., *Decisive Battles of World War II: The German View*. New York, G. P. Putnam's Sons, 1965.

King, E., and Muir, W., *Fleet Admiral King*. New York, W. W. Norton & Company, Inc., 1952.

Lewin, R., *Ultra Goes to War*. London, Hutchinson & Co. Ltd., 1978.

Lenton, H., *German Submarines*. Garden City, N. Y., Doubleday & Company, Inc., 1965.

MacIntyre, D., *The Battle of the Atlantic*. London, B. T. Batsford, Ltd., 1961.

MacIntyre, D., *U-Boat Killer*. London, George Weidenfeld & Nicolson Ltd., 1956.

Morison, S., *History of United States Naval Operations in World War II*, Vols. I and X. Boston, Little, Brown and Company, 1947, 1962.

Rohwer, J., *The Critical Convoy Battles of March 1943*. Naval Institute Press, 1977.

Roscoe, T., *United States Destroyer Operations in World War II*. Annapolis, Md., U.S. Naval Institute, 1953.

Roskill, S., *The Navy at War*. Glasgow, William Collins Sons & Co. Ltd., 1960.

Roskill, S., *The War at Sea*. London, Her Majesty's Stationery Office, 1954.

Ruge, F., *Der Seekrieg*. Stuttgart, K. F. Koehler Verlag, 1957.

Schull, J., *The Far Distant Ships*, Ottawa, Canadian Department of National Defence, 1950.

United States Submarine Losses, WW II. Washington, Naval History Division, CNO, 1963.

Wemyss, D. E. G., *Walker's Groups in the Western Approaches*. Liverpool, Liverpool University Press, 1948.

Willoughby, M., *United States Coast Guard in World War II*. Annapolis, Md., U.S. Naval Institute, 1956.

Winterbotham, F., *The Ultra Secret*. New York, Harper and Rowe, 1974.

INDEX

Boldface references are to names of Allied Vessels, U-boats, and Convoy designations.